Control, Abuse, Bullying and Family Violence in Tourism Industries

Full details of all the books in this series and of all our other publications can be found on http://www.channelviewpublications.com, or by writing to Channel View Publications, St Nicholas House, 31-34 High Street, Bristol, BS1 2AW, UK.

Control, Abuse, Bullying and Family Violence in Tourism Industries

Elisa Zentveld

CHANNEL VIEW PUBLICATIONS
Bristol • Jackson

DOI https://doi.org/10.21832/ZENTVE8717
Library of Congress Cataloging in Publication Data
A catalog record for this book is available from the Library of Congress.
Names: Zentveld, Elisa, author.
Title: Control, Abuse, Bullying and Family Violence in Tourism Industries/Elisa Zentveld.
Description: Bristol, UK; Blue Ridge Summit, PA: Channel View Publications, [2023] | Includes bibliographical references and index. | Summary: 'This book explores control, abuse, bullying and family violence within the tourism system using autoethnography. It reveals the impacts of family violence and is an important and under-researched area in the tourism literature and will be of interest to researchers and practitioners in tourism, events, family violence, social work, health and law' – Provided by publisher.
Identifiers: LCCN 2022051513 (print) | LCCN 2022051514 (ebook) | ISBN 9781845418700 (Paperback) | ISBN 9781845418717 (Hardback) | ISBN 9781845418731 (epub) | ISBN 9781845418724 (pdf)
Subjects: LCSH: Tourism – Social aspects – Case studies. | Family violence. | Domestic relations. | Ethnology – Research.
Classification: LCC G156.5.S63 Z46 2023 (print) | LCC G156.5.S63 (ebook) | DDC 362.82/92091 – dc23/eng20230210
LC record available at https://lccn.loc.gov/2022051513
LC ebook record available at https://lccn.loc.gov/2022051514

British Library Cataloguing in Publication Data
A catalogue entry for this book is available from the British Library.

ISBN-13: 978-1-84541-871-7 (hbk)
ISBN-13: 978-1-84541-870-0 (pbk)

Channel View Publications
UK: St Nicholas House, 31-34 High Street, Bristol, BS1 2AW, UK.
USA: NBN, Blue Ridge Summit, PA, USA.

Website: www.channelviewpublications.com
Twitter: Channel_View
Facebook: https://www.facebook.com/channelviewpublications
Blog: www.channelviewpublications.wordpress.com

The policy of Multilingual Matters/Channel View Publications is to use papers that are natural, renewable and recyclable products, made from wood grown in sustainable forests. In the manufacturing process of our books, and to further support our policy, preference is given to printers that have FSC and PEFC Chain of Custody certification. The FSC and/or PEFC logos will appear on those books where full certification has been granted to the printer concerned.

Typeset by Riverside Publishing Solutions.

I dedicate this book to my four children: James John Zentveld, Chantelle Rose Zentveld, Jonathan Alexander Zentveld and Sebastian Alexander Zentveld, for all their love, support, encouragement and inspiration.

I also dedicate this book to my late father, John Zentveld. While he passed away before this book began, his role model to me as a father and to my children as a positive male role model had been exceptionally helpful. While he was an older European (Dutch) man, not once did I feel inferior in his eyes because of my gender. He was calm, positive no matter what went wrong, generous to the community, and remains a constant reminder of what a good father can be.

Many years ago my late father wrote:

> *I was almost eight years old that day in May 1940. They sang as they marched down our road, thundering jackboots the only accompaniment. Behind the curtains we wept. The Germans had arrived in Holland sentencing us to five years of hunger, fear, and anger. Searchlights replaced stars, nighttime lullabies the drone of bombers heading East. Returning later the drone threatened by the staccato screaming sounds of fiery trailed broken planes.*

> *Peace at last. I turn thirteen. Hardship without hope replaces victory's euphoria. A new life beckons in Australia. Reborn aged twenty in a land of freedom, hope and love.*

> *They took our dignity, our possessions, our freedom but they couldn't take our souls.*

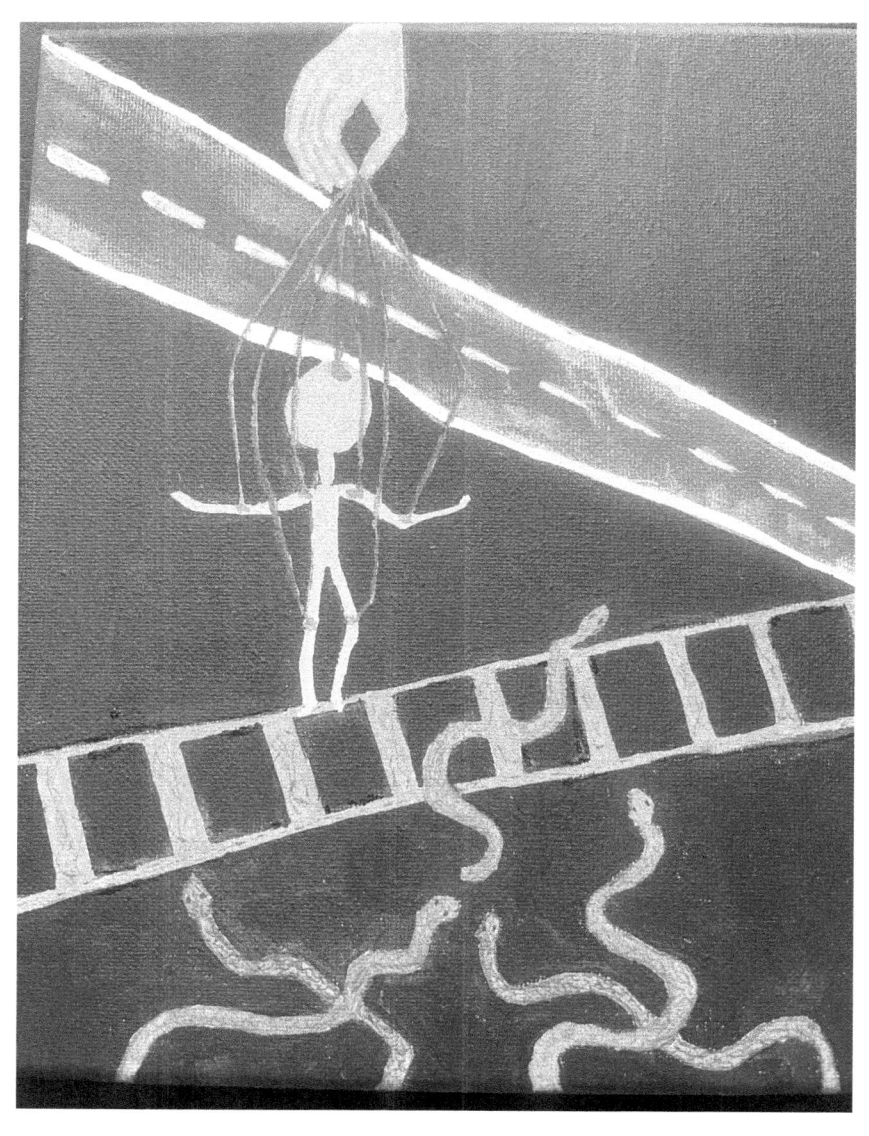

Image and front cover image credit © Chantelle Zentveld

Contents

Tables and Figures

Acknowledgements

I would like to acknowledge my four children: James John Zentveld, Chantelle Rose Zentveld, Jonathan Alexander Zentveld and Sebastian Alexander Zentveld. My children have been huge supporters of this book project and were also involved in reading various sections, and I thank them very much for their support and input. I would also like to acknowledge Dr Brad Mitchell, who encouraged me to write this book for years and read many of the sections and provided feedback. I also thank Dr David Brennan, who supported me through many of the journeys that I write about in this book and also read drafts of some of the sections and provided feedback. I would also like to thank the reviewers of this book and the publisher, who enabled this book to be published.

As a journalist I have heard countless stories of women who have experienced family violence which has left physical scars and lasting psychological trauma, not only for her but also her children. The constant fear and state of hypervigilance, not knowing what may come next, is all-consuming, exhausting, relentless and identity stripping. Victims say they feel they will never be free from control and abuse, even after separation, which is considered among the highest risk times for victims. Each individual's story is unique, but the lasting and intergenerational effects are common. It is important that victims' voices are heard, their stories are shared and members of society become aware of issues in the legal system and experiences of violence after separation which are not well understood. This book also reveals a dark side of the seemingly bright and positive tourism industry by shining a light on the experiences of family violence victims while travelling which has not been acknowledged in the industry before.

Rochelle Kirkham
ABC News Reporter

Overview

'No passion so effectively robs the mind of all its powers of acting and reasoning as fear'

Edmund Burke, *A Philosophical Enquiry into the Origin of Our Ideas of the Sublime and Beautiful*

Most books are structured to be read from beginning to end. Each chapter connects and flows. This book, however, does not need to be read from beginning to end, it does not need to be read in sequence. Some readers may only be interested in one chapter that is relevant to their interests or needs. While this is an educative book that is technical in nature and aimed primarily at an academic readership, it is hoped that the readership may be broader.

This book employs autoethnography as its method and includes 'storytelling'. The style is deliberately set in a manner to be relevant to a readership of academic researchers, but also, beyond this, includes stories to make it more relatable and readable. This book discusses problematic behaviour and some confusing and poorly understood legislative aspects. While discussed in the context of tourism industries, the key message is generalisable to anybody (not just tourists), and to any workplace (not just those that serve tourists).

This book discusses control, abuse, bullying and family violence. It discusses these matters as they are, as well as how they impact the tourism system. Family violence can be especially difficult to understand as it tends to happen behind closed doors, and some of the problems with family violence relate to the judicial system, which is also behind closed doors. Thus, this book explains the various aspects of legislation and presents stories about what family violence is like. Such knowledge is important for those working in tourism industries, as well as for anyone considering separating from a perpetrator of family violence. Decisions made without important legislative knowledge will impact many aspects, of which mobility and undertaking travel will, potentially, be among those most impacted.

Uniquely, this book presents an inside account of a number of events including the Family Law Court. These occurrences are behind closed doors and present a mystery to the outside world. Family law legislation tends to work similarly in many countries, where people are prevented from disseminating what occurred in a proceeding. Some people have tried to work around this by sharing their events anonymously through the media or blogs. However, this book provides the reader with the inside experience. While this is banned in most cases, there are a few exceptions. As this book is an educational work that is of a technical character primarily intended for professionals, it presents an opportunity to share a perspective of proceedings normally hidden from the world.

Such knowledge is important for understanding what might evolve through the justice system. People can end up having 'blind faith' in a form of justice that they expect but do not receive. It is not uncommon for victims of family violence to regret leaving their abusive partner (not for emotional reasons but because of the orders made by the courts). Victims may leave a perpetrator of family violence and be seduced into thinking they will be free, only to learn that their abusive ex-partner is likely to have equal responsibility on the major decisions for their dependent children, which can impact employment, mobility, and even travel plans.

For those living with a perpetrator of family violence, tourism conceptual frameworks describe touristic activities as being a time for escape and relaxation. None of these models takes into account what holidaying away from home with a perpetrator is like. The holiday, which is meant to be about escape and relaxation, is not escaping a primary source of stress. Tourism models omit family violence and, as such, are a type of Trojan Horse where the dark hidden secret comes along for the journey but people outside the Trojan Horse only see the illusion, not what is going on inside. Therefore, this book explains family violence so that readers have some context of how tourism (and other things) are impacted by family violence.

An Overture is included. This presents my story of family violence, which I tell for the reader who may be looking for context. Various legislative aspects within the book link to 'journeys' in the Overture. The reader can duck in and out of various sections to provide context if they desire. Sometimes it is difficult to understand how tourism (and other things) can be affected by family violence and court outcomes after separation. Therefore, the Overture aims to provide some authenticity and context for the reader. Depending on decisions made and outcomes from family law courts, the ability of an individual to even undertake touristic experiences can be reduced. To understand why holidaying away from home with a perpetrator of family violence is not necessarily relaxing (and in fact may be worse), it is important to know what living with family violence might be like: the Overture attempts to present this. Therefore, the Overture may serve to assist some readers. In some cases, as is shown in this book, mobility can be negatively impacted post-separation from family violence.

Finally, the book attempts to be a standalone book, so that readers have no need to undertake other reading (e.g. reading about family violence or bullying in the workplace) in order to understand these matters. As a whole, the book takes a tourism systems approach, explaining the impacts of control, abuse, bullying and family violence within various elements of the tourism system. It explains the partial industrialisation in tourism, as the dimensions of tourism are extremely broad. At its centre, there are obvious examples of businesses that serve tourists, such as motels and theme parks. However, as the often-used expression 'Tourism is everyone's business' tries to explain, there are few businesses that do not serve any tourists. Looking at some fringe beneficiaries, even dentists will correct teeth for tourists, and medical doctors will have tourists as patients. Some people have said to me that a funeral parlour is a good example of a business that does not benefit from tourism: on the contrary, many friends and relatives will travel (often great distances) for a funeral and, as such, the celebration of a life that has ended through a funeral is part of what is known as Visiting Friends and Relatives (VFR) travel.

I draw attention to the quote at the beginning of this section: 'No passion so effectively robs the mind of all its powers of acting and reasoning as fear.' The employee who lives with family violence, also lives with fear. This will impact them. We need to understand that as employers. For the victim sitting in court trying to articulate their story while overwhelmed with fear, their ability to explain the situation clearly may be affected, while the perpetrator, devoid of fear, can play the game much better. If this was better understood, we might see better decisions in our judicial systems.

This book provides three unique aspects for the reader. Firstly, it explains how control, abuse, bullying, and in particular family violence, impact the tourism system. Family violence does not go on a holiday. Secondly, the book focuses on post-separation aspects to reveal that separation from family violence is not necessarily 'freedom'. Escape is more complex than is understood and the control and abuse often continue but simply outside the house instead of within it. Thirdly, the book offers a rare glimpse of several types of cases to help guide interested readers through those processes. Uniquely, experiences from family court proceedings are presented, to share events that are normally hidden from view. I hope the readers find this helpful and interesting and also hope that some of what is shared will lead to further change. A world with less abuse, less controlling behaviour, less bullying and less family violence would be a better world. Education about what happens may assist in generating micro steps towards a better world. My hope is that readers will find this book beneficial.

Overture

'How many times can I break 'til I shatter?'

Source: 'Shattered', O.A.R

Sometimes, a person uses up all the forgiveness cards in the pack we set aside for that person and there are none left to hand them. I do not forgive my ex-husband for what he did to me and the children; the internal and external scars live on years later. However, I do believe in two things – accept, and be thankful. I accept what happened and there are many things to be thankful for.

I decided to include an Overture to this book after reading Jordan Peterson's *Beyond Order*. Peterson's Overture added context and authenticity, which, as a reader, I valued. In my book, I have also provided an epilogue, which serves to offer interested readers some concluding points regarding perspectives and attitudes.

Many of the issues I raise and the questions I set about answering in this book came from various pathways in my life. Some readers may wish to know more background from the snippets that pop up through the chapters. Therefore, this section sets about providing a summary of my story. While personal experience is relevant to many aspects that I cover in this book, the important thing to share with readers is that much of what I learned about the issues with the Family Law Act came from riding through it and seeing its ugliness. My experiences of living with family violence may provide context for interested readers. They may also provide some comfort to readers: for all of us who look at ourselves and wonder how we ended up trapped in a life of family violence, there is some sort of comfort in knowing we are not alone, and that others have also been trapped. Perhaps, also, when we look at others who are, or were, trapped in family violence, we may be less likely to judge after understanding more about it. Reading this Overture may also help explain why family violence serves as part of the tourism underbelly. Various aspects relating to family violence impact the tourism system.

Ironically, while having expertise and qualifications in tourism, I developed a firm dislike for travel. My colleagues used to find that extraordinary. Reading this Overture may help to explain why I developed a dislike for travel. Living with a perpetrator of family violence is awful. Even worse is being in unfamiliar closed quarters with them and travelling in a car with them. Does family violence impact tourism? Absolutely it does.

The idea of camping or caravanning might be worse than staying at home because it may mean being confined in very small quarters with a perpetrator of family violence and being more isolated. For me, travelling by plane ended up with arguments because all the children would fight over being seated with me on the plane. This resulted in more problems. While travelling can always be stressful, especially with young children, such stress increases when that family is living with a perpetrator of family violence. Family violence doesn't take a holiday.

Writing this Overture also meets a recommendation from an incredible friend, Brad Mitchell. Brad was a colleague of mine at Federation University. He was one of the very few people who knew that I was living with family violence. He was aware of my journey through the brutal family law system. He was aware that I uncovered loopholes because I read and asked questions and pushed painfully for the best outcome possible. Brad kept telling me I needed to tell my story. While writing this, I told him that I had decided to write my story by way of an Overture to this book, rather than bury it in snippets throughout. I asked Brad why he believed I should tell my story. He told me:

> I have always thought that it would be of tremendous help to others. It is a most unusual story of overcoming abuse because of your doggedness in tackling the system. You were not content to just get out of the situation by working within the system – you challenged the system and in so doing have provided precedents that will empower others … victims of abuse should not be victims of the system. (B. Mitchell, 20 March 2022)

The Overture will hopefully provide the reader with a sense of what it is like to live with family violence and why this contributes to a tourism underbelly.

I will also journey through the three court battles I had after I finally managed to separate from a perpetrator of family violence. Those three journeys are important because they are journeys that explain the problems with the family courts. Two of those journeys are ones that victims of family violence will likely go through as part of the separation journey. The three journeys are: getting an Intervention Order; settling parental matters; and changing the surname of children.

In this Overture, I will refer to my ex-husband as Mr Ex rather than provide his name. One person who read a draft of this book suggested

I should call him something else because Mr Ex was too respectful. That might be a fair point but my purpose is simply to explain what can happen to raise awareness. Mr Ex is merely a by-product in that narrative. I don't think it matters if the term seems respectful, which to me is better than disrespectful.

The surname belonging to me and my children is not the same as Mr Ex's surname. How I changed their surnames was a mission in itself, which created new case law and accordingly was published in AustLII. In terms of the name of my ex-husband, I do not provide his name as the purpose of this book is to provide education and not to denigrate any particular individual. My purpose is to tell a story of what can go wrong, how things go wrong, and how to work with broken legal systems to try to achieve the best possible outcome.

In terms of the accuracy, particularly in quotes, I referred back to my notes, screenshots, emails and documents to check the details to ensure accuracy. I had learned to keep everything and to have records, and would also write notes after events in a notebook to ensure I had an account of matters that I knew I might need to rely on for court battles in the future.

Living with and Separating from a Perpetrator of Family Violence

In many ways, my story begins on the 20 September 2017. It was a Wednesday. That is the day I separated from my husband. It was a day I had been knowing was in front of me for a long time. Looking back, really the signs that I had married a controlling and abusive man were there from the beginning. There were some red flags that I wasn't aware of at the time. For example, he spoke disrespectfully about women. He would say that 'all the stupid women turn up at the local primary school half an hour early to get a good car park'. He would also say that 'all the stupid women can't park properly'. He had been married twice before and spoke very poorly about his first wife. There were various controlling and abusive indicators. However, it was only when we had children that things really soured. I think that he saw them as competitors. They consumed my focus. I will provide a few key aspects during that time of being married to an abusive and controlling man.

A key marker was in 2005 when I discovered I was pregnant for the third time, carrying identical twins. Upon learning of the pregnancy at around 13 weeks gestation, Mr Ex told me that I had two choices – abort the babies or divorce. I told him: one I could live with (i.e. divorce) while the other I could not. He didn't talk to me for three days or attend to the needs of the two existing children, telling me to 'get used to doing everything on my own'. It was from that point that the relationship worsened and, during pregnancy, Mr Ex choked me in the kitchen and I thought I would die. I lay on the floor coughing and inhaling deeply as

I struggled for breath after he finally let go. I set up a bed for myself on a fold-out couch and Mr Ex yelled at me that I had to sleep in the bed with him. This was the commencement of an era of abuse comprising yelling, choking, belittling, as well as Mr Ex abusing the children physically and psychologically.

It is probably important that I mention that Mr Ex had told the children on more than one occasion that he had never wanted so many children and hadn't wanted 'the twins'. The reason this is important is that, had he not made this quite clear to them, I would not include the statement in the previous paragraph about him not being supportive of the pregnancy. The youngest two were sadly aware of this from the candid comments from their father. I don't suppose he thought about how it might make them feel. His intent was probably to garner sympathy as to these things I had put him through and that this was not the easy comfortable life he had imagined for himself. So, I genuinely don't believe he disclosed this to the children to hurt them. I just think that he didn't think. He thought about it from his perspective. After all, anyone who engages in family violence cannot possibly be thinking of the impact of their actions and words on others.

In the marriage, I endured psychological and physical abuse. Another serious choking event occurred in late 2008, when I was unable to lecture at work the next day and was referred to a counsellor by my line manager after she offered to take over my teaching that day. This event traumatised me for some months and impacted my work and studies. I had reported the event in my PhD progress report without naming who the abuser was. Many years later (in 2017) that report became the first piece of documented evidence that I became most grateful for. I could never have foreseen this in 2008 but remembered it after separating and it became a marker in the evidence I used in my separation battles.

Another significant choking event was witnessed in its entirety by my daughter Chantelle, who watched it in the reflection of the bathroom mirror as she cleaned her teeth. She had asked me to fix her iPod and I was in her room doing a factory reset (at that time her bedroom was across the hall from the bathroom). Mr Ex became enraged that I had been asked to fix the iPod rather than him and tried to take over. I told him I was fine with doing it and then he threw me on Chantelle's bed and started choking me. This event was less significant for me but became a significant event that traumatised my daughter, who had flashbacks of traumatic events for years (reported in notes from her psychologist) of which this was one of the feature ones.

While I was the main target when my behaviour wasn't suited to what Mr Ex was expecting, the children were also victims – both by way of living with what was happening to me as well as enduring treatment toward them. When I was not present, the children regularly reported things that con- stituted hitting, yelling and other various behavioural aspects that all fall under what is family violence. There were bruises and at times handprints, burst capillaries, and belt buckle marks on the children.

I was regularly criticised and belittled. Mr Ex would often stand over me and yell at me while thrusting a pointed finger in my face. I was also at times physically abused and choked. Strangely, I was choked from the front, while the children were gripped from behind their necks. This suggests a calculated approach. I was told I was a 'stupid bitch', as was my daughter. My eldest son was told he was a 'mongrel bastard'. One time, in November 2013, Mr Ex hit me in the head, which resulted in a swollen black eye, a cut eyebrow and a perforated eardrum. My eldest son, James, who was then aged 10, called 000 (Australia's main emergency service number).

The police came to the house and took away the perpetrator. I didn't sleep at all that night because I kept thinking he was going to come back to the house and be angry that the police had been called and I was so frightened. I remember the leaves of the plane tree, blowing against the house, and I kept thinking he was trying to get into the house. I can still remember the fear and the sound with intense clarity.

When the police interviewed me I told them something was wrong with my ear as I could not hear properly and there was ringing and pain. They recommended I go to the Emergency Department. The next day, when I did go, I was told I had a perforated eardrum. My eye was swollen and black. I was exhausted and I was frightened.

I took solace in writing some days later, in a desperate attempt to make sense of the foggy world I was now in. Since the day I was hit in the head was so close to White Ribbon Day (aligned with the International Day for the Elimination of Violence against Women), the irony of this led me to write the following poem:

White Ribbon, Black Days

Dark.
Sunlight shines on my face,
But darkness clouds my mind.

Fear.
I close my eyes and remember.
The pain pierces my thoughts.

Pain.
My ear and eye hurt,
And I think about the hand that caused it.

Crushed.
Words from the past flood my head;
I feel like I am drowning.

Sorry.
The words register,
But is it really enough?

Exist.
Hours turn into days,
And normality is attempted.

Silence.
The secret remains,
For to speak of it causes judgement.

After that night, my daughter Chantelle developed a sleep disorder. For years she had difficulty sleeping and for those years she went to therapists and a child psychologist. I was told by the child psychologist treating her that the sleeping problem was because of family violence and that the abusive father was causing the problem. The answer was there in black and white.

Looking back at this, most people viewing this from the outside would wonder why I stayed and why I couldn't see the problem before me. The reason I stayed is the same reason I left. I stayed because I was living with family violence. I left because I was living with family violence.

That probably sounds like it makes no sense. However, because of the way the family court system works, I stayed. If there had been no children, leaving would have been simple. Leaving is not simple when there are children involved. There were times I did try to leave. But I would accept his apologies and promises to change and take him back. But in a sense, I chose to live with family violence because I was afraid of what might happen if I separated. With four young children, I expected that in all probability the courts would give the father of those children equal rights and equal time. It could have gone even worse than that because, one year after being married, my then-husband stopped working and for the vast majority of my married life I was the sole income earner. In terms of parenting rights, I could find myself with few parental rights. It could be argued that the father, as a non-income earner, was the primary carer. I had little faith in the court system for any type of justice. Anyone who has set foot in a family court will appreciate that these courts are far from family-friendly.

I found myself stepping back from myself and asking myself whether the father was likely to get at least some substantial time with the children on his own. I could only see that the answer was yes. The courts have a pro-contact mentality and do not seem to understand the risks to children and the victim from this forced contact with a perpetrator of family violence. And so, what might that mean for the children? Children … with no voice in court and no rights – being minors – to speak against it and no way to protect themselves? What might that mean for them? And so … I stayed because it seemed safer for the children than leaving. But I nearly left several times before I finally did leave.

I remember sitting in court when they assessed what Mr Ex had done to me, and remember considering the prospect of returning to the family home. A policewoman sat beside me and said, 'Are you sure you want to take him back, because you look really frightened?' I was not only frightened of him, I felt nauseous. The prospect of having to share not only a home but a bed with this person who was capable of behaving the way he did made me feel deeply sick. A bed is meant to be for rest and recovery. A bed is the vilest place to be when it is shared with a person who is a perpetrator of family violence. These were very dark and very ugly days for me. No words can outline how I battled internally every single day.

For readers familiar with the movie (and book) *The Shawshank Redemption*, it may give you a sense of what living with family violence is like. You feel imprisoned. You did nothing wrong to be imprisoned. There is no escape. There is brutality and fear and you are trapped. You can only find joy by living with hope, which nobody has the power to take away.

Staying came with so many costs. Costs to me. Costs to the children. My daughter was unable to sleep properly and had started to engage in deliberate self-harm. I was contacted by the school counsellor about this, and the child psychologist made me aware that this was because of family violence. I had to leave to save my daughter, but leaving could put her and her three brothers at greater risk. I could lose her if I stayed. I could lose her if I left. These are terrible scenarios to face but this can be the picture when living with family violence.

In some ways, I lied to myself and pretended things would get better. In other ways, I tried not to see what my life was. In other ways, I knew what my life was and knew it was damaging my four children, but I was unsure how to escape it. I had also genuinely hoped that the court-mandated men's behaviour change programme would change him. However, he did not see that he belonged there and resented me for his having to go. Hope was a large part of what kept me going. I hoped he would change. I hoped things would get better. My friend Brad Mitchell once said to me that hope is what keeps a lot of people going: farmers stay on the land despite the endless drought because they hope there is rain in the approaching clouds. Hope was what kept the main character of *The Shawshank Redemption*, Andy Dufresne, going. Andy, who was wrongly sentenced to life in prison in Shawshank for the murder of his wife and his wife's lover, remained calm and positive no matter how bad each day was. A famous line in the movie (said by Andy) is: 'hope is a good thing, maybe the best of things, and no good thing ever dies'.

Over the years, I experienced some moments of wisdom when I kept records, documents, notes and photos. At times I had entrusted a few people with snippets of my life. A friend of mine, who was an ex-barrister, told me that separation was riskier when children were under 12 as they had no voice and were likely to be made to spend time with their father even if they did not want to and did not feel safe. While not entirely accurate, there is some truth to that. Essentially, that became a marker for me: I needed to keep going until the two youngest of my four children were both 12. I did not quite make it to that time but came close.

In 2016 I was contacted by a child protection agency. This was triggered by one of the children's teachers after one of the children mentioned to the teacher that their father was violent. Marriage counselling in early 2016 brought too many buried memories to the forefront and my days became even harder after that. Mr Ex would be angered by my lack of passion towards him and tell me that there was something wrong with me for not feeling more passionate towards him. He told me I must be missing some vital hormones and should take medication to make me more interested in him. I was regularly called a 'stupid bitch', told that I was 'an arrogant academic', and that I was 'full of myself'. Mr Ex would ask me who I was texting, who I was emailing, and, when I had coffee with a male friend, he told the children I was having an affair with the man. As a result, I stopped seeing friends because it only brought anger and abuse from Mr Ex. I felt very alone. I was living a lie and I felt ashamed and I felt trapped.

In the year 2017, the effects of living a lie, sharing a bed with an abusive person that I did not feel safe around, walking on eggshells, and the emotional labour involved in all of that, started to take their toll. I was worn out and I was sick. I developed pneumonia. Being unwell presented a wonderful opportunity for me to sleep on the couch and it was such a treat. I relished the freedom of sleeping in a place that was not shared by someone whose behaviour I could not respect. Those nights of freedom were a sanctuary and gave me a little strength, and I felt that my sickness was a sign that I could bear my life no more.

I also started to observe that my three sons were increasingly treating my daughter with disrespect. I knew these were very clear signs. The final moment was presented in September 2017 over dinner. I still recall the dinner conversation. Mr Ex had denigrated me in front of the children. He seemed to enjoy highlighting to them how pathetic I was. If he sent me a grocery shopping list but I didn't follow it strictly he mocked me in front of the children, saying that I wasn't even capable of grocery shopping since I bought things that were not on the list.

On this particular evening, he was making fun of the fact that I regularly exercised and told them that I was 'obsessed with exercise'. I remember him standing in the kitchen spraying this latest criticism for the children to absorb while they sat at the dinner table for their meal. My daughter muttered under her breath, just loud enough for everyone to hear except Mr Ex, 'obsessed is a word the lazy use to describe the dedicated'. I couldn't help but feel a bit proud of her. It was rather brave and funny.

Mr Ex was in a real storm that evening. People who live with family violence often report that there is a pattern, and the behaviour gets worse and worse and builds up and then there is an explosion. The eruption is usually when the worst words are said or there is physical violence or both. On that evening, Mr Ex said to me in front of the children 'There is nothing about you I like'. I was a little bit shocked and calmly asked, 'What … nothing?' and he roared, 'NO…NOT ONE THING!' And so I said, 'Well, I guess you really should think about separating, then, as there is no point staying with someone that you don't like'. This seemed to make him angrier and he said, loudly, 'WELL, THERE IS NOTHING ABOUT YOU THAT I LIKE.' The strange thing is that he kept repeating this line. It was like a record that had a scratch in it and kept repeating. After he had said this about 12 times I said, 'Yes, you have already said that. I have heard you already' but he said it again anyway because he always had to have the last say.

That explosion served as a segue into having the separation conversation. It was in some ways a type of gift. Instead of me announcing a separation, I could simply follow up on the fact there was nothing about me he liked and therefore separation was immensely sensible under such conditions. It was a bit hard to argue against, so it was a gift and I had to take it.

Separation day was 20 September 2017. On that separation day, that Wednesday, I drove to work and my then-husband said he would drop the children off at school and then leave the house. I went to work wondering all day whether they would be safe. When I returned home from work, I opened the garage door and, as the garage door went up, one of my youngest children, Jonathan, was in the garage waving madly and smiling broadly to greet me. I remember feeling the most wonderful sense of relief and joy. He bounced around and told me that he and Sebastian (his identical twin brother) had grated cheese and got some sausages and bread rolls ready so that we could have hot dogs for dinner. I can still see it now. It became an imprint and a confirmation that I must not 'turn the car around' (i.e. take him back). It was a line I told myself: 'Don't turn the car around … keep moving ahead … one day at a time.'

A song I regularly played to myself in those initial days was 'Shattered' by O.A.R., as I found the lyrics provided me with confidence to continue being strong, not 'turning the car around' and allowing Mr Ex back into my life. Too many times, far too many times, I had accepted his apology and 'turned the car around'. He said he was sorry. He said he would change. There were reasons to explain why he 'snapped' and he would get help. He had counselling, he went through a court-mandated men's behavioural change programme. Nothing changed. I kept letting him back into my life. My biggest fear at that early stage of separation (which wasn't my first attempt at separating) was falling victim once again and letting him back into my life.

An earlier attempt to separate, in 2014, had gone well, with an agreement to separate for seven days to see how it went. After four days

I was feeling free although I was incredibly busy juggling four primary school-aged children with a full-time job. I went out to buy a broom as our house broom was very worn. I felt so alive buying that broom. I still remember how good it felt. It's a broom. Pretty boring, I know! But I happily chose it, bought it, and brought it home knowing I wasn't going to be abused for buying a broom.

I made two mistakes in that first separation.

Mistake one: I had told my line manager that I was separating from my husband. I thought that was honest and appropriate so that he might understand the situation I was in. The next day, my line manager came into my office and said,

> 'I've been thinking a lot about your situation since you told me what was going on yesterday.' I felt very happy to know that he was concerned about my welfare. No. That was not it at all. He then said, 'I don't think you are going to be able to do this. You have four children and a job. I don't think you can do it. I think you should ask yourself in what way you are at fault and contributing to the problem. Instead of looking at where the other person is wrong, perhaps look at what you are doing to cause the behaviour.'

The life sucked out of me, as if one of those Dementors from Harry Potter had just swooped upon me.

Mistake two: Mr Ex had kept calling me. On day six, I had my phone off because I was being X-rayed for my back. When I turned my phone back on and had so many messages from Mr Ex asking why I wasn't answering, I stupidly was honest and said my phone was off because I was having an X-ray done. A few hours later he appeared at the house. We had an agreement to separate for seven days and then discuss what the next step would be. It was day six. Mr Ex arrived unannounced and uninvited and I was shattered. I had decided we would separate and I was so much enjoying feeling free and alive. I asked why he was back when it was day six and that was not the agreement. His response: 'You said you were getting an X-ray done and I was so worried about you so I thought I should come back immediately to help you.' Did I mention those Dementors from Harry Potter? Well, they were back again. They sucked the joy and life right out of me once again. I was shattered and trapped once more.

So, when 20 September 2017 came around and I was trying once again to separate, the song 'Shattered' provided me with some sort of inner channel not to turn the car around. The lyrics were very powerful for me.

The beginning of the chorus is (Wattenberg & Roberge, 2008):

> How many times can I break 'til I shatter?
> Over the line can't define what I'm after
> I always turn the car around

This spoke volumes to me. I felt broken. I wondered how much longer I could go on before I was shattered and it was too late. I felt I had always turned the car around and allowed Mr Ex back into my life. I wanted so badly to 'make my own pattern'.

Other words in the song that were meaningful to me were 'but I'm good without you'. And so I told myself that I could do this. I was capable and could raise the children and re-finance and be free. The final lines of the song are:

> Don't wanna turn that car around
> I gotta turn this thing around

Over and over I told myself, quite literally, not to turn the car around. I needed to turn 'this thing' (i.e. my life) around. I couldn't do that if I turned the car around. I had to keep going … one day at a time.

Each day felt long. My friend, Brad Mitchell, said to me to just take each day at a time. Each day you move forward is a big achievement. Just focus on the day. Count each day. And before long, you will be counting weeks instead of days. He was right. But the first few days did feel like I was looking up at Mount Everest and had to climb to the top of it.

For anyone trying to imagine what someone is facing internally when they contemplate leaving a perpetrator of family violence, visualise Mount Everest. You are about to climb it. If you reach the top it will be amazing. But climbing Mount Everest is not simple and not everyone reaches the top. Not everyone returns. Mount Everest takes lives. The climb to the summit of escape from family violence carries risks. Life is on the line. So, for all those people who say 'Why didn't she just leave?', it is like saying, 'Why didn't she just climb Mount Everest?'

Each day, climbing Mount Everest is a challenge, just as each day of separation from family violence is a challenge. The early days were the hardest for me and I was frightened of turning the car around and letting Mr Ex back into my life.

On Friday (i.e. two days after separation) I received a text message from Mr Ex asking if I was working from home as he needed to talk to me. I *was* working from home, and I became alarmed that he asked me this. I felt he knew that I was home. I became overwhelmed. I felt sick. I felt dizzy. He said he wanted to talk. I reached out to a friend and said I was frightened he was going to turn up at the house and what should I do. She told me to tell him I was not ready to talk yet and then get the hell out of the house so I wasn't there if he did show up. And that is exactly what I did.

Those early days were challenging and frightening. Four days after separation, Mr Ex rang and spoke to each of the four children individually, asked each of them if they missed him and instructed them to get me to take him back. There were many of these efforts, either through the children or through me. He even rang my parents and asked my mother to get me to take him back and said he didn't understand what went wrong.

There were times that Mr Ex had access visits with the children. They were the worst times of all. The children became anxious and unsettled in the lead-up to those events as they didn't want to go. One of my youngest boys would complain of feeling nauseous. The behaviour of the children leading up to access visits was awful, and then, when they came back home, it was more awful. I was told that they were suffering from anxiety and therefore it was only when they returned home that they felt 'free' and able to reveal their emotions and that, while their behaviour was difficult for me, it meant they felt safe enough to release it.

The cycle was dreadfully difficult for me. The worst behaviour was from Sebastian, who was so angry with me. At one stage he just yelled at me, 'Why didn't you leave him earlier? Why did you make us put up with living with abuse for so long?' He was filled with anger and was a very difficult child to parent. He hated me for not leaving Mr Ex earlier. I hated myself for it as well. Did I want to leave earlier? Absolutely. However, looking back on my failed attempts to separate, and the risks of separating earlier, I think that, awful though it was, my result was improved by not leaving earlier. Younger children would likely have been made to spend time with the abusive parent. The Family Law Act in Australia and the comparable framework in other countries are in my view responsible for victims living with family violence longer than they want to and for the cycle of violence into next generations. I explain this later in the book so I will not do so here. But it is a delicate balance between staying and leaving, thanks to the broken system that claims to act in the best interests of the child.

During these early days, many difficulties arose. One was the children's behaviour. Another was that I developed a recurring dream where Mr Ex had managed to get into the house and stood over me, mocking me and saying, 'Did you really think you could prevent me from coming back?' I had this same dream over and over. I rang a family violence organisation to ask why I was being haunted by a dream when I had separated from Mr Ex. They explained to me that, when people live with family violence, the brain is holding on to emotions because it is unsafe to express them. My dreams were a sign of healing because the fear that had been held back over so many years was finally being released.

Those dreams were very traumatic for me but gradually, over the years, the interval between them widened. I did notice they re-emerged during the three different court battles I had with Mr Ex.

***

Back to those early days of separation. As my friend Brad had said to me – at first you will be counting each day and then those days become weeks. There was much to absorb. Emotionally I was dealing with four children who were going through a difficult time, I was dealing with my own emotions, including fear, and then there were the sheer pragmatic aspects that had to be resolved ... and fast.

I found myself constantly thinking about what Mr Ex's next moves might be, so that I could be one step ahead. One thing the children noticed when their father had cleared out his belongings for separation day, is that he also took with him two large jars filled with gold coins that were actually for the children. They were a bit sad that he took their money. This was also a red flag for me – he felt entitled enough to take anything, including money belonging to the children. I raced into action knowing that each child had around AU$4,000 in their bank accounts, which totalled more than AU$16,000. Part of my salary had been going into those accounts since they were born, and they had also each been gifted $1,000 each by their grandmother when they were born. Both Mr Ex and I were signatories to those accounts. I knew I had to move fast. I was fortunate enough to speak to a bank manager who knew what I was going through and went through the steps for me. I also had to deal with my shared bank account that my salary was going into and which Mr Ex had access to. But I had to think strategically. If I locked him out of the joint account that my salary was going into first, he might then focus on the children's accounts. I figured I needed to deal with the children's accounts first.

I went into the bank with the four children and their accounts were promptly closed down and then their money was moved across into new accounts. After this was done, I then dealt with my accounts – locking up everything and then contacting my employer to have my salary go into an individual account. It was only a matter of a day or perhaps two when Mr Ex asked me what happened to the children's accounts. I told him that they had new accounts now, where he no longer had authority. He was not at all happy about this and said he needed access. When I asked why he required access to their accounts, he said he would like to put money into those accounts. I told him I was very happy to provide the account numbers to allow such transfers for the children. Needless to say, this conversation did not come up again and not one cent has ever been transferred from him to any of those accounts.

Things became even nastier after that point. The utilities were in Mr Ex's name and this presented a point of immense vulnerability for me. I asked him numerous times to transfer ownership but he refused. It was very difficult for me to do this but, eventually, I was able to speak to the right people to find workarounds, which involved setting up new accounts for the property. Everything was a bit more difficult though.

I also tried to get Mr Ex to sign forms to unlink our Medicare card, but he refused to cooperate with that as well. I created my own with the children linked to mine. Sadly, I found out not long ago that he still had not only the children attached to his Medicare card but me also.

This had to be actioned from our end as well. Everything was just a little harder.

The first time that Mr Ex took the children for a visitation day, the children came home distraught. They said he was texting while driving, and playing mournful love songs, and said that he would need to find a 'rich widow' to marry. He was already thinking about what would be a fourth wife for him. The children also told me that on two occasions their father had said to his family (whom they visited in Geelong – about a one-hour drive away) that, when he received the settlement money from me, he was going to buy a gun. This unsettled the children as they were unsure what the gun was for.

In another of those early days, Mr Ex came to the house to pick up the children for an access day. He made a point of entering the house to track me down and abuse me because I had disconnected him from my private health fund. Of note, I had had that private health fund for decades – it pre-dated my marriage. I had added him to my account. It was my account and the payments came from me. He abused me for disconnecting him, yet I was paying the bills for it and it was in my name. When I explained that he was not one of my dependents and I was no longer responsible for his costs so there was no reason to retain him on the account, he became enraged. He said that I was responsible for maintaining him and that his lawyer had said that he should claim spousal maintenance from me. My daughter ended up diffusing the situation by saying they should go now. She told me later that she thought he was going to hit me, which is why she suggested they just go.

I suspect that Mr Ex had already been fuelled with anger because I had sent him a message previously to advise him that only three of the children would be participating in that particular access day. In the days leading up to the event, Sebastian, who was 11 years and 8 months, told me he didn't want to go because he always felt so sick on those access visits. I had contacted an organisation to seek advice about this and I was told that he was suffering from anxiety and not to make him go. I was also told that since he was almost 12 years of age, he was able to make an informed decision about these types of matters.

Mr Ex had tried very hard to make Sebastian go when he was at the house to pick up the others. Mr Ex directly asked Sebastian, 'Why don't you want to see me?' to which Sebastian very calmly said, 'I didn't say that; I just said I didn't want to go.' The conversation repeated several times and everyone could feel the tension. Jonathan sidled up beside me and asked me if I thought it was safe for him to go. It was unsettling to see Mr Ex drive away with three of the children. As always, I was unsettled until they were returned.

Various attempts to have me take him back continued. He tried to arrange opportunities to talk about things concerning the settlement, but what he proposed was a one-on-one discussion rather than through an external mediation avenue. I declined any such offers. He sent text messages and he sent emails. He told me it was my fault because I needed to realise that it was my job that was creating the stress that resulted in me being cold towards him and, because I had no passion for him, it resulted in him behaving as he did. He probably actually believed that. Amazingly, a person can be abusive and expect it to result in passion.

More than two months after separation, on Wednesday 29 November 2017 at 3:08 pm, Mr Ex sent me a long email saying that separation was a 'huge mistake' and that it wasn't too late to take him back. He continued to blame me for the reasons for separation.

The next day, Thursday 30 November 2017 at 11:15 am, Mr Ex turned up unexpectedly. I was working from home and was at the computer in the room at the front of the house and I saw through the window his car pull up. I immediately got up from my desk and ran around the corner and hid. I heard him knock on the door. I ignored the knock and stayed hidden from sight. He knocked again and I remained hidden. I sent text messages to two friends and one advised me to contact a family violence organisation. I did that, and they advised me to seek an Intervention Order against him. They also advised me to set up a second mobile phone that was dedicated to communication with the children's father and then to block him from my main number.

A few days after that, on Monday 4 December 2017, Mr Ex rang my parents (this was the second time he had done that) and spoke to my mother. He asked her if there was any chance I might take him back. She told him there was no hope of that.

The next day, Tuesday 5 December 2017, I was in the Magistrates' Court, relating to the matter of requesting an Intervention Order. An interim Intervention Order was granted that day, which protected me, the four children and my parents. It was interim, which means it was temporarily in place, but a hearing would be scheduled for Mr Ex to have the opportunity to respond to determine whether it should continue and, if so, for how long.

Shortly afterwards, on Thursday 7 December, I set up a second mobile phone number and sent a message to Mr Ex to advise him of the new number. I then blocked him from my main number. I cannot explain how empowering and liberating that one simple action was. I could check the other phone when I felt ready to, and I wasn't constantly afraid of what text message had just come through. I cannot emphasise enough how powerful this was. This was truly a defining point for me and I highly recommend anyone going through what I went through to do this. It is well worth the expense. It gave me so much strength and freedom. This is very beneficial. If you are reading this and you know someone going through what I went through, then please help them get a second phone. There are cheap basic phones and it only needs to be a basic credit system rather than a plan. Do not underestimate the power this small action will have.

The interim Intervention Order was served on Friday 8 December 2017. I felt safer knowing it was in place. However, there were numerous times when he tested this. Sometimes, perpetrators of family violence will push the boundaries of these orders. Accepting some things that seem trivial can then lead to further breaches. I was advised to report it no matter how minor the breach was. There were various minor breaches, but some were circumstantial, although unsettling. One example was that early one morning when I went to go for my morning run, I noticed a pair of my daughter's worn-out school socks in the letterbox. They had been dropped off during the night. There would be nobody else other than Mr Ex who would have done that, but I had no proof. In addition, a few days later, my daughter received a message from the eldest child from Mr Ex's first marriage (who lived thousands of kilometres away) to say, 'bet your (sic) missing the house lights … they were beautiful'. The only way she would know that we had not put any outside Christmas lights up is if her father had been there at night time (breaching the interim Intervention Order) and told her. On the balance of probabilities, I would say that Mr Ex was there, breaching the order, putting a pair of worn-out school socks in the letterbox probably to make a point that he was there.

I reported every single breach, no matter how small or how circumstantial. I wanted to send a message that the line would not be crossed. Two weeks later, Mr Ex moved interstate, which resulted in there being no requests for access. Communication stopped at that point.

Journey One: Seeking an Intervention Order

As mentioned above, I sought an Intervention Order, which was initially granted as an interim order. I then returned to the Magistrates' Court a few weeks later for a hearing to determine whether that order should be granted and, if so, for how long.

Mr Ex, as the respondent, recruited a legal firm to represent him. As such, he was not in court but was represented by his lawyer. I chose to represent myself. I did this because, concurrently, I was also involved in a legal matter relating to the financial and parenting arrangements for the children, which was increasingly drawn out and looking unlikely to be resolved soon. I was 100% financially responsible for the four children and knew I would be needing to re-finance and possibly have to sell the house. I did not have money to spend on lawyers, which can become a bottomless pit.

I had been advised that, if I did not have legal representation, a person would be allocated to me on the day. However, it seemed that every community law firm within and outside the region had been contacted by Mr Ex meaning they could not help me.

To explain this, if someone has an appointment with a law firm, it means that the other party cannot be represented by that same law firm, even if the person does not choose to be represented by them. It is a tactic to be aware of. Some people (not just perpetrators of family violence) will make appointments with as many firms as possible. In some cases, they visit every firm in the area. This can result in the other party not having access to legal representation because the other party has spoken to every firm in town.

In my situation, no community lawyer could assist me – they were all unavailable based on a 'conflict of interest'. I had not been prepared for that one. However, a person from a family violence organisation sat with me so that I was not alone.

The lawyer for Mr Ex requested 'further and better particulars'. This was granted and timelines were set out. I walked out in a daze. I had no idea what 'further and better particulars' were. When I asked at the court reception I was told to ask my lawyer. I was feeling overwhelmed. The only way to get the Intervention Order was to get 'further and better particulars' and I didn't know what that was and it seemed to mean I needed a lawyer. It was starting to sound expensive. The person from the family violence organisation told me this was a common tactic because it means the person has to come back to court yet again, take another day off work, arrange childcare, and spend money on a lawyer. The only way to escape this horror is to drop the application, which is precisely the outcome desired by the other party.

I felt like those Harry Potter Dementors had just come back and paid me another visit. I went home feeling awful and then started to google 'further and better particulars'. Despite the confusing terminology, I realised it was essentially, just a report. I felt buoyed by this realisation. I knew how to write a report … this would not be impossible after all.

And so, knowing that this had been a tactic intended to make me drop the application, I thought to myself: 'You want further and better particulars … I'll give you further and better particulars.' And so I started pulling together all my evidence, all my key points, and who could be called in as a witness to verify my allegation. The document ended up being more than 40 pages in length. As a final coup, I decided to have the document thermal bound. I thought that might be a nice touch, whereby it would be just a little bit of a nuisance for the legal team to have to pull it apart and copy it all so that they could send their client a copy. I figured it was about time I sent one of those Harry Potter Dementors to visit someone else.

In this book, I do explain the mechanics of this process more, to assist the reader. In terms of my story, I will say that I felt a little bit more comfortable when I had to go back to court again, this time on

27 February 2018. The sheer size of the document, with a total of 23 allegations against Mr Ex, made a bit of a statement. It also had appendices complete with screenshots, photos, a police report, and case IDs. I was quite proud of that document, and I must say that they did me a favour by asking for further and better particulars. The exercise I went through to pull all the evidence together was helpful on other occasions. Even in writing this book, I have referred back to it for dates and accurate quotes.

On that day, the Intervention Order was granted. I remember the magistrate asking me how long I would like the order for. I did not know and simply said 'One year' because that had been the duration of the Intervention Order that the police had issued back in 2013. The magistrate said to me that the offences in the history (i.e. punching me in the head) were very serious and one year was not very long. I asked how long Intervention Orders could be in terms of range, and she said they can be infinite. So, I said I would like one of those, then. She said to me, 'How about we make it five years. By that time, the youngest of your children will be almost 18 and then you will never have to have anything to do with him [Mr Ex] ever again.' The thought of never having to have anything to do with Mr Ex ever again gave me a feeling of inner peace. That sounded very good indeed.

The magistrate was clearly aware of the 'type' that Mr Ex was and she ensured the orders included very plain and clear statements about what he could not do and what type of messaging was allowed. I remember her saying, 'Since Mr Ex is not present to hear this, I will make this very clear for him so that there is no misunderstanding.' This became a very important document for me in so many ways. I have been told numerous times by police, family violence workers and school staff, that they don't need to be told anything about my life except that I have a 5-year Intervention Order against my ex-husband to know what I went through. I have been told numerous times that it is uncommon to see one for so long. I attribute this in part to how bad things were but also to my evidence. Someone could have the same experiences but no evidence. This is a really important tip for people, which I outline in this book. Evidence, evidence, evidence. That evidence may even take the form of telling people – friends/family or a therapist.

Journey Two: Financial and Parenting Agreements

While the above matters were going on (i.e. working out separation and applying for an Intervention Order), I was concurrently trying to reach an agreement with Mr Ex for the financial and parenting orders. An early step in that process is to have mediation and, to begin with, each person meets separately with the mediators. Mr Ex had met with them first and I had then been contacted to meet with them. Two women were present – one was the interviewer and there was a second observer person. I remember being asked:

'What emotions did you first feel when you separated? Some people feel confused, some people feel angry, and there are all sorts of emotions. How did you feel?'

My answer was one that clearly surprised them, based on their shocked faces. I said:

'I felt like a dark cloud had left the house.'

I think they knew at that moment that I had escaped family violence. After I answered some additional questions, they granted an exemption from mediation certificate, recognising that mediation was unsuitable given the power imbalance present when there has been family violence.

I was in a rush to finalise financial and parenting agreements. I wasn't thinking clearly in those early months. In my blur I thought that ticking this off would get rid of a major connection between me and Mr Ex and help me feel free. The amount of money I initially offered him was ridiculous (50%) and went against legal advice. I wasn't thinking and I know that now. However, what I was thinking is that I had demanded sole parental responsibilities. This is very important and the mechanics and importance of this are discussed in this book. Importantly, the only reason I knew to seek sole parental responsibilities was that I read the Family Law Act. I was spending my evenings reading case law and the Family Law Act, trying to figure out a pathway to freedom. I remember when I told my lawyer that I wanted sole parental responsibilities she told me that nobody gets that. I remember saying that maybe nobody gets it because nobody asks for it, and if they do, they are told that nobody gets that. Maybe nobody is told there is a clause in the Family Law Act where you can rebut the default position of equal shared parental responsibilities.

I made it clear: I would negotiate on money but I would not negotiate on this point. One thing I knew inside myself was that I would never really be free from Mr Ex without this. I would need his permission to relocate, to travel anywhere with the children, to change schools for the children, for any health issues. I would constantly be connected to a person who had demonstrated he did not act in the best interests of the children. He was controlling and abusive and to give him that sort of power was nothing short of irresponsible. I did not want to ask his permission every time I wanted to go on a holiday out of town. I wasn't budging. I knew what was ahead for me and the children if I didn't stand firm on this point.

I also asked for an agreement that, should I need to relocate for work purposes, there would be no objection. Looking back, I am unsure why I asked for that because if someone has sole parental responsibilities, they are not required to seek permission from the other parent to relocate. This is one of the tourism traps I discuss in this book.

The amount of money I offered was rejected: the amount he wanted was 60%. This was despite me having all the costs of raising four children. Not only was it preposterous – it was unaffordable. He also did not agree to granting me sole parental responsibilities or allowing me to relocate if I needed to for work purposes. We were nowhere. The months rolled by, the tactics got dirtier, and letters from the other side were nasty. I had reduced my costs by drafting letters that at times included case law. The threat of going to court was made often by the other side. One of the swords I ended up wielding was the 'Kennon agreement' – a case (*Kennon and Kennon* [1997] FamCA 27) I found very relevant. I said to my lawyer that this case was to be mentioned in the letter to the other side. I said that we would be using the Kennon agreement – which comes from a key case where the wife ended up receiving a booster allocation of the settlement funds because her marriage was made more difficult by enduring family violence. I remember my lawyer telling me that the other lawyer would already be aware of that case. I said, 'That's good. Now let's remind her of it.'

By this stage, we were heading towards one year of fighting over financial and parenting matters. The emotion for me was reduced and the early erratic offer demonstrating poor thinking was gone. Delays served me well because I was able to think more objectively and treat the case more like a negotiation rather than a desperate act of fear and escape. I was like a broken record. I was not budging. As time went by it became almost a nuisance rather than anything else. I remember making an offer (much lower than my original) and then finding out that Mr Ex had lied about not having a job, so I dropped my offer by AU$10,000. My lawyer thought I was completely mad.

It was almost 12 months to the day after separation when the financial and parenting orders were made. Painfully, I had to give him money, but far less than I was originally going to. But the most important thing of all: I became one of the very few people who had been awarded sole parental responsibilities.

My tips from this are:

(1) Don't rush to settle. Victims of family violence are in a highly emotional state of fear and cannot make sound decisions. They could agree to things they shouldn't. I almost did. No matter how smart and rational a person is, separating from a traumatic living arrangement takes years, not days, to recover from. Quick early decisions may be poor decisions that affect the rest of your life and that of your children.

(2)   There is a clause in the Family Law Act to rebut the default position of equal shared parental responsibilities. Chapter 9 in this book outlines why this matters. You will never be able to travel without permission from the perpetrator of violence against you if you do not have sole parental responsibilities. This is a tourism trap.

Journey Three: Changing the Children's Surname

Changing a child's surname is discussed in Chapter 9. In this Overture, I will present my journey, which sits alongside the discussion in Chapter 9 to provide a fuller context for the reader wanting to capture my lived experiences as well as the more technical discussion.

This journey was my most challenging. As mentioned earlier, the children had been affected by long-term exposure to family violence – most especially my daughter. While her sleep issue was resolved after separation, other problems remained. She was still suffering from flashbacks of traumatic episodes. Counselling was unsuccessful because she didn't want to talk about it. We tried art therapy. She was struggling internally. She told me she wanted to change her surname because she had flashbacks whenever she wrote her birth surname. She was refusing to use her birth surname at school, including on test papers. The school staff were very good about it and even changed her surname informally to assist her. I sent Chantelle to a child psychologist, hoping they could assist her with making peace with her birth surname so that she might view it differently. Instead, the psychologist told me that I should change her surname, as it might empower her and reduce her flashbacks.

And so the project began as to how to go about changing a child's surname. The three boys asked to change their surnames while I was at it, and my eldest son also wanted to change his middle name (because it was his father's first name). I started to make some enquiries about how to change a child's surname, only to find out that this was very niche. I was unable to locate a local lawyer who had experience in that field. I figured I didn't want to pay a lawyer to learn, so I would learn instead. That proved to be a wise choice. The matter ended up being complicated due to appeals from Mr Ex and multiple hearings and would have become very costly. I also do not think that I would have obtained the outcome I did if I had not run the case myself. Only I knew my life, and once I familiarised myself with the processes, it meant I could figure out what to do when it seemed it had all gone pear shaped.

The project began during the Christmas period of 2019. I took six weeks off work to map out how to do this project. While processes within a state are reasonably straightforward, my situation was complicated by the fact that the four children were born in two different states, neither of those states being the state we resided in. When I examined the legislation for the state process (Victorian County

Court), I could not see how it could have the legislative authority to order changes within other states (Births, Deaths and Marriages are state legislation).

It seemed there were two ways: one would be to go to each state court and process the relevant children for each state body. The other would be to try at a commonwealth level and try the Family Law Court. However, name changes are not included in what the Family Law Act does. And Births, Deaths & Marriages are not a party to the proceedings and so really can't be ordered to do anything.

I looked for case law, examined the legislation for the relevant state bodies and re-read the Family Law Act. I made an application to the Family Law Court, ex parte (meaning, without the other party). Family law involves two parties – someone as the applicant and someone as the respondent. In my case, I had sole parental responsibilities and, according to the Family Law Act, parental responsibility means the responsibilities that parents have for major long-term issues for the child. This includes a child's name. Given I had sole parental responsibilities, I was applying to do something within my set of responsibilities.

I spoke regularly to a good friend of mine, David Brennan (who is a lawyer), about this. He was less optimistic than I was. He could see where I was coming from but also felt that conservative judges wouldn't want to do anything new and might prefer the father to have an opportunity to comment. Mr Ex had no parental responsibilities, and name change comes under parental responsibilities, so this surely was clear? David told me he shared this conundrum with his magistrate friends at the local dog park in Melbourne. He said they were quite intrigued and considered it could go either way. They saw it as a 'grey' area. I didn't. But they were right.

When the hearing came up, David sat beside me. We waited for my turn and watched the long, sad faces of so many before us. One woman looked worn out and trundled in with a suitcase. She had clearly come straight from the airport. She looked like one of those Dementors had visited her.

When my turn came, I could see that the judge was uncertain. This was a case that she had not come across before. There was no other party. There was no case law. She said she thought the father should have an opportunity to comment. I didn't even know where he was. He had moved interstate two weeks after the interim Intervention Order and we were not sure where he lived. I was told to make every attempt possible to locate him so that he could be served papers and invited to comment. The Dementors were surrounding me.

Not only did the Dementors return but so did my recurring nightmare. I was devastated. I started to try to locate Mr Ex. He had a mother who was in a nursing home about an hour's drive away so I googled her name, which is when I learned that she had died. She had died during the time that Mr Ex and I were negotiating parental and financial arrangements. The grandmother of the children had died and we were not informed. Keeping that sort of information away is a whole-of-family affair. They were all in on that one.

There was only one explanation for why we were not told, and why the children were not given the opportunity to go to the funeral of their grandmother: we had not finalised the financial agreement and, technically, the inheritance would have had to be disclosed on his assets. He went underground to avoid disclosing his finances.

I ended up being able to make contact with Mr Ex and I asked him for his residential address to send him legal documents. He sent me a false address: he sent me the address of his eldest daughter from his first marriage. He was still playing possum.

By this time, Covid-19 had hit and the courts were largely closed down. Priority cases such as family violence were being run via Teams video conferencing or telephone conferencing. I had served the documents to Mr Ex. Based on the timelines in family law, responses are required from the respondent at least seven days prior to the hearing. A few hours before the hearing, Mr Ex bombed my email with a copy of the response papers. Since they were well outside of the court deadlines, I didn't take too much notice of them but thought that possibly he or his lawyer may dial in for the hearing, which was held via teleconference.

Mr Ex did not dial in for the hearing and neither did his lawyer. The hearing took place on the basis of him not being represented, and orders were made based on the papers. The wording of the orders was as I had requested. It had taken me a while to map out the wording, As mentioned above, Births, Deaths and Marriages cannot be ordered to change a name as they are not part of the proceedings. I had a series of orders, which also included that the children 'be known as' their new names as a backup strategy.

My case, as with other cases selected for publication, is published under pseudonyms. The Family Law Act Section 121 does not allow for publication of descriptive factors such as home addresses, work addresses, occupation, religious affiliation or real estate owned. Once the orders were made, I filled in the paperwork to have the children's names changed. The processes were slightly different for each state.

Twelve days after the hearing, I received a letter from Mr Ex's lawyer asking me to consent to set aside the orders made. The letter said that if I did not consent that proceedings would commence without further notice. By that time, I already had two of the new birth certificates in my possession and the other two were being processed. I ignored the letter.

Sometime later, I was served papers advising of an application in a Family Law Court in a different state to the hearing for my case. I was amazed that Mr Ex's lawyers thought that they should commence a new application in a completely different court when what they were wanting to do was appeal, which needed to be through the same court.

I was confident they were wrong so I ignored it. Some weeks later I was served again, with a note that the other papers were not correct. This time they were notifying me of a hearing with the same judge and at the same court as the orders had been made. They were appealing the orders made.

It all seemed rather pathetic to me. A father who had not notified his children that their grandmother had died, who had not been in contact, who had not sent any messages of Happy Birthday or Merry Christmas, and who provided no emotional support, wanted to challenge a name change. Worse, he had submitted papers well and truly outside the clear deadlines in the court. I was amazed that they were entertaining this.

The hearing came three-and-a-half months later. The hearing was held virtually, using 'Teams' software with webcams. I might add that the prospect of having to stare directly into the face of the man who was abusive to me and the children was very distressing. He, however, was in his element. These people are very fine storytellers and I have often thought of them as con men. They are very convincing. He looked destitute as he explained tearfully how much his children meant to him but I had torn his world apart. Tearfully he said, 'I just want to talk to my children.'

Earlier in this Overture, I mention the movie *The Shawshank Redemption*. In that film, the main character, Andy Dufresne, is regarded in court as guilty of murder – despite his claims of innocence – because he was seen as being so cold. He lacked emotion and so appeared to be a coldhearted killer.

In court, I was Andy. While Mr Ex was there with his tears and looked forlorn, I was poker-faced. From the outside, if you don't understand what family violence does to a person, I might have appeared cold and distant. This is a by-product of being a victim of family violence. The only way for me to survive was to be numb. Like Andy Dufresne, I was regarded as guilty because I wasn't showing any emotion.

The judge was very sympathetic to Mr Ex and told him that a 5-year Intervention Order was a very long one indeed, and told him he could apply to have that taken away and explained how. I felt horror, although my face remained like Andy Dufresne's. The judge then created an order for him to ring the children each week and she said that this order trumped the previous one. I couldn't believe what was happening. This hearing was appealing a name change application made on behalf of the children. Suddenly the perpetrator was being told how to undo all the previous work, by a judge who hadn't been privy to all the evidence. She was relying on this con man in front of her. She also ordered another hearing four weeks later to ensure I had been complying with the order to facilitate weekly phone calls at the convenience of the perpetrator.

The order about Mr Ex being able to ring the children each week, and me having to provide him with suitable times and days, was ambiguous in that having a weekly call with the four children could be interpreted as a call with all four children or four one-on-one calls.

This order was also under a heading of 'Consent Orders'. I had not consented to that at all. It was not linked to the original orders. It was extraordinary. When people talk about some of the horrific things that happen in family law courts, they often sound exaggerated and untrue. I have seen it and lived it. It absolutely happens.

Since children are not allowed in court, the children had submitted affidavits to explain in their own words why they wanted their surname changed. This was actually their project. Their case. I was merely the messenger for them because I was their parent and they were under 18. Their affidavits spoke of the family violence they had endured, but Mr Ex successfully requested that their affidavits (their only voice in court for their very own name) be struck out.

The nature of research is that researchers tend to remain within their own discipline. Law is law. Law research tends to be doctrinal analysis – i.e. reading cases and legislation. Legal research is not focused on the practical application of the law. The reading of law cases does not reveal the underbelly. This underbelly is out of sight. Nobody will read about my case despite it being printed in AustLII. The published case stops after the first hearing where the orders are granted. The appeal, based on a nonsense claim of procedural irregularity because non-filed response papers (lodged a few business hours before the hearing) were not considered, is not included in the published case. The case in its printed version stops where it should have stopped in its living version.

I had to share the news of the forced weekly phone communication with the children. They were horrified. They did not understand how they could be made to speak to someone when they didn't want to and that, if they didn't, I could be in breach of the court orders. It was putting me in a difficult position. It is hard enough to get a teenager to clean a bedroom. This was highly unreasonable.

My daughter said, 'I wanted to change my name to unhook me from my past and now I have been reconnected to it.' A few days later she said, 'I feel like I will never be free.' She spiralled down and was a mess. She was in tears. She refused to eat. Shortly after, Chantelle overdosed on a cocktail of painkillers and ended up in hospital. To this day, I hold the judicial system entirely responsible for that happening.

The phone call

As the children were opposed to the phone call but knew I could be held in contempt of court if they did not comply, we were faced with a difficult situation. They made it absolutely clear that they would not speak to him. In trying to find a solution, I proposed that all four children be present for the phone call but that James, as the eldest child and at 17 years of age, be responsible for the 'purple phone' (the phone dedicated to communication with Mr Ex) and be the spokesperson for the children. As all four children would be present, they could decide what they wanted to do during the call.

The phone was on speakerphone so that all children were involved. Unknown to me at the time, my daughter recorded the entire call. While writing this book, I asked my daughter if she still had that recording and I listened to it and transcribed some parts of it. The call lasted 42 minutes. At no stage did Mr Ex ask anything about school, health, interests or activities. His entire focus was on denigrating me and trying to create a false truth.

James kept telling Mr Ex that nobody wanted to talk to him because he had been abusive and they had no desire to have any communication with him. Mr Ex said to James on so many occasions: 'You've been brainwashed', 'I never treated you poorly', 'Your mother has put all this in your heads', 'There is only one person that you were under the control of and so was I', 'I never choked you children. I grabbed you from the back of your necks', 'Your mother has brainwashed you beautifully', 'You've been brainwashed into believing that a smack on the bum is abuse', 'She's had two-and-a-half years to brainwash you and she's done a bloody good job', 'you're making up stuff that doesn't exist', 'you're remembering something that doesn't exist.'

This is a form of gaslighting, which is discussed in Chapter 11. Perpetrators of family violence will often use this tactic to gain more control and power. Confusion weakens people and so the perpetrators tell blatant lies and tell you that you are imagining things. In the 1944 film, *Gaslight*, a young woman is manipulated by her husband into believing that she is starting to become insane. It is important to keep in mind the ages of the children, who were aged between 14 and 17 at the time of the phone call and who at separation were aged almost 12, 13 and almost 15. This is important in terms of memories and their ability to make judgements.

Listening to that call, which at the time of writing was almost two years ago, I am amazed at how well James handled the call and how he remained calm but firm. As many times as Mr Ex said that James had been brainwashed and was remembering things that hadn't happened, James would repeat that he recalled the abuse, the yelling, the hitting, the belt-whipping and choking. James said, 'It would be best if you just left us alone, to be honest.' Mr Ex wasn't pleased and threatened with, 'I'll let the courts decide on the 28th if you don't want to talk to me.'

The day I had asked Chantelle if she still had the phone recording and she sent it to me (24 March 2022), she listened to it herself. She sent me a poem she wrote after she listened to the recording. She has permitted me to include it in this book.

You said it was nice to hear our voices,
It was awful to hear yours.
I had forgotten what you sounded like,
But now I remembered.

I remembered you screaming every day,
Your voice echoes throughout my brain.
All the terrible things you would say.
Hearing you cry you love us all so much,
While memories of you yelling you hate us flood my mind.

And in these thoughts, I am drowning,
Close my eyes so that I can be blind
Which version of you do I trust and believe?
Be blind to your lies, you try and deceive

At deception, you were the game-master,
It's hard not to fall for your crocodile tears.
But to be so foolish always ends in disaster,
The false hope of your lies, so many fears.

I hope for you to change,
And I cling to that hope.
Hope is all I have when you left me to drown,
Falling deep beneath the murky waters.

My chest feels so heavy,
Trying to breathe feels so strange.
But my chest doesn't feel as heavy
as the weight you left me with.

Oh, the strength I have gained,
from carrying you with me all these years.
Carrying your lies, carrying the silence.
I'm done carrying your burdens.
Done carrying your violence.

I include a summary of the court-ordered phone call to highlight the problem created by the Family Law Court. Giving a perpetrator of family violence that sort of control and power over victims of their abuse is scandalous and shocking. We were victims of Mr Ex's abuse and we were victims all over again because of the Family Law Court, which was focused on the perpetrator's best interests and not the children's. All the reports and journal articles about family violence build up each year, and the cases continue. The reports and journal articles ignore where the underbelly is ... it is in the darkness of the courts and behind closed doors. People are not allowed to talk about what happens, but this educational book for academe is one of the few exceptions to the restrictions. While there are some judges who have been trained in family violence and who understand it, there are still too many who don't understand it. With the discretionary nature of the Family Law Courts, the outcome is a lucky dip.

I said earlier that undertaking this law case myself was my saviour. Because I knew my life and I also needed to learn processes, I had an idea. There was a scheduled follow-up hearing in four weeks' time to check up on my behaviour, that I had ensured Mr Ex was able to communicate weekly with the children. This was appalling but it was also my lifeline. I mapped out my strategy.

I contacted two family violence organisations that had worked with the children over the past two years, and I also contacted a counsellor. They all submitted letters to the court that essentially said the same thing: any future contact with Mr Ex would not be in the best interests of the children and may increase the likelihood of trauma regression in all four children.

In my affidavit, I requested that the order relating to forced phone contact be struck out. I submitted more than 60 pages, including the police report of when Mr Ex hit me in the head and a close-up photo of my swollen black eye. I force fed the old evidence to the judge. The hearing lasted a couple of minutes. The judge asked Mr Ex if he had read my responses. He said, 'I couldn't be bothered. She ignores orders and I have wasted thousands of dollars with nothing to show for it.' At that moment the judge got to see the real Mr Ex.

The order was struck out, and the previous orders (that by then were already fully realised by way of full name changes in all forms of ID and birth certificates) were unchallenged. The whole process was distressing for the children and disgraceful. I was already a victim and was then treated poorly by the courts. Not a trace of this can be found in the AustLII case. What is printed is an illusion that does not reveal the true underbelly.

For an example of this, I recommend reading (or watching) *Into the Wild* (Krakauer, 1996). It is a true story (with the abuse removed). Then read *The Wild Truth* (McCandless, 2014). The abusive father refutes the contents of *The Wild Truth*. They always do. Read both and be a judge of the truth. It is a good example of how the truth is covered up.

Concluding Thoughts

Family violence is a field that is studied from many disciplinary perspectives. People often focus on the behaviour of the perpetrator and how to work with them to improve their behaviour. People also focus heavily on the counselling and support side for victims. There is an incredible focus on supporting the victim to leave the perpetrator. If the victim does leave the perpetrator they are referred to as 'survivors' or 'victim–survivors'. For me, this term misunderstands family violence. I left an abusive and controlling man and do not consider myself a survivor, yet I came out of this so much better than most others because I have sole parental responsibilities and so don't need his permission to relocate or take the children out of town on a holiday. At the time of writing this, I had separated five years before. The children and I have not seen him for almost that same period. The courts awarded me sole parental responsibilities (very rare to get). There is a 5-year Intervention Order against Mr Ex. This situation is probably as close to separation utopia as it gets, but I still wouldn't brand it 'victim–survivor'. I spent 17 years in an abusive and controlling marriage and spent much of the following 3 years in three separate court matters. So, for essentially two decades – what constitutes two-thirds of my adult life – I was either trapped in a hopeless marriage or dealing with a hopeless court system. I don't believe it is possible to go through what the children and I went through and pop out the other side all shiny and new as if nothing happened. These experiences stay for ever. My daughter remains traumatised with flashbacks from particularly unsettling moments, although far less often since the surname change. The concept of 'victim–survivor' is discussed in Chapter 1.

Despite all that I have just said, I do not regret my choices. I married a man who was a perpetrator of family violence. There were moments of terror, and they grew in intensity each year. However, like many perpetrators, he was not constantly bad. Most importantly, I have four children who I am grateful for. Had I not married the man I married, those children would never have been born. So, it is not possible to have regrets knowing what beauty came from the hardship.

Do I regret not leaving sooner? No. Because had I left sooner, the outcome may have been worse. The children would have been younger and would not have had a voice to say they did not want to spend time with their father. I don't know what that would have looked like for them. A longer period of growing up and being exposed to family violence had its costs. But they also may have been exposed to more of it if forced by the courts to spend time with him. It is hard to know.

I often think of the movie *Sliding Doors*, where a woman's pathway in life is determined by whether she caught a train or not. The movie shows in parallel both pathways, based on which event happened. And similarly, at times, I do wonder what that alternative pathway may have been. Maybe it was better for the children and me. Maybe it was worse. What I do know is that, relatively speaking, given the atrocious discretionary disaster that the Family Law Courts are, I came out the other side better than most – and that troubles me. So while I don't know what the alternative pathway might have been, I know that it could have been a lot worse.

A few risk factors relating to separating when children are younger are:

- They have less personal power to make choices about spending time with the perpetrator.
- They are not allowed to be left home alone when under 12 years of age, which can make it difficult to retain employment.
- Younger children are more at risk if they are spending time with the perpetrator. This risk is both physical and psychological.
- Younger children can be at risk of siding with the abuser, as they may be too young to see through the abuser.
- Courts may be more likely to allocate more time to a perpetrator when the children are younger.

On balance, when these things are considered, I have no regrets. I could not have stayed any longer. I was dying inside in so many ways, and the environment was starting to impact the behaviour of the boys towards their sister. I also genuinely remain unsure whether my daughter Chantelle would be alive to this day if I had left it any longer. Shortly after separation, she handed me a note from the psychologist. The warning of Chantelle being suicidal due to it representing for her the only way she was in control of freeing herself from family violence, was there in black and white.

Shortly after separation, Chantelle started sleeping again. I acknowledge that was a very clear indicator for me not to turn that car around. However, we all still live with many scars. Internal scars as well as physical ones. I also believe that the journey the children and I have been on, as unfair and sad as it has been, has so much good to it. We have an acute understanding of difficult situations. We do not judge others, because we know that some people have had pain in their past that may make things difficult for them. We know what can happen behind closed doors and the children and I can all use that experience for making the world a bit better. The children may be better in their jobs because they make better judgements due to their experiences.

I have always said to the children to remember two things: accept and be thankful. There is no value in being resentful. As Malachy McCourt said: 'resentment is like taking poison and waiting for the other person to die' (Witchel, 1998). There is no point in looking backwards and wishing for a different life. It is as it was. And whatever shortcomings can be felt and observed, there will always be things to be thankful for in their lives. If they focus on those two things, then the pain of the past has less power. And pain can be used to guide us to a better place.

I hope this book, and the knowledge and experiences I encountered, provide some benefit to others as they try to find a pathway to some type of freedom from abuse. Perhaps in time, when courts are considering whether perpetrators of abuse should be empowered to make decisions for their children and act in their best interests, those courts will be concerned with the best interests of the children, and not the best interests of the perpetrator.

1 Introduction

'I am not what happened to me, I am what I choose to become.'

– attributed to Carl Jung

Introduction

Family violence does not take a holiday. Nor does bullying, control or abuse. This book discusses these problems using a whole tourism system model. Tourism is more than a person's holiday experience. The person who works for a business that serves tourists is also in the tourism system. Therefore, the impacts on the employee working for a café that might serve tourists, the medical practitioner who serves a tourist, the airline pilot transporting tourists, the tourists themselves, are all part of the tourism system. This book discusses these aspects through the whole tourism system.

This book is an educative book but is not overly weighed down by heavy statistics and excessive references. It uses autoethnography as its method and there is storytelling to bring real stories to life. A single story that resonates with a reader can be more powerful than a statistic showing how often something happens to someone. The emotion from that 'someone' can sometimes be a better way to explain things.

Although this book is set out in chapters and there is a structure to those chapters, by no means does the reader need to read every chapter, nor do they need to read them sequentially. Reading the book sequentially is ideal because some of the key concepts are discussed at the front end of this book. However, this book is designed to benefit a wider readership and therefore a single chapter or two from later in this book may be read in isolation to serve the needs of some readers. Although at its heart, this book is of a technical nature designed to spotlight issues that require further understanding by professionals and for raising awareness and through that, aim for improved outcomes and better processes.

This book is about the underbelly of tourism. It discusses control, abuse, bullying and family violence in tourism industries. The early chapters set the foundation for understanding tourism. They establish what is meant by tourism industries, the legislative framework that impacts many industries relevant to tourism, as well as explaining tourism systems, which is the framework for this book. These earlier chapters deal with frameworks, systems, theories, and employment law. Later chapters focus heavily on family violence. Some of what is discussed are thoughts and opinions and things that happen. These issues are much more personal and traumatic. Each case is different. Each case can be traumatic. Every case is important. As such, there is storytelling alongside some objective discussion. Chapters can be read out of order and in isolation.

Control, Abuse, Bullying and Family Violence

Tourism cannot occur without a number of elements. If there are no businesses that serve tourists, no destinations, no transit routes, no tourists, then there is no tourism. Imagine a remote island but there is no way to access it and no businesses located on that island nor any food sources. If nobody can reach that island, then tourism cannot occur on that island. So, while a determined individual could arrange their own private transportation and bring their own food, water and tent and stay on that island, that does not make it a tourist destination. In the absence of the infrastructure – the industries to support the needs of tourists – and a transit route, the remote island is not a tourist destination. It is not part of the tourism system. In other words, tourism requires more elements than just a place to go and a person who wants to go there. To understand tourism we need to understand it through all its elements.

This book outlines the impacts of control, abuse, bullying and family violence on the elements of the tourism system. In other words, it is about more than the abuse of violence when on a holiday. It is also about the bullying in businesses that serve tourists. A workplace filled with bullying will affect employees who serve tourists. It is all part of the system. To understand control, abuse, bullying and family violence in tourism industries, we need to discuss these matters through the tourism system.

This book focuses on family violence, which can be complex and difficult to understand for those who have not experienced it. Typically it happens behind closed doors. Many victims do not talk about what is happening to them (or, if they do, they may mention little about it, and to few people). The events from family law courts dealing with separation or intervention orders are also behind closed doors and it is difficult to understand what happens to the victim while living with the abuser, and while trying to gain protection from the abuser, and trying to separate from the abuser and protect the children. It is therefore important to understand what these aspects may be like, so that as a society we keep better notice of what is happening, and have better systems. If employers do not understand the nature of family violence, they may not design the best processes to support employees.

This book discusses problematic behaviour and some confusing and poorly understood legislative aspects that affect people within the tourism system. While discussed in the context of tourism industries, the key message is generalisable to anybody (not just tourists), and to any workplace (not just those that serve tourists).

Autoethnography

This book is written from knowledge and research but is not filled with heavy tables of complex statistics. Tables and references are included but the book is not overly weighed down by them: I want it to be accessible to a wider readership group, and many of the components covered come from my experiences or from people I know, and from reading about family violence. Some aspects shared in this book come from reading as well as from experiences with the tourism industries. At times those experiences include personally working through legislative aspects, such as components of employment legislation, family law, as well as observation at various court hearings related to family violence. The discussions of family violence in this book come also from the stories that victims told me and from information that was shared with me by those who work with victims of family violence. The stories come from various sources, including published victim's stories (which are anonymous or use pseudonyms), media sources, reports, or comments provided in the capacity of a research project with ethical approval. Some components also come from lived experience.

I was once told by a researcher in family violence who used to run men's behavioural change programmes that most people who research family violence do so because they have experienced family violence and want to change the future for others. Some of the research gaps that I uncovered, and the problems that I have identified, have arisen because my situation led me to research in that area. Some of the learning contained within this book comes from my own lived experience. Family violence not only affects 'some' people: it can happen to anybody.

One of my friends, who is a professor of tourism, told me that an academic tourism conference paper he submitted in 2018 required an editorial change regarding a comment made about family violence before it was accepted. The paper's topic was around barriers to attending conferences and he had mapped out solutions in the paper. He had commented that some female academics may be unable to attend conferences because they live with family violence and may not be allowed to attend, or they may be in fear of the treatment of their children in their absence. This professor friend related how he was told by one of the reviewers of his paper to remove the statement since those things don't happen in academe. He shared with me his dilemma in believing it was wrong but feeling he wanted to share his research and so he complied while recognising the problem and struggling with that decision.

I should also say that, when I discuss the education and legal systems in this book (family law and employment law), I will be discussing mainly those that exist in Australia. It would be a complex and highly time-consuming task to navigate the equivalent systems in every country, although I do discuss some aspects in a number of other countries. While the legal framework will concentrate on that of Australia, the reader can seek to reference the legal framework in their own country and compare key aspects to determine similarities and differences. The aspects relating to employment law focus on Australia but also raise issues that can arise in other countries. Matters such as the casualisation of the workforce in industries that relate to serving tourists (such as hospitality, retail and fast food) are global matters, although they are especially bad in Australia. While the detail of the legislative frameworks varies across countries, the key points made are relevant globally.

Discussions about the legal framework are important because it can be what keeps a victim from separating, and it can be what allows the abuse to continue after separation. The ongoing cycle, or secondary victimisation, can impact any element of the tourism system. It can impact the person who works for a business that serves tourists. It can prevent a person's mobility. Without understanding the legislation, we cannot see the whole picture. What happens in court is a secret and this is part of the problem. As Jane Matts says:

> I advocate to change the family law system, both in government and within the system itself. Terrible things are happening in our family law system – children are being ordered to live with parents who have been assessed by child protection as a 'risk of harm' to them. I have worked on these cases – the outcomes are shocking. But the public generally does not hear about them, because family law is a place of secrecy; thanks to privacy legislation, it can be difficult to report on. To make these issues real, we need stories – that is how we will change the system. (Hill, 2022)

In terms of the discussions I share about family violence from personal experience, I want to make it clear that I was not brought up in a household of family violence. My late father was an incredibly fine human being whom I deeply respected and he was always hard-working, positive, calm and kind. He never saw me as inferior because I was a female. My experience in family violence came from my marriage and I experienced firsthand the slow progression into what I refer to as 'the perpetrator's web' (discussed in Chapter 3). Leaving is not as easy as those on the outside might think. Like a web, it feels like being stuck and, in many ways, a person *is* stuck – especially once children are involved; and the judicial system can make this worse in some cases.

Hearing the stories of other victims, while each was different, they involved many key similarities. Most particularly, injustices exist in legal systems where victims of family violence can find themselves connected to the perpetrator and unable to escape (psychologically). Separation from a perpetrator of family violence appears to be a poorly understood component as there seems to be an attitude (even among some of those who work in family violence) that separation is synonymous with freedom. Sometimes, staying with a perpetrator is a deliberate strategy for safety. Sometimes, it is safer to stay. And sometimes, as I decided in my case, it is safer to stay until the children are old enough to have an externally accepted choice of whether to spend time with the perpetrator.

Often, people refer to the victims who separated from living with family violence as 'survivors' or 'victim-survivors'. In my view, this misunderstands family violence, and the impact on children during and/ or post-separation is greatly misunderstood. As has been reported, there is a strong correlation between people who have been a victim of family violence and people who then perpetrate violence against others: 'we saw a staggering overlap between young people's experiences of family violence and their subsequent use of family violence in their childhood' (Price, 2022). Research further indicates that around 20% of adolescents use violence against a parent/sibling/carer and around 66% of those who used violence admitted to using it against their mothers. In other words, even for those who manage to separate from a perpetrator, the impact on the children from that environment could result in the victim experiencing family violence not only from the perpetrator (but outside the home rather than inside it), but also potentially from their own children as a result of that exposure. Is that survival? In many cases, the education 'system' may also compound the problem, which is discussed in Chapter 6. Sadly, so very sadly, it is no wonder we see the volumes of family violence we see.

This book's contents come from many sources including lived experiences from me, and others, combined with reading and drilling into complex terminology and explaining it in an easier language and using storytelling to provide examples. Of course, good research can come from various sources. In fact, in a tourism paper written by Michael Hall and Stephen Page about the late tourism scholar Neil Leiper (Hall & Page, 2010: 300–301), it was stated that, for Neil, 'empirical "evidence" often came from personal experience and observation that would be incorporated into an overall argument rather than via empirical research per se'. Neil Leiper was undoubtedly a great leading tourism scholar, whose ideas still serve as critical frameworks in understanding tourism. His Simple Whole Tourism System Model remains the key framework for understanding tourism in almost every tourism textbook. Leiper's Simple Whole Tourism System Model is the conceptual framework used for this book, and tourism systems are discussed in Chapter 2 of this book.

Discussing research and understanding research is not always undertaken in the same way for it to be relevant, accurate and meaningful. Much of this book has stemmed from lived experience in various ways and, as such, uses autoethnography as its method. I have used cases to bring life to complex matters wherever possible. Some of these cases are publicly available, some cases are ones that I was involved in (at least in some way if not entirely). As this book is of a technical character and intended primarily for the academic community my experiences with the judicial system can be presented as part of the educational nature of this book. This may help to shine a light on matters that are ordinarily hidden from view because of legislation restricting the publication of court proceedings. This hidden judicial system is part of the problem.

Definitions

While definitions can seem purely academic and mundane, there can be differences in what is included within the legislation. In Australia, each state and territory has its own legislation and there can be differences as to who is included and excluded within the scope of the legislation. Therefore, when referring to particular legislation, it is very important to check the scope (Alexander, 2018). In some states of Australia, domestic violence tends to be regarded as violence within one's domestic setting. In that sense, it may be between housemates; or between people with a disability in a group home; or even a person with a disability in their own home with a support worker perpetrating the violence. In family violence, people may not live together for the violence to be experienced. In other words, it becomes about the relationship between the people rather than the setting. Family violence is about familial relationships.

Family violence terms

Some common terms for family violence include:

Batterer – 'an individual who has abused a current or former spouse, or current or former cohabitant' (Law Insider, 2022).

Domestic Abuse – 'a pattern of behavior in any relationship that is used to gain or maintain power and control over an intimate partner' (United Nations, 2022).

Domestic Violence – 'acts of violence that occur between people who have, or have had, an intimate relationship in domestic settings. These acts include physical, sexual, emotional and psychological abuse' (Parliament of Australia, 2011).

Family violence – 'any threatening, coercive, dominating or abusive behaviour that occurs between people in a family, domestic or intimate relationship, or former intimate relationship, that causes the person experiencing the behaviour to feel fear' (Safe Steps, 2022).

Intimate partner violence – 'one of the most common forms of violence against women and includes physical, sexual, and emotional abuse and controlling behaviours by an intimate partner' (World Health Organization, 2012: 1).

Partner abuse – 'a systematic pattern of behaviors where one person non-consensually uses power to try to control the thoughts, beliefs, actions, body, and/or spirit of a partner' (The Network la Red, 2018).

The term family violence 'is the preferred term in many indigenous communities' (Parliament of Australia, 2011). It is also the term used in Australia's Family Law Act. From the Family Law Act 1975 Section 4AB, family violence is defined and explained as follows:

(1) For the purposes of this Act, family violence means violent, threatening or other behaviour by a person that coerces or controls a member of the person's family (the family member), or causes the family member to be fearful.
(2) Examples of behaviour that may constitute family violence include (but are not limited to):
    (a) an assault; or
    (b) a sexual assault or other sexually abusive behaviour; or
    (c) stalking; or
    (d) repeated derogatory taunts; or
    (e) intentionally damaging or destroying property; or
    (f) intentionally causing death or injury to an animal; or
    (g) unreasonably denying the family member the financial autonomy that he or she would otherwise have had; or
    (h) unreasonably withholding financial support needed to meet the reasonable living expenses of the family member, or his or her child, at a time when the family member is entirely or predominantly dependent on the person for financial support; or
    (i) preventing the family member from making or keeping connections with his or her family, friends or culture; or
    (j) unlawfully depriving the family member, or any member of the family member's family, of his or her liberty.

This book adopts this definition of family violence. The focus is specifically on family relationships, namely between a couple.

Understanding what the terms mean can also have implications, because it determines how people self-assess their situation. All too often victims of family violence and children are enduring family violence but do not know they are. I have spoken to people who have experienced appalling treatment but they have not regarded their situation as family violence. Such perception, or misperception, is a significant block to people accessing available support systems. Children remain in unsuitable situations, which damages the receptors in the brain. And, sometimes, these situations remain simply because the impacted people do not understand that they are living with and experiencing family violence.

Terms can also impact how someone feels. For example, in 2021 I had a conversation with a person from the human resources department of a large organisation. The person mentioned to me that the organisation had excellent processes to support staff, including the opportunity for staff to take family violence leave, instead of using their annual leave, to deal with matters relating to family violence. They explained that staff did not use this and they were wondering why. My suggestion was that instead of calling it 'Family Violence Leave', they could call it 'White Ribbon Leave' or something similar. Whether this was technically accurate in this situation may not be so important, compared to the way a term may make someone feel. Applying for 'Family Violence Leave' is very confronting. It would involve acceptance and disclosure. It may take time for someone to be at that point. It can be more comfortable to remain in the shadows and take a 'normal' type of leave. Taking 'White Ribbon Leave' has a different flavour and may seem easier. Just as we use softening phrases when someone passes away, some thought around the use of terms in businesses (not just tourism businesses) can perhaps be useful. It is also noteworthy that, among thousands of staff at that organisation, nobody had taken family violence leave. Statistically, there would absolutely have been staff eligible for that type of leave. Nobody had taken it. This also highlights the hidden nature of it, where many people choose not to divulge what they are enduring.

Survivor

In the Overture, and the previous section, I mentioned the term 'survivor'. In family violence, the terms 'survivor' as well as 'victim–survivor' are used. As with other things, the terms may mean different things in different locations and may also mean different things to different individuals. Some discussions around the use of victim/survivor include that it is a term to 'describe women and their children who have experienced domestic, family and sexual violence by a male perpetrator' (Council of Australian Governments, 2015: 3). I do wonder whether the term 'survivor' may present an impression that the person is now 'free'? When we look at definitions of 'survivor', phrases such as 'overcoming' hardship, or 'gets through' might be used. The *Macmillan Dictionary* mentions that a synonym for 'survive' is 'escape' and means 'to get out of a situation' (*Macmillan Dictionary*, 2022). It is also said that a survivor is 'someone who manages to continue a successful life despite very bad experiences' (*Macmillan Dictionary*, 2022). It seems that this notion of 'coping successfully' is inherent in the use of the word 'survivor'. I wonder how many women and children who have escaped abuse would consider that they are indeed coping successfully – and what does 'successful' mean in this context?

For the mother who cannot relocate in order to retain employment because the abusive ex-partner will not approve it, and who consequently becomes unemployed, I wonder if she feels like a survivor. For the mother who cannot take her children on an international holiday to visit their maternal grandparents, because the abusive ex-partner will not allow it, I wonder how much of a survivor she feels.

I think it is fair to say that there is already a misunderstanding by some people that, when a person has separated from family violence, they are 'free' and it is behind them. As will be discussed through some of the cases in this book, in many instances the family violence continues (sometimes through legislative practices), and sometimes even gets worse. Sometimes, separation from family violence results in death. In many cases the family violence continues but is simply outside the house instead of within it. This doesn't sound like survival.

The employee who tries to look cheerful when greeting tourists at the 5-star hotel they work for might be assumed to be a 'survivor' by their workplace because they separated from their abusive partner. However, they might still be receiving threatening messages; they might be unable to take the children overseas to visit the maternal grandparents due to restrictions; they might be unable to relocate because the abusive ex-partner does not agree to it. Is this surviving? Is it all behind them? They might live with children who then re-enact what they observed in their childhood and use abusive tactics on their mother. Is she a survivor? Has she escaped? Is it all behind her? Is she still living with it? Is she now a victim in her home but through her children being abusive towards her?

I spoke recently to a person whose father killed his mother after she had finally made the difficult decision to leave the situation of family violence. The research is quite clear in this area that risk can actually increase when a victim attempts to separate from a perpetrator of family violence. This person admitted to me that 22 years after the death of his mother at the hands of his father, he is still weighed down by complex feelings of hopelessness and inferiority and has not been able to hold down a relationship successfully. I have heard from others that they cannot hold down a relationship because of how they feel about themselves, or because of the fear of going through it all again. Some people may fear they will get caught in the perpetrator's web once more and maybe it will happen again. Some may feel that it can be safer to be alone.

Family violence can continue after separation. It can worsen. It can continue through various tactics including court orders So, does the term 'survivor' present a misleading perspective that may reduce the ability of society to understand family violence? This book does not try to answer this question but merely presents it as a point to consider. The term perhaps is trying to make people feel empowered but, if it contributes to a misunderstanding of the difficulty of life forever after, then maybe it is doing more harm than good for people. For those who are alive but not living, are they really a survivor? Particularly if the world assumes they are. Maybe it needs more thought. Someone who survives a shark attack may still be traumatised after the event but they won't have to wonder if that shark might find its way into their home. Someone who fell off a very tall building or wind turbine and survived may carry all types of physical and mental scars, but they won't have to wonder if the event will be repeated in their home. A person who has lived with family violence and separates from that person may continue to be plagued by them, especially if they share children.

Unlike any other crime, the victim may still have to communicate with the perpetrator and likely has to make decisions jointly with the perpetrator with regard to the children. At family events, at the future weddings of their children ... it is likely that the perpetrator is there. So, should society be using that umbrella term of 'survivor' on behalf of those who have had no say in the term? Someone lived with family violence. Someone separated from family violence. Why not call it as it is. If we accept that, as a society, we need better understanding and education, maybe the post-separation component requires more understanding and education as well. A term that possibly misleads and misunderstands what it is like living with family violence after separation may not be as helpful as intended. As discussed in Chapter 9, many people regret deciding to leave the abusive relationship because they are left with a court order that puts them and their child/ren at risk of harm (Kivela, 2020). Some people have told me they thought the justice system would provide them with justice and that, had they known what the result would be, they would never have left the situation of family violence. Does that sound like surviving, given some would have preferred to stay trapped had they known what being a 'survivor' would look like? I think we have it very wrong. I also fear that using the term 'survivor' inflates the situation of the victim and may contribute to poor decisions in the judicial system since the victim is apparently a survivor.

Family violence suffers from a misunderstanding in many ways, including that it must be physical violence. Understanding the definitions can aid education and improve society's awareness.

Bullying, control and abuse

Terms such as bullying, control and abuse are perhaps better understood. These matters can be associated with family violence (i.e. family violence involving control and abuse) and can also involve the workplace, schools or other environments. Below are the definitions selected for use in this book.

> *Bullying* – 'when people repeatedly and intentionally use words or actions against someone or a group of people to cause distress and risk to their wellbeing. These actions are usually done by people who have more influence or power over someone else, or who want to make someone else feel less powerful or helpless' (Australian Human Rights Commission, 2022). The word 'repeatedly' is critical, as one-off events are not considered as bullying. It may give rise to a grievance (which can be a separate process in workplaces) but it is not bullying if it happens once.

> *Control* – 'to command, direct, or rule' (Hanks, 1986: 342).

> *Abuse* – 'any intentional action that harms or injures another person' (Slater and Gordon Lawyers, 2022). It is important to note that there are different types of abuse and no legal definition, but it is generally understood to mean that the action is deliberate and that harm comes as a result of that action. Different forms of abuse include child abuse, sexual abuse, financial abuse, elder abuse and institutional abuse. Within family violence, the different forms of abuse can include – verbal, psychological, emotional, financial, physical, sexual, spiritual/religious, reproductive and technological. One or more types of abuse can be present.

Control and abuse can sometimes be better terms to explain family violence, as many victims may relate to those terms for themselves but not relate to there being any 'violence' where matters are not physical, or perhaps not regularly or severely physical. But these matters can also exist in workplaces, at times in quite a discreet way. The loopholes that can exist in employment law, combined with the employment of vulnerable groups such as teenagers, can be a platform for taking advantage of their naivety and having employment conditions that are out of date and unfair. This aspect will be discussed in Chapter 5.

Bullying and controlling behaviour occurs in many workplaces and, like family violence, is one of those undercurrents in society that can be hard to garner support for and people (in the workplace) may find themselves trapped. In many ways, bullying in the workplace resembles family violence in the home. In both cases the person feels unsafe: unsafe in the home and walking on eggshells; unsafe at work and walking on eggshells. This book discusses bullying as well as unfair work environments. Tourism and hospitality industries often heavily employ staff on a casual basis, which can make the employees quite vulnerable to poor workplace conditions. In particular, the hospitality and fast-food industries will employ teenagers and other vulnerable groups and may take advantage of these employees through having unfair workplace conditions. Attention is given to explaining some of the key workplace matters.

Let's Assume We Have a Can Opener

I am going to share a joke told to me as an undergraduate economics student:

> A physicist, an engineer and an economist are stranded in the desert. They are hungry. Suddenly, they find a can of corn. They want to open it, but how?
>
> The physicist says: 'Let's start a fire and place the can inside the flames. It will explode and then we will all be able to eat.'
>
> 'Are you crazy?' says the engineer. 'All the corn will burn and scatter, and we'll have nothing. We should use a metal wire, attach it to a base, push it and crack the can open.'
>
> 'Both of you are wrong!' states the economist. 'Where the hell do we find a metal wire in the desert? The solution is simple: let's assume we have a can opener ...'

The purpose of the joke is to make fun of experts who attempt to resolve real-world problems by making unrealistic assumptions that bear no relationship to the problem at hand.

I often think of separating from a perpetrator of family violence as a case of 'Let's assume we have a can opener'. That's partly because I think the process is a bit like a can of worms (or actually snakes, which is explained later in this book in Chapter 3). But more so because some of the processes involve making assumptions that are unrealistic, like the economist's non-existent can opener.

For anyone who has been able to finally leave an abusive relationship and begin to navigate the legal system to work through parenting matters to separate, they will soon discover that the Family Law Act has an inherent mechanism for 'equal shared parental responsibility'. This is based on some unrealistic assumptions.

In 2006 the Howard Government changed the Family Law Act (1975) to state that separated parents would have 'equal shared parental responsibilities'. The underlying principle in the Family Law Act is to ensure 'that the best interests of children are met'. It is assumed that the best interests of children are met if they have meaningful involvement from both their parents.

The inherent assumption in this is that both parents are rational and 'normal' and motivated by the children's best interests – that both parents will put aside whatever ill feelings they may have for each other for the sake of the children. This assumption is very much like the economist's can opener – helpful in theory but often useless in reality. If there is no can opener or the can opener doesn't work (that is, one person is not rational but is instead abusive and controlling), then the whole assumption is flawed and the parenting orders may be far from in the best interests of the child.

Watching Shadows on the Wall

The chapters in this book attempt to unpack and explain various legislative flaws, loopholes and gaps. There are discussions on aspects relating to family violence, as well as employment law, and policies and procedures in general workplace settings including natural justice. Many of these are components that it is important to have an understanding of – not necessarily a deep understanding, but sufficient to know the basics and at least where to look or who to go to for answers to things that should not be mysterious. Much of our understanding of matters such as workplace practices, employment law, and family violence, suffers from a lack of clarity of rights and processes.

In many ways, I am reminded of Plato's 'Allegory of the Cave'. This forms Book VII in Plato's famous work, *Republic* (Plato, 380 B.C.E.). The work is written as a dialogue between Plato's mentor Socrates and Plato's brother Glaucon (narrated by Socrates). In the allegory, there is a description of a group of people who live chained to the wall in a cave with 'their legs and necks chained so that they cannot move, and can only see before them, being prevented by the chains from turning round their heads' (p. 306). The people watch shadows that are projected on the wall from objects passing in front of a fire that is behind the people 'like the screen which marionette players have in front of them, over which they show the puppets' (p. 306). The people in the cave only see the shadows, not the real objects, because they cannot turn their heads. The names of those shadow objects (e.g. a book) become their version of reality. They have never seen a book: they have only seen a shadow. Leaving the cave and seeing things clearly is difficult and the inmates of the cave in many ways do not want to leave their prison because they are accustomed to their life. Facing the reality can be too uncomfortable.

Conclusion

People in difficult work environments, people living with family violence, or perhaps living with the memory of family violence, may find comfort in the shadows rather than the reality. Sometimes the reality can be too much to face. Plato believed that facing the difficulty of seeing reality through light was the pathway to becoming a philosopher. Similarly, facing the reality of whatever the difficulty is (or the memory of it) through clarity, acceptance and knowledge, while difficult, is the pathway (even if it is bumpy, confronting and uncomfortable) to the light in front of us. Sometimes, the most difficult thing for someone to acknowledge is that they are living with family violence. The idea that it will get better, and accepting the excuses presented for the behaviour, is often far more palatable than accepting what the light shows is actually before us.

Xavier Legrand, the director of the award-winning French film *Custody* has been quoted as saying that the film set out to answer the question: 'Can a violent husband be a good father?' Perhaps, as readers of this book journey through the chapters, they may consider that question, and also a related one: 'Will a violent and abusive husband set aside his behaviour for the sake of the children?' And perhaps, in time, that question will be at the forefront of decisions regarding 'the best interests of the child'.

2 The Tourism System

'Systems thinking is a discipline for seeing wholes. It is a framework for seeing interrelationships rather than things, for seeing "patterns of change" rather than static "snapshots".'

Peter Senge, *The Fifth Discipline: The Art & Practice of the Learning Organization*, pp. 68–69

Introduction

This chapter will introduce the reader to the tourism system. To fully understand tourism, it is important that those who are interested in understanding the nature of tourism are introduced to tourism systems theory. The structure of this book takes a tourism system framework, and, accordingly, this chapter will assist the reader in understanding the structure of the following chapters.

General Systems Theory

Before the discussion on whole tourism systems is presented, an overview of general systems theory is provided. This then leads to a more complete understanding of whole tourism systems, which will enhance comprehension of the Underbelly of Tourism Model presented at the end of this chapter.

General systems theory was originally considered to be a 'radical movement in science' (Klir, 1972: v). While general systems theory has been said to have begun in the 1930s (Leiper, 2004), writing in the general systems theory field in fact began much earlier. A leading contributor to this field, Ludwig von Bertalanffy, began publishing in general systems theory in the late 1920s (Bertalanffy, 1928). Bertalanffy progressed the development of systems theory by integrating multiple disciplines. He proposed general systems theory as being 'a model of certain general aspects of reality' (Bertalanffy, 1972: 38) and explained that systems can be either open or closed (Bertalanffy, 1968). This aspect of being open or closed is especially important for understanding tourism.

General systems theory should be considered a type of 'methodological maxim' (Bertalanffy, 1972: 38) since it allows things to be looked at that may ordinarily be overlooked or bypassed. Bertalanffy believed that general systems theory commenced well before his contributions and that it can be regarded as being as old as European philosophy. As Bertalanfly (1972: 21–22) argues: 'Aristotle's statement "The whole is more than the sum of its parts" is a definition of a basic system problem which is still valid', since general systems theory concerns studying the 'wholeness' of something (Bertalanffy, 1972: 30). If we accept that Aristotle's writings should be considered to be early writings in general systems theory, then this posits general systems theory as far back as the mid-300BC period.

Around two hundred years ago Friedrich Hegel (1770–1831) made four key statements regarding systems: 'the whole is more than the sum of the parts; the whole defines the nature of the parts; the parts cannot be understood by studying the whole; and the parts are dynamically interrelated or interdependent' (Skyttner, 2001: 45–46). A system can be described as being 'a model of general nature' (Bertalanffy, 1972: 31). It can be defined as 'a set of elements standing in interrelation among themselves and with the environment' (1972: 31). As such, systemic models show the elementary components necessary for a particular system to exist.

Whole Tourism Systems

Tourism itself can be regarded as a system (Baggio, 2008; Gilbert, 1990; C.M. Hall & Butler, 1995; Leiper, 2004). A system that is isolated from its environment is a closed system (Bertalanffy, 1968). Therefore, tourism is an example of an open system, because it is not isolated from its environment. 'A systems approach in tourism has been used as a framework for quite a number of texts' (Hall & Butler, 1995: 101). Many core tourism textbooks include a discussion on tourism as a system in their early pages.

While Getz (1986) can be credited with first using the expression 'whole tourism system', Leiper (2004) greatly expanded the use of this term through the development of his whole tourism system models. Models of whole tourism systems are useful tools to examine tourist flows in a holistic and systematic way. The elements of the whole tourism system and the relationships between them can be described through a whole tourism systems model.

Tourism Models

A model can be described as a representation of reality, used to guide thoughts, and often action, in relation to some sort of ideal or actual phenomena. While 'no model is a perfect representation of reality' (Leiper *et al*., 2008: 214), models can be considered to be intelligible versions of reality (Leiper, 2004) that depict how certain relationships, processes or features operate (McKercher, 1999). Some tourism models are specific to particular aspects of tourism, such as Butler's (1980) destination lifecycle model, which describes how destinations change and develop over time. Similarly, Doxey's (1976) Irridex model describes how resident attitudes change as tourism develops within a destination. Fodness and Murray (1999) developed a model to describe the tourist information search strategy process. Murphy (1985) developed a community approach to tourism management model. Other tourism models exist as specific models to describe particular aspects of tourism.

However, few models aim to describe tourism as a system. Perhaps the best known of these are Leiper's (2004) whole tourism system models. One of the reasons for the popularity of these could be linked to Leiper's adherence to Occam's Razor. William of Occam (c.1285–1349) commanded his famous razor, 'entities should not be multiplied unnecessarily' (Blumer *et al*., 1987: 377), against the superfluous writings of his scholastic predecessors. This principle is still considered important by some scholars and practitioners. Leiper's (2004) Systematic Whole Tourism System Model formed the foundation of the VFR Whole Tourism System Model adopted as the conceptual framework for this book, which will be introduced in this chapter.

A Simple Whole Tourism System Model

While Neil Leiper has developed three whole tourism system models, perhaps the best-known of these models is his Simple Whole Tourism System Model (Figure 2.1). Although this model was first published more than forty years ago (Leiper, 1979) many tourism textbooks continue to use it in an early chapter to outline the traditional view of tourism as a system. As such, this model has become a common organising framework for the study of tourism.

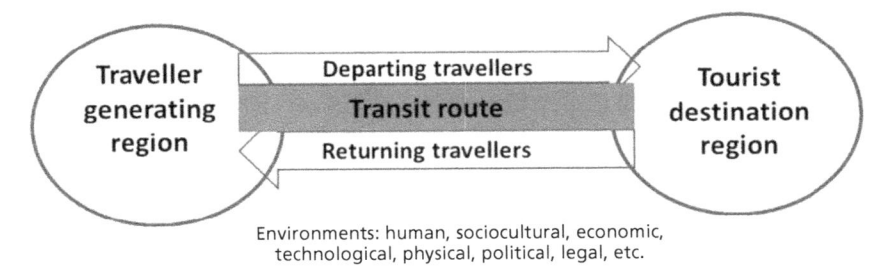

Figure 2.1 Simple Whole Tourism System Model
Source: adapted from Leiper (2004: 53).

Whole tourism systems comprise five elements – tourists, tourist generating regions, transit routes, tourist destination regions, and tourism industries. It is all five of these elements and the relationships between them that make up a whole tourism system (Leiper, 2004). The Simple Whole Tourism System Model is considered a basic whole tourism systems model, useful for explaining the tourism system for a trip involving one tourist destination and the return back to the usual residence. It recognises that tourism involves three geographic elements: the generating region, the destination and the transit route. It also shows tourism as an open system, acknowledging externalities in the environment that influence touristic trips. In addition, it recognises two other tourism elements: the tourist, as well as tourism industries, which exist along the shaded section of the model. This shaded area exists along the transit route as well as in the generating region and destination region, highlighting that these elements can exist in any of the three geographic elements. However, this model does not depict the relationships between the elements. While the grey zone depicts tourism industries, this may not be immediately clear to the reader.

The Whole Tourism System Model Conceptual Framework for this Book

This chapter has discussed systems theory and tourism systems. The conceptual framework for this book is adapted in part from Figure 2.1 above, as well as Figure 2.2 below. Notably, the mixed terminology of traveller and tourist used in the Figure 2.1 model differs from that in Figure 2.2, which uses tourist and not traveller.

The terms tourist and traveller are not substitutes for each other. While travellers engage in a range of activities that are also undertaken by tourists, they are not entirely the same. Travellers and tourists both

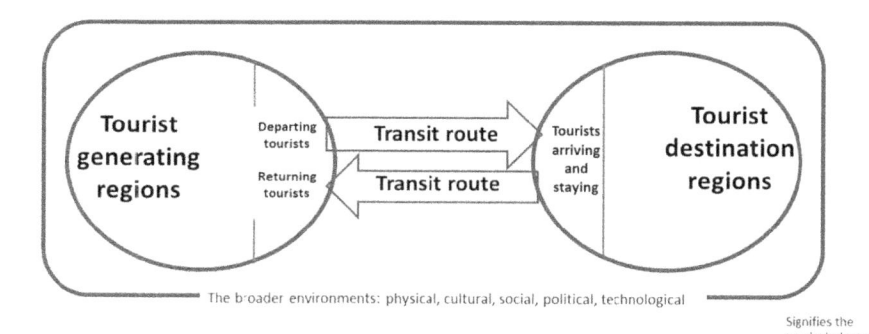

Figure 2.2 The Tourism System
Source: adapted from Leiper (1979: 404).

depart a region, they travel to a destination, they travel along a transit route, and they engage in industries involving the consumption of services and products during their trip. However, travellers and tourists are not the same. A tourist must consume tourist activities that are leisurely (Leiper, 1979). That is:

> Leisure is usually recognised as an essential factor contributing to the demand for tourism and recreation … it is the anticipation of leisure which is operational as a demand factor, whereas the subsequent use of leisure is a factor of supply. Leisure time is the fundamental resource input consumed in the tourism process. (Leiper, 1979: 398)

Notably, Visiting Friends and Relatives (VFR) travel literature (e.g. Backer & Morrison, 2017) argues for the term 'VFR traveller' instead of 'VFR tourist' since some VFR trips contain no leisurely component (e.g. travelling for a funeral might not include leisure activities).

The structure of this book follows the Whole Tourism Systems framework. The framework adopted for this book is illustrated in Figure 2.3. It is an adaptation of Leiper's model depicted in Figures 2.1 and 2.2. This book examines problematic behaviour (bullying, control, abuse, family violence) along the pathway between the tourist generating region (where the tourist resides) and the tourist destination (both to and from). The transit route represents the path that takes the tourist from their generating region to their destination; and the return journey. The transit route and mode of transport may be different for each departing and returning trip. Tourism industries supply services and products to the tourist to consume for their trip, and those services and products might be consumed in their usual residence (i.e. the tourism generating region), such as booking a trip through a travel agent, buying a plane ticket, buying items for the trip, and consuming food at the airport or bus station. Services and products can be consumed along the journey to and from the destination. Services and products are also consumed at the destination itself.

━ ━ ━ ━ = tourism industries

Figure 2.3 Whole Tourism System Model
Source: adapted from Leiper (2004).

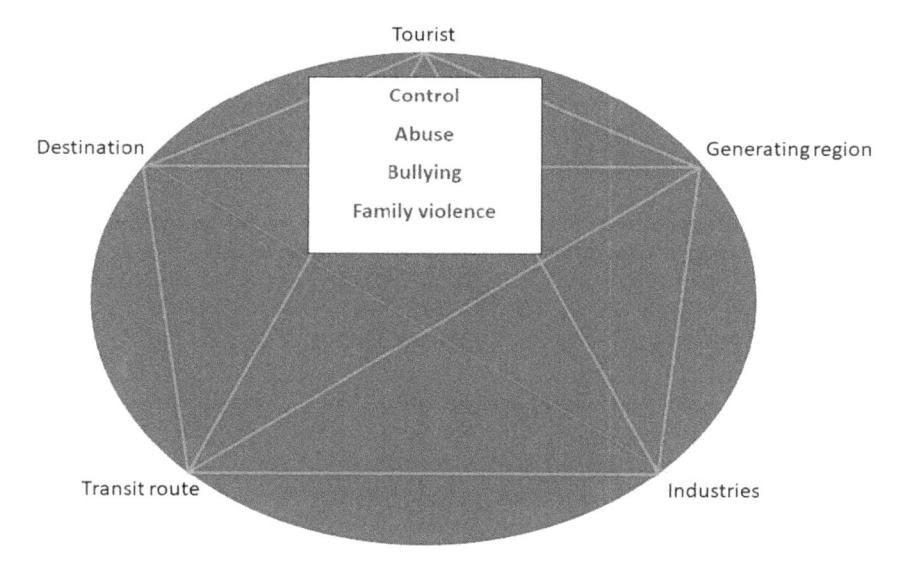

Figure 2.4 The underbelly of tourism

The Underbelly of Tourism

Following on from the previous section outlining the whole tourism system model, this section explains the focus for this book conceptually. As previously described, tourism has five elements:- a tourist, industries, a generating region, a transit route, and a destination region. There are linkages between each of the elements. This book focuses on the underbelly of tourism, i.e. what are the dark aspects that might be encountered either by a tourist or an organisation that serves tourists.

Importantly, tourism is considered to be positive and relaxing; however, for some people, it may not be. From the tourist's perspective, their relationship with the other tourism elements of the generating region (the region in which they reside) – the destination they are travelling to, the industries they are served by, and the means of their travel – can be negatively impacted by control, abuse, bullying and family violence. As represented in Figure 2.4, any of these four areas can impact their relationships with the other tourism elements.

Conclusion

This chapter has introduced the reader to the topic of the tourism system. A discussion of general systems theory was followed by an explanation of whole tourism systems. The chapter then explained tourism models and the whole tourism system model. The adaptation of the whole tourism system model is used as a conceptual framework for the book. Each element of the whole tourism system is connected and is impacted by control, abuse, bullying and family violence. One of these elements – industries – can be impacted either through serving tourists or by having tourists working for them. The scope of those industries is broad as many businesses can serve tourists but they do not have distinct business strategies to target tourists (e.g. a dentist, a medical practitioner) and, therefore, are only partially in tourism (discussed in Chapter 4). Before taking the reader through each of the elements in the tourism system, we need first to deepen our understanding of family violence.

3 Control, Abuse and Family Violence

'I want to tell everybody that family violence happens to everybody, no matter how nice your house is, no matter how intelligent you are.'

– Rosie Batty, quoted by Wendy Tuohy in *The Age*

Introduction

This chapter will explain the aspects of controlling and abusive behaviour in the context of family violence. The key concepts and a series of conceptual frameworks are presented to provide tools for understanding – visually and via text – how family violence might feel and occur. The components introduced in this chapter will help the reader to develop a foundation of understanding for the later chapters, which explain how these aspects interrelate with each element of the tourism system. As this book is primarily for academics, it is also hoped that these frameworks may assist with future research and education in the field.

Family violence has become a term that is used in mainstream forums; however, the term, while well known, is not known well. This chapter attempts to allow readers who may be unfamiliar with family violence to gain some further understanding about how it may feel and present, how it might impact people in the workforce who live with family violence, and to provide an opportunity to reconsider whether our understanding of going away on a holiday applies to victims of family violence or whether we have our tourism motivation theories wrong.

While it is recognised that there are some cases where men are subjected to abuse and control from women, these cases are extremely rare (Bancroft, 2002; Our Watch, 2018). It is also acknowledged that family violence exists between same-sex couples. Given the significant proportion of cases of women as victims of family violence where the male is the perpetrator, it is also noteworthy that 'violence against women has been a weapon in men's arsenal for centuries' (Stark, 2007: 172).

Women with children are in a particularly vulnerable position as victims of family violence. This is partly because the children are essentially an umbilical cord connecting the victim to the perpetrator for life. However, it is also partly because family violence is perpetrated toward mothers at higher rates than it is toward women without children (Denham *et al.*, 2007; McDonald *et al.*, 2006).

Gender Inequality

When seeking to understand the undercurrents of family violence, it is important to recognise the existence of gender inequality. Essentially, when a male has the casting vote all the time, we have to accept that being male gives him superior decision-making. As much as we want to believe that society is progressing, we still have a long way to go.

By way of a very recent example, 8 March is International Women's Day. Only three days prior to that day, I was at a parkrun event. I was volunteering at that event and so I had the neon orange volunteer top on. A man called out to me and said he was wanting to speak to the race director, and asked me where 'he was'. I pointed to the race director (who was in fact a she). Another volunteer, on hearing this and understanding that the race director was needed, proceeded to call out to her and pointed to the man who was asking to speak to the race director. The man then muttered that he only wanted to know if the race had started. The underlying assumption when asking where 'he' was, was that only a male could be undertaking that role.

There are similar stories all too regularly. A female friend of mine is a futsal coach at the nationals for boys. She told me that she is at times shunned by the men, who choose to seek advice from a child's father rather than from her as a coach. Yet, her husband can coach girls and nobody questions his ability.

I have heard many female academic colleagues tell me that when they make a booking for 'Dr XXX plus one', upon arrival the greeting of 'Dr XXX' is assumed as belonging to the male. These stories are common. Gender inequality is a critical area and it is not my intention to discuss this in any detail here but simply to highlight this as being an undercurrent in family violence. Gender inequality continues to exist in the naming of children, which is discussed later in Chapter 9 under 'Changing a Child's Surname'.

Statistics

As already mentioned, I have sought to avoid weighing this book down with heavy statistics. However, in this section I present a few key family violence statistics to provide some context. This will assist the reader in understanding the depth of the problems faced by society.

Firstly, family violence in its various forms is prevalent and is probably far more common than some people realise. There are different statistics for different cultures, different countries, different genders and different ages. However, I deliberately will not provide a wide range of statistics as my notion for this book is to let storytelling explain the problems. As such, a few examples are provided to illustrate the prevalence within a certain context. Some key statistics to highlight prevalence (White Ribbon Australia, 2022) are:

- On average, one woman each week is murdered by either her current partner or her former partner.
- Since the age of 15, 25% of women have experienced emotional abuse from a current partner or a former partner.
- Almost 40% of women experience violence from their 'partner' while they are temporarily separated.
- Stalking is experienced by 1 in 6 women from the age of 15.

Some further statistics from the Australian Institute of Criminology are (Tuohy, 2022a):

- One-third of Australian men who kill their female partners are high functioning elsewhere in their lives. Their partners were also middle class, employed, and may not have recognised themselves as victims of family violence.
- The 'killers' are often 'typically middle-class men' who were well respected in their communities and had low levels of contact with the criminal justice system.
- Intimate partner homicide is the most common form of homicide in Australia.
- Intimate partner homicide accounted for 21% of all homicides in 2018–2019.
- There has been an average of 68 cases of intimate-partner homicide each year since 1989–1990, mostly perpetrated by a male offender against a female partner.
- A key stage in the journey to fatal violence was if the woman challenged her partner such as by separating, returning to work, or attempting to maintain relationships with family members.

Another critical statistic is the correlation between non-fatal strangulation (NFS) and attempted homicides in family violence, which is regarded as 'the biggest sign domestic abuse will turn deadly' (Stacey, 2021). In almost 45% of attempted homicides in family violence, non-fatal strangulation had been reported (Stacey, 2021).

Workplaces need to have awareness of these issues, as many workplaces are likely to have many victims of family violence in their employment. Some small tourism businesses may have long operating hours and this may present a risk to victims who have separated from a perpetrator, as the perpetrator may attempt to confront them at their workplace.

How Does the Perpetrator Know Where I Am?

Sometimes, when people leave abusive relationships, there are significant attempts by the perpetrator to locate the victim. This can also mean that an ex will know where someone is holidaying. Some examples are:

- A woman who escaped family violence and left her car near a women's refuge with a smartwatch in it. She was tracked by the watch.
- Spyware on a victim's computer.
- Tracking software on children's phones.
- Cameras installed in the victim's home.
- Social media – to humiliate, punish and stalk.
- GPS tracking device in a child's toy or backpack.
- Dog's collar (which lists the phone number).
- Electoral roll.

In terms of the last bullet point, in Australia, once a person is aged 18 or over, they are required by law to have their details on the electoral roll and to keep those details up to date. An electronic copy of the current electoral roll can be viewed by any member of the public at any Australian Electoral Commission (AEC) office. Victims of family violence can apply to be a 'silent elector' so that their address does not appear alongside the surname on the electoral roll. People who apply for this must provide a detailed explanation regarding why their family's safety, or their safety, is at risk. A statutory declaration must be completed and witnessed by a person who is eligible to witness statutory declarations.

Some other opportunities for abuse if the victim cannot be located include bank transfer deposit descriptions. A perpetrator of family violence may leave intimidating messages through the deposit description mechanisms of online bank transfers, often with minuscule bank transfers. Various words and phrases have been blocked by banks as a result of this occurrence. It is now so common that one bank, National Australia Bank, stopped 10,000 of these types of messages from reaching 6,800 customers in March 2022 alone (Tuohy, 2022b). Abusive ex-partners may use making payments, such as child support payments, an opportunity to leave abusive or threatening messages. Instead of making the required payment, they might choose to make around 500 small payments and leave an abusive message for their ex-partner on each deposit as the deposit description (Tuohy, 2022b).

Another example: a woman called Rosemary who found a cutting of the herb Rosemary on her front doorstep. She considered this a sign from her ex-husband to let her know that he knew where she lived, in order to terrorise her. The extent to which efforts are made to use messages to exert power and to intimidate victims of family violence cannot be underestimated.

The Iceberg: A Conceptual Framework

Following on from the discussion introduced in Chapter 1 about the hidden aspects of family violence, Figure 3.1 depicts how I see the public versus the private person in family violence. It is like an iceberg. The exposed section of a person who is a victim of family violence is just a small part of them. It is what the world sees. It is what the person allows the world to see. Remembering that family violence largely happens behind closed doors, the real person (their emotions, their fear, their life) is partly submerged from view. It can also be useful to consider that the exposed part of icebergs can shrink. Early in a relationship of family violence, the exposed part of the iceberg is large. Over time, the

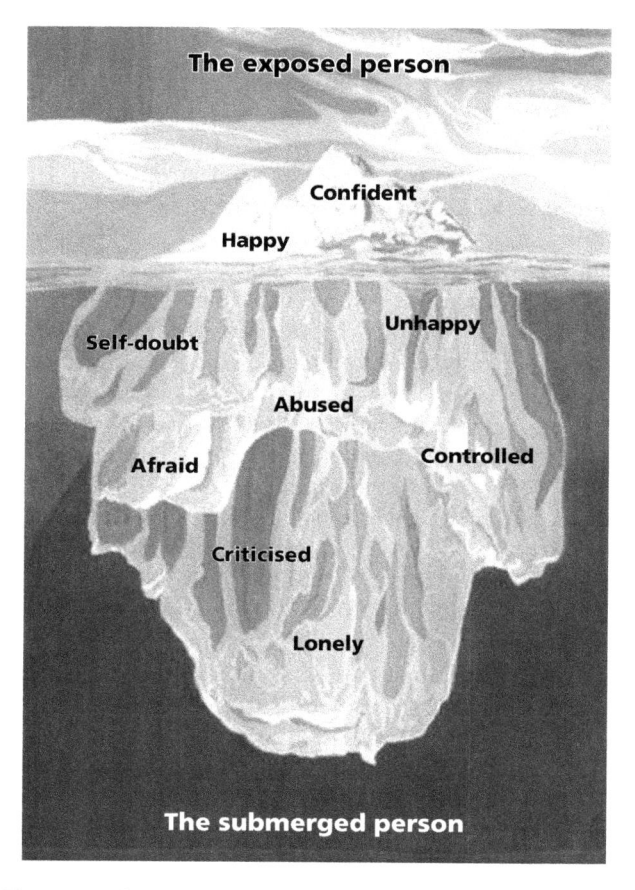

Figure 3.1 The exposed versus the hidden person in family violence. Iceberg base image from Haamer, K. (2021); model concept and design is the author's own

submerged portion of the iceberg continues to grow, pulling the person down. The exposed portion shrinks, sometimes until there is nothing left.

The Perpetrator's Web

In the Introduction to this book I mentioned what I call the Perpetrator's Web. Others who have experienced family violence may be able to relate to the Perpetrator's Web, although it may not represent everyone's story entirely or exactly. For those who have had no experience with family violence, the concept of a 'web' should help explain how people end up in a situation where they are living with family violence.

The traits a perpetrator of family violence exhibits when they meet their next victim are not the same as what is revealed over time. The early stage is 'the Garden of Eden', and the traits exhibited in the early stages are depicted on the outside of the web (Figure 3.2). The victim is free and not trapped (i.e. not caught in the web). The victim is drawn closer to the web. The victim thinks they have found an incredible person. As the victim spends more time with the perpetrator the victim starts to become trapped. The victim at this point is on the edge of the web.

Some early signs of controlling and abusive behaviour might begin, but then the perpetrator is sorry and it is easy to accept the apology. This is often called the 'hearts and flowers' stage, as the person might buy flowers or some other type of gift and say how sorry they are. Being with an abusive person does not mean they are only and always angry and demeaning. They still show positive traits. When things go their way, they can be kind and supportive. However, if the victim isn't operating

Figure 3.2 The Perpetrator's Web

to the perpetrator's expectations, the abusive cycle is rekindled. Early signs of the perpetrator being possessive and jealous are exhibited, but the victim is able to dismiss these signs and to think that perhaps this behaviour is something temporary. These signs continue as the victim gets closer and closer to the centre of the web.

At the centre of the web is the label 'Kids'. Once the couple has children between them, the victim is heavily entangled in the perpetrator's web. Escape may seem impossible and, in many ways, there is no true escape because children connect the victim to the perpetrator for life. The risks to personal safety and the risks to the children become central. The Family Law Act can make true escape almost impossible. The trapping nature of the Family Law Act is introduced later in this chapter in the 'Snakes and Ladders' discussion and is outlined in detail later in this book (Chapter 9) in discussing the binding nature of 'equal shared parental responsibilities'.

The Perpetrator's Web is a concept I developed for this book. In summary, getting into abusive relationships is like getting into a comfortable bed. They are easy to get into but difficult to get out of.

When I have been asked to explain how I married a controlling and abusive man, I explain that how he conducted himself when I met him was not who he revealed himself to be over time. The types of traits I observed early on were positive personality traits. He was charming and generous. He was charismatic. He also shared with me stories of being misunderstood and badly treated in past relationships, by his siblings and by his parents. He had been married twice before. The claims he made about his first wife were very shocking to me and I could not help but feel sorry for him. I look back on this now and feel guilty for believing his stories about his past. I viewed these people through the eyes of the stories he told me, which I believed. It is entirely possible that nothing he told me about those people was true.

A person speaking with disrespect about past relationships is a warning sign to be on the alert as the person could be an abuser. As Bancroft, who has treated thousands of men in men's behavioural change programmes, says:

> Beware of the man who is very focused on his bitterness or who tells you about it inappropriately early on in your dating. Be especially cautious of the man who talks about women from his past in degrading or condescending ways. (Bancroft, 2002: 114–115)

The early stages of a relationship with a perpetrator can trap the victim due to four key reasons (Bancroft, 2002):

* Friends and family are informed about this amazing person she has met; after 'talking him up so much, she feels embarrassed to reveal his mistreatment when it begins, so she keeps it to herself for a long time' (p. 110).
* Given how the abusive person behaves in the beginning, when behaviour changes, she thinks that something 'has gone wrong inside of him' (p. 110) and tries to work out what went wrong.

- As 'she' believed she found someone so perfect, it is difficult to let go of that dream.
- She wonders if she did something wrong or has a personal deficit that caused the problem and tries to find the solution.

As such, the early stage of the relationship (i.e. the outer stage of the web) is incredibly powerful (just like a real web). Because the early stage is so wonderful and cements thoughts and dreams, and results in positive conversations about the person who ends up being abusive, the victim becomes trapped.

Bancroft (2002) lists a series of 'warning signs' that abuse could be ahead in a relationship. I list these as follows:

- Speaks disrespectfully about former partners.
- Disrespectful towards you.
- Does unwanted favours for you or is overly generous.
- Controlling.
- Possessive.
- He does not believe that anything is his fault.
- Self-centred.
- Consumes a lot of alcohol or abuses drugs.
- Pressures you for sex.
- Gets serious about the relationship quickly.
- Intimidates you when he is angry (e.g. points a finger at you, blocks your passage, shouts you down).
- Double standards.
- Negative attitudes towards women.
- Treats you differently in front of people than in private.
- Attracted to vulnerability (generally women much younger than him).

Abusers may have some, most, or all of the traits. Signs of any of the items on the list could be warning signs to be on alert. As outlined in the Perpetrator's Web, once in the web it can be difficult to escape. Knowing the signs before entering the web is a safe strategy. Just as a spider's web is a trap because it has a secretion that sticks the caught insect to the web, the perpetrator's web can stick its victim through children, financial dependency, legal systems and isolation from others. These items are highlighted in the next conceptual framework: Snakes and Ladders.

Snakes and Ladders: A Conceptual Framework

Academic readers will be familiar with the notion that academic works tend to be positioned on a conceptual framework. In simple terms, it can be useful to provide a visual representation of the variables connected. This can provide structure to the research and/or a way to explain things visually. It can help to ensure the aspects that serve as key elements are put together and covered. This can ensure nothing critical is left off.

By way of background, the conceptual framework developed to explain separation from family violence was progressively developed over some time, before the first word of this book was written. A series of 'tests' was then undertaken to limit the chances of overlooking a key element. That does not make the framework exhaustive of everything that happens; it just comprises the essential components (i.e. the elements).

Testing of the snakes and ladders conceptual framework was through several meetings and discussions with representatives working in the frontline of family violence. This included a journalist who worked as a court reporter for family violence matters, numerous family violence court network officers, and representatives from organisations that work to assist women and children impacted by family violence.

The conceptual framework developed to explain separating from family violence is based on a combination of the ancient game of *Snakes and Ladders* (called *Moksha Patam*) and the Family Violence Power and Control Wheel. The conceptual framework will be explained after first explaining *Moksha Patam* and the Power and Control Wheel.

Moksha Patam

The original *Moksha Patam* game was created by Indian poet Saint Gyandev, who developed the game to teach moral instruction and values to children. The original game had 100 squares. Snakes represented vices, ladders represented virtues. There were more snakes than ladders to represent that journey of life – that there are more vices to overcome and that rising above them is a more difficult journey. Good deeds take us to evolution, while evil results in a cycle of rebirths.

In the original game, ladders could be found as follows:

- The 12th square was faith.
- The 51st square was reliability.
- 57th was generosity.
- 76th was knowledge.
- 78th was asceticism.

In the original game, snakes could be found as follows:

- The 41st square was for disobedience.
- 44th for arrogance.
- 49th vulgarity.
- 52nd theft.
- 58th lying.

- 62nd drunkenness.
- 69th debt.
- 84th anger.
- 92nd greed.
- 95th pride.
- 73rd murder.
- 99th lust.

The 100th square represented nirvana or *Moksha* – liberation. Reaching the 100th square signifies that you have attained *Moksha* (liberation and enlightenment).

In one adaption located by this author (Figure 3.3), the 12th square represents non-violence, which has a ladder to catapult the player up to square 91 – universal love.

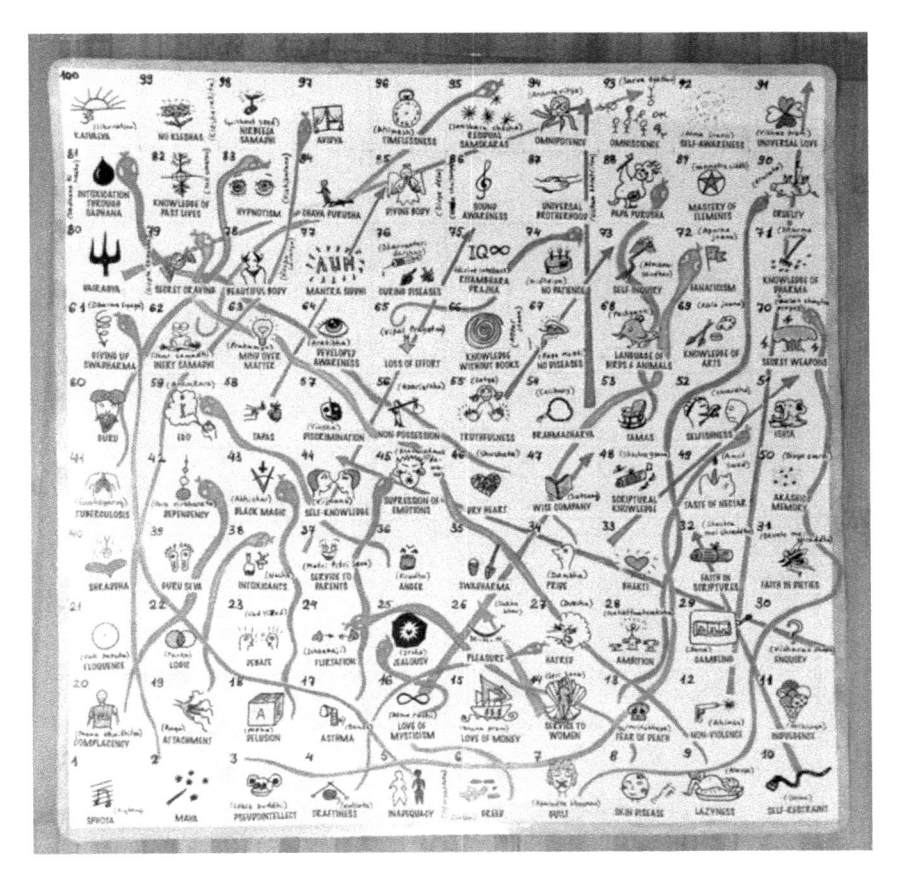

Figure 3.3 *Moksha Patam* board game
Source: Walk Through India (2010).

The Power and Control Wheel

The Power and Control Wheel (Figure 3.4) demonstrates the various tactics that an abusive partner employs to generate and maintain power and control in the relationship. Perpetrators may use some of the tactics or all of them.

Figure 3.4 is an adapted version of the wheel, simplified to show the core eight segments without the details listed for each segment. The Power and Control Wheel (also called the Duluth Model) was developed in the city of Duluth through a domestic abuse programme. There are critics of the wheel, who say it is not representative, and curious readers may like to pursue deeper reading if interested. However, the purpose of introducing the model here is to present the eight components of the wheel, which can be a useful way of understanding the different types of power and control that may be employed by a perpetrator of family violence. In the original model (Domestic Abuse Intervention Programs, 2017), examples of tactics can be seen under each heading in the wheel segment (e.g. 'playing mind games' sits under 'using emotional abuse'). If each of those tactics mentioned in the wheel model was placed on a *Snakes and Ladders* board, it would fill many squares (Table 3.1).

Figure 3.4 The Power and Control Wheel (Duluth Model)
Source: adapted from Domestic Abuse Intervention Programs (2017).

Table 3.1 Common tactics in family violence

Making or carrying out threats	Threatening to leave her or commit suicide	Making her drop charges	Making her do illegal things	Making her afraid through looks, actions, gestures	Smashing things
Destroying her property	Abusing pets	Displaying weapons	Putting her down	Making her feel bad about herself	Calling her names
Making her think she's crazy	Playing mind games	Humiliating her	Making her feel guilty	Controlling what she does and who she sees and talks to	Limiting her outside involvement
Using jealousy to justify actions	Making light of the abuse	Saying the abuse didn't happen	Shifting responsibility for abusive behaviour	Saying she caused it	Making her feel guilty about the children
Using the children to relay messages	Using visitation to harass her	Threatening to take the children away	Treating her like a servant	Making all the big decisions	Acting like 'the master of the castle'
Being the one to define men's and women's roles	Preventing her from getting or keeping a job	Making her ask for money	Giving her an allowance	Taking her money	Not letting her know about or have access to family income

Escaping Family Violence: A Conceptual Framework

I developed a conceptual framework to explain visually the steps that may be involved in trying to escape from family violence. It is outlined in Figure 3.5. This framework is briefly introduced in this section but discussed in more detail in Chapter 14, as this framework captures the key components discussed in this book that result in an understanding of 'The Great Escape'.

The bottom level indicates the vices. These are the elements from the Power and Control Wheel. These aspects provide control to the perpetrator.

The middle layer of the model is made up of the knowledge elements, and knowledge can assist the victim to reach the 'ladder' faster/safer (and/or be useful for friends/family to assist the victim to reach the ladder). The first aspect is that family violence is the 'perfect crime', where both perpetrator and victim tend not to disclose what is happening. This ensures the vices continue (i.e. slipping back down into the 'snake pit' situation). Lack of knowledge about what drives family violence can create a situation where victims 'feed the beast' – pampering to them, which can allow the perpetrator to 'grow'. Knowledge can also lead to the 'ladder' towards escape, to separation. In the knowledge row is also an element, 'Dr Jekyll and Mr Hyde' – to understand how a perpetrator can be one type of person to their partner yet may, to others, be the person who is the best neighbour who volunteers regularly

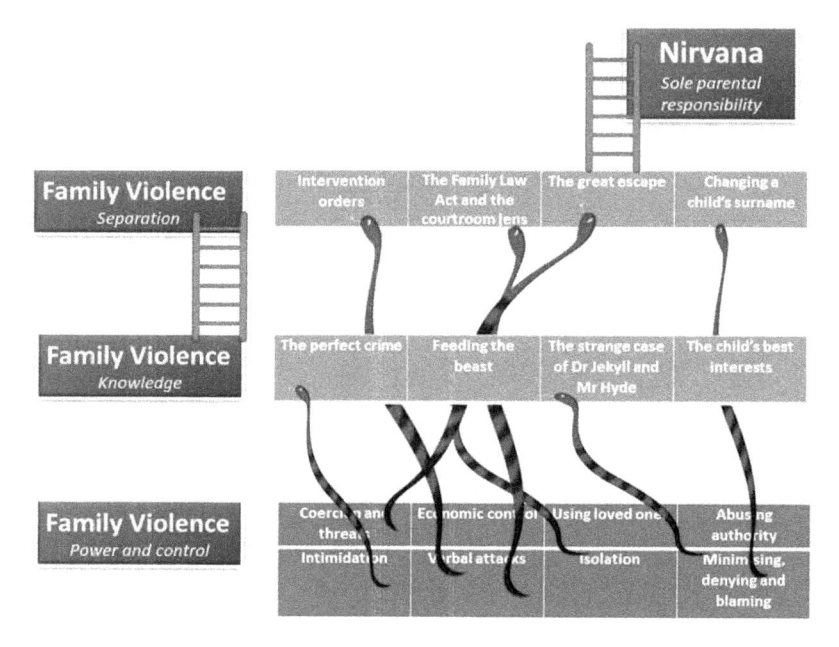

Figure 3.5 Escaping family violence framework

at a sports club. This dual aspect can be confusing and can result in attempts by the victim to seek support being dismissed as not credible by others who know the perpetrator. However, knowledge of this duality can empower a victim to climb the ladder towards escape. The fourth element in the knowledge row is the child's best interests.

In the top row sit the aspects relating to the separation stage. The first aspect is intervention orders. The second aspect is the Family Law Act and the courtroom lens. While these may also be viewed as knowledge items, they are essentially separation tools and, when used and understood, can assist with separation. The great escape is located third – because escape does not occur until the matters relating to parenting agreements and financial settlement have been resolved. While these aspects do not require court orders, true freedom will not happen without a legal process, which is discussed in this book. The final step is changing a child's surname. This is not relevant to all cases but is a matter that is relevant in some cases of family violence. It is a convoluted process and the mechanism is an important aspect of separation in some cases.

It is useful to keep in mind through the separation framework that the process will be difficult. The 'snakes' that send a victim back down to the 'snake pit' as they try to locate a 'ladder' to freedom, capture what they might face. This is discussed in more detail in Chapter 14.

A key point to remember is that trying to be rational and reasonable with a perpetrator of family violence is unlikely to be effective. Many of the behaviours of perpetrators are also seen in people who have narcissistic personality disorder, and there is research to indicate an overlap (i.e. many perpetrators of family violence also have narcissistic personality disorder). The notion of being able to see the victim's point of view requires empathy. Empathy means we are separate from the other person's feelings but can identify with those feelings. We are capable of stepping back and understanding their perspective. We can feel compassion and 'turn down the noise of our own preoccupations and open ourselves to what the other person is expressing' (Hotchkiss, 2002: 23). If the perpetrator is exhibiting signs of narcissism, then these signs might be: shamelessness, magical thinking, arrogance, envy, entitlement, exploitation and bad boundaries (Hotchkiss, 2002). Understanding that narcissistic personality disorder involves an inflated concept of entitlement and supremacy, a lack of empathy, and a strong need for validation and adoration, can help us in understanding the perpetrator's perspective because abuse and narcissism can appear to be similar. However, research has shown that men learn abusiveness from other men and not from their experiences with women. While narcissistic personality disorder stems from emotional injuries during childhood, abusive behaviour is learned from key role models and the 'misogyny of the society at large' (Bancroft, 2022b).

Conclusion

This chapter introduced the reader to control and abuse in the context of family violence. It began by briefly mentioning gender inequality as a contributing driver in family violence, and then discussed a small number of key statistics relating to family violence. A series of conceptual frameworks was introduced to help portray visually what living with family violence might be like, how a victim gets caught, and why just leaving is not as simple as it sounds. The next chapter is the first in the sequence discussing how family violence impacts every one of the five elements (generating region, destination, industries, tourist, transit route) in the whole tourism system model.

4 Tourism Industries

'Not all those who wander are lost.'
– 'The Riddle of Strider', *Lord of the Rings*, J.R.R. Tolkien

Introduction

This chapter is the first of four chapters that discuss matters within one of the five elements in the tourism system/tourism industries. Tourism industries are represented by the dashed line in Figure 4.1. Tourism industries can serve the tourist along any or all of the three elements the generating region, the transit route, and the destination. This chapter will introduce the reader to the complex nature of tourism and provides a foundation for defining industries, explaining tourism industries, and outlining partial industrialisation in tourism. Understanding partial industrialisation in tourism and tourism industries (plural) requires some understanding of strategic management. Understanding that not all readers will be familiar with strategic management (or even want to be), this chapter introduces some key aspects in a simple manner to aid comprehension of these complex but important matters.

As with all chapters in this book, some key theoretical aspects are provided where these are important but the chapter deliberately avoids the heavy referencing to be found in academic journal articles. Key references are provided, and these sit alongside other forms of evidence

▬ ▬ ▬ ▬ = tourism industries

Figure 4.1 Whole Tourism System Model
Source: adapted from Leiper (2004).

including observation, lived experience, as well as deciphering and interpreting legislation and cases. Stories are included wherever possible, to help personalise and bring life to the key material.

Tourism comprises multiple industries and is not one single industry; and tourism is partially industrialised. Readers will be forgiven for being confused by the notion of tourism industries being plural. We are constantly exposed to messages in the media regarding 'the tourism industry'. It is as if to suggest that every business that serves tourists must belong to some giant industry, and those collective businesses comprise 'the tourism industry'. From a common language perspective, this is fine. However, researchers should have awareness of why tourism is not one giant industry but multiple industries; and why tourism is partially industrialised.

These concepts become important as matters relating to employment law issues in retail, hospitality, and fast food are discussed in the next chapter. Such industries are industries in their own right. However, businesses in those industries serve tourists as well as non-tourists and some do not have business strategies that target tourists as a distinct segment. In fact there is a great range of different types of businesses as well as recreational facilities and public services that service the needs and wants of tourists but do so incidentally as their main clientele are local residents (Leiper, 1979). If a restaurant serves a tourist it is 'tourist expenditure', but the same meal served to a local resident is not. This creates an overlap with industries that are defined based on the services or the good that the business produces rather than who consumes them. Therefore, understanding foundational matters relating to industries and partial industrialisation is important for discussions throughout the later chapters of this book. It is important to be clear on what is meant by an industry. Accordingly, this chapter commences with a detailed discussion about defining and understanding industries.

Defining and Understanding an Industry, Tourism and Holidays

This section will explain how to define an industry. Understanding what an industry is will be especially important for the next chapter, where various industries including the 'hospitality industry' and the 'fast-food industry' are discussed.

Readers may already be familiar with terms such as 'monopoly' and 'oligopoly'. This is a good starting point for understanding an industry. An oligopoly is 'an industry where only a few firms operate' (Corporate Finance Institute, 2022b). Typically, the industries in which oligopolies exist are those where the goods produced are extremely similar. Airlines (domestic and international airline industries are separate industries) and pharmaceuticals are oligopolies. A monopoly has many buyers but only a single seller in the market (Corporate Finance Institute, 2022a). Therefore, there is no competition in the industry and buyers have no choice of supplier.

Following on from these simple examples of industries, a broad definition and explanation of industries is needed. A simple and clear definition of an industry is that it comprises 'a group of products that are close substitutes to buyers, are available to a common group of buyers, and are relatively distant substitutes for all products not included in the industry' (Bain, 1968: 124). Bain goes on to explain that this definition is for a 'theoretical industry' (p. 124).

An important point of distinction that Bain (1968) offers is that an industry comprises products (which might be services) but that an industry does not comprise firms. This distinction is important because a firm might produce a number of different products. Each product may belong to a different industry from that of the other products the firm produces. Therefore, the industry comprises similar substitutable products. Those products are created and supplied by firms.

Accordingly, to measure industry concentration means to measure seller concentration. Measuring the industry means measuring the 'number and size distribution of firms supplying a given group of close-substitute products, the size of each firm being measured by the proportion of output it supplies within the given product group' (Bain, 1968: 125). It is noteworthy that statistical and census measurement data of industries may not match the definition of an industry (i.e. the theoretical industry). Measurements of industry are often for convenience rather than accuracy, and Bain refers to these as being a 'Census industry' (1968: 125). Such groupings may comprise firms with similar processes although those processes may involve numerous products that are not close substitutes (Bain, 1968). An example would be 'bread and bakery products' in the US. Another example (also from the US) is the 'accommodation and food services' industry. This is not an industry (in the theoretical sense) but the grouping of fast food, cafes, coffee shops, caravan parks, hotels, restaurants, motels and nightclubs among others is a convenient grouping of information.

Looking at the types of firms included in the 'accommodation and food services industry', we see cafes, caravan parks, hotels, motels and other types of firms that we understand are used by tourists. Such businesses are apparently also in 'the tourism industry'.

As was discussed in the previous chapter, tourism is a system. Within that system, tourists make tours (i.e. temporarily depart their residence and make tours to return to their point of origin). Therefore, in understanding tourism, it is crucial to understand that it comprises five elements of which a tourist is only one of those elements. In terms of defining a tourist, 'a tourist can be defined as a person making a discretionary, temporary tour which involves at least one overnight stay away from the normal place of residence, excepting tours made for the primary purpose of earning remuneration from points en route' (Leiper, 1979: 396). Leisure is a major feature of tourism, and as such it is useful to note that a definition for a tourist will also involve 'a search for leisure experiences from interactions with features or characteristics of places they choose to visit' (Leiper, 2004: 35).

It is probably useful also to discuss holidays, because while a person might be a tourist when on holiday, they might take holidays (i.e. time off work) but not go anywhere. When people talk of taking a holiday, the underlying assumption is that someone is taking time to get away. Get away from work. Get away from routine. A holiday can be defined as 'a period in which a break is taken from work or studies for rest, travel, or recreation' (Hanks, 1986: 730). Similarly, the *Cambridge Dictionary* defines a holiday as 'a time when someone does not go to work or school but is free to do what they want, such as travel or relax' (*Cambridge Dictionary*, n.d.).

We see from these two dictionary definitions the commonality of a holiday as representing time away from something. Notably, *The Collins English Dictionary* defines a holiday as being 'for rest' (Hanks, 1986) and the *Cambridge Dictionary* states that a person on a holiday 'is free to do what they want'. No wonder a holiday sounds so wonderful to so many people.

But what about those who are living with family violence? As I mention in the Overture, family violence does not take a holiday. And, as also described in the Overture, a holiday with a perpetrator of family violence can mean feeling even more trapped. Whether or not someone decides to travel somewhere or whether they spend their holiday at home, the lack of a break from family violence can result in the same thing. The next section takes the reader through why tourism is not one single industry but comprises multiple industries.

Understanding Tourism Industries

Understanding that tourists will frequent cafes, but so will people who are not tourists, it is critical to outline that tourism is partially industrialised. The concept of partial industrialisation in tourism is explained in the next section. However, to begin with, in simple terms, partial industrialisation means that many businesses are partially in tourism (i.e. they serve tourists as customers as well as belonging to other industries). Accordingly, many different businesses sit across more than one industry that may partially include tourists as a market. Such businesses also sit quite rightly within another industry: such as retail, restaurants, fast food or education.

The previous section took us through what is an industry. Looking at this specifically for tourism, it can be seen how tourism became known as an industry, and why it isn't an industry. Seven approaches have been used to critique tourism as an industry (Leiper, 2008b):

(1) *Authoritarian decree* – by leading institutions referring to 'the tourism industry' it can be viewed as a type of authoritarian pronouncement. In other words, if leading organisations keep using the term 'the

tourism industry' it becomes engrained and accepted without question. It is noted that International Standard Industrial Classification (ISIC) refers to 'tourism-related activities' instead of an industry.

(2) *Impacts on economies* – measuring the value of 'the tourism industry' requires aggregating the economic impacts from expenditures made by tourists. That involves examining tourism from a demand side (i.e. consumption of activities). However, industries are measured from a supply side, and the demand-side data of tourism expenditures cannot be assumed to represent 'the tourism industry'. Of note, many suppliers of goods and services consumed by tourists do not have strategies targeting tourists, who are simply part of their customer base (e.g. a restaurant or supermarket). This is discussed in more detail later in this chapter in the section Partial Industrialisation.

(3) *Competition among suppliers in markets* – businesses within an industry compete with each other. They compete to gain an advantage or to defend and retain a position within an industry. For example, manufacturers of cars will compete with other manufacturers of cars within the motor vehicle industry; manufacturers of soft drinks will compete with other manufacturers of soft drinks within the soft drink industry. However, the Hilton Hotels in Chicago are not competing with the British Museum in London. Both may serve tourists, but they are not competing with each other. They are not in the same industry.

(4) *Substitutes in markets* – operating in the same industry means that there are substitutes. If a particular soft drink is not in stock, an alternative soft drink can be substituted as there is a soft drink industry comprising substitutes. An industry comprises a number of sellers who are offering substitutes to a group of buyers (Bain, 1968). The Backpackers Inn in Byron Bay Australia is not competing with the Grand Royale London Hyde Park in England. These are not substitutes. These businesses are not competing for the same buyer and are operating in different industries.

(5) *Cooperation among suppliers in markets and wider systems* – industries comprise a collection of suppliers. Aside from some forms of behaviour in industries such as price-fixing, organisations within industries tend to cooperate. The global oil industry highlights cooperation. More than a century ago, when separate and independent suppliers provided oil, engines would fail because the technical composition varied. The standardisation of fuel/petrol/gas was instrumental in creating a successful industry. Similarly, organisations such as IBM and Nokia cooperated to create an industry that competed but also cooperated to develop Bluetooth technologies. Cooperation transforms unique individual suppliers and transforms the collection into an industry. As another example, when coffee began to be grown in northern New South Wales in Australia, farmers needed to cooperate and share the

costs of buying a mechanical harvester (which would only be used for a few days across a few weeks each year but was very costly). The cooperative purchasing and sharing of the mechanical harvester allowed for a coffee-growing industry to develop. The costs of a mechanical harvester on an individual farmer basis would have prevented most if not all farmers from moving into the coffee industry in northern New South Wales as the entry costs would have been too great.

(6) *Strategic management* – a fundamental theory in strategic management is Porter's (1979) 'five forces model'. This theory is well known and is considered a foundational teaching component in strategic management at universities. The model sets out to identify the factors that shape an industry. The five forces are: competitors, buyers, suppliers, new entrants and substitutes. The strength of each force needs to be assessed to provide an overall view of the industry. The model can help determine whether to enter an industry. Anyone who has attempted to apply Porter's five forces model to 'the tourism industry' will quickly realise the problem. The whole concept of substitutes, buyers, suppliers, new entrants and competitors is completely different for a business such as Disneyland compared with the Colosseum tour operator.

(7) *Estimated numbers of tourists* – when reports are published that outline the number of tourists in 'the tourism industry' there is confusion between supply and demand. Industries supply to a market. Tourists consume products and services. Essentially, reports of tourism numbers, which are a flow, cannot be considered to be the same as a collection of suppliers providing tourists with products/services. The number of tourists does not measure an 'industry'.

According to (Leiper, 2008: 249):

> Once the fetish with a singular industry is abandoned, commentators can more readily recognise that certain tourism industries are capital intensive and others are labour intensive. This should reduce the incidence of comments about 'the tourism industry' being simultaneously labour intensive and capital intensive, which is like saying that a person is simultaneously small and large.

To summarise, the key point regarding why tourism comprises multiple industries and is not one 'giant' industry can be captured by reminding ourselves what an industry is. While it is easy for a term that is regularly used to be conveniently adopted, when properly interrogated it can be seen that tourism is not one giant industry. Again, using the term in everyday speech is not necessarily problematic. However, for the purposes of certain academic and industry pursuits, correct terminology and understanding are important. For example, if a Destination Marketing Organisation is misusing the components that comprise tourism (e.g. including all expenditures across all industries that tourists may use, or using tourism data, which is a flow to claim value to a local economy), this can result in local government providing funding (which comes from ratepayers) disproportionately such to the inflated result of 'the tourism industry' claim. Similarly, if industry practitioners are looking at entering an industry, they need to have an understanding of what an industry is to assess barriers and potential profit. Practitioners could arrive at flawed findings, resulting in potentially expensive business mistakes.

Essentially, as has been outlined, what is meant by an industry is that it comprises a group of sellers who are competing for the same buyer. In other words, the companies within an industry are producing substitutes. By way of a simple example, certain car models can be considered to be substitutes. A buyer can select from various options. They may have a preference but may shift their preference based on availability or price. The pharmaceutical industry is another example. Paracetamol is the active ingredient in Panadol. It is the same active ingredient in many other brands (e.g. Hedanol, Herron). Similarly, ibuprofen is the active ingredient in the brand Nurofen, as well as Advil, Motrin and IBU. Hedonal is a clear substitute for Herron and Panadol. Advil is a clear substitute for Motrin and Nurofen. In essence, any of those over-the-counter pain relief medications are substitutes in that if a person was wanting Panadol but the only thing they could purchase was Nurofen, in many cases (allergies and other similar reactions aside) each item would be a substitute for the other item. These items are positioned in the same industry. The backpackers in Byron Bay are not competing with Disneyland. These are not in the same industry. These are not substitutes and these companies are not competing for the same buyer.

Partial Industrialisation

Following on from the discussion in the previous section, an awareness of the issue of industries is important in terms of the partial industrialisation in tourism (PIIT). As one of the key foci of this book is on examining bullying, control, abuse and family violence in tourism industries, it is important to recognise the theory of partial industrialisation in tourism. This concept is especially relevant in the next chapter (Chapter 5), where employment law legislation is discussed.

Partial industrialisation is a way to explain how and why tourism systems differ in their use of tourism industries. Forty years ago the concept of PIIT was first raised by Leiper (1979), who stated that 'the process of tourism is ... inherently ... partially-industrialized' (1979: 390). As such, PIIT should be considered an important element in under-standing the whole tourism system, as it has implications for understanding tourism, tourism-related jobs, destination competitiveness, tourism management, sustainability and seasonality (Leiper *et al.*, 2008).

The importance of understanding whole tourism systems by acknowledging PIIT was demonstrated by Hall (2007), who discussed these connections through his discussion on the tourism system. Tourism systems were discussed in Chapter 2 of this book.

While raised initially by Leiper (1979), partial industrialisation has attracted few researchers since. The most recent work on partial industrialisation in tourism was in 2013 (Backer & Barry, 2013), and was only the third study to undertake empirical testing of the theory. As such, this discussion necessarily centres around the work by Leiper (1979) and Leiper *et al.* (2008). The lack of recognition of PIIT was acknowledged by Leiper *et al.* (2008), who provided five reasons for this neglect.

Firstly, PIIT has only been mentioned briefly by a handful of researchers and therefore there has been a lack of serious discussion in the field through international research journals (Leiper *et al.*, 2008). Therefore, the information on PIIT has not filtered through to a wider selection of government agencies and tourism officials.

A second reason may relate to the notion of tourism industries as a plural, rather than a singular entity, linked to the understanding of PIIT theory. Since 'PIIT challenges the widely accepted idea of tourism as "an industry" … a general recognition of PIIT could disturb interest groups' (Leiper *et al.*, 2008: 208). Many tourism researchers have to date resisted adopting the plural variant: this may be a contributing factor in limiting the interest and application of PIIT.

In explaining PIIT, Leiper *et al.* (2008) highlight that 'an industry is a group of sellers of close substitutes to a common group of buyers' (Bain, 1959, cited in Leiper, 2008: 241). Similar definitions are supplied by Porter (1985) and Gilbert (1990). An industry is where businesses are competing with each other, by focusing on 'structural heterogeneity within an industry' (Porter, 1985: 272). This point is also targeted by Tremblay, who says (1998: 840) that tourism 'is not really an industry'. A definition of industries provided by Gilbert (1990: 58) states: 'Industries are made up of firms which produce the same product or groups of products so that the consumer regards these as ideal substitutes for one another even though the products may differ slightly.' As such, tourism comprises multiple tourism industries. Some of these are actively targeting tourists in their business strategies; others are passively accepting them. Such a concept was empirically tested by Backer and Barry (2013), who found that all commercial accommodation operators interviewed reported having a strategy that distinctly targeted tourists, although tourists were not the only market for some operators. Some commercial accommodation operators relied heavily on short-term residency for contract workers and travelling sales representatives (Backer & Barry, 2013). Backer and Barry (2013) also found that retailers and operators of cafes and restaurants were serving tourists as part of their market but did not have distinct business strategies targeting them.

A third reason provided is that understanding PIIT requires some grasp of strategic management, which 'some researchers on tourism have treated casually and superficially' (Leiper *et al.*, 2008: 208–209). Fourthly, it has also been suggested that the complexity of the original (Leiper, 1990) PIIT model has put off interested parties (Leiper *et al.*, 2008). A fifth reason is that it is difficult to measure industrialisation in tourism and, as such, PIIT has necessarily been confined to academic discussions (Leiper *et al.*, 2008).

In seeking to understand PIIT theory, it is useful to consider how industries are measured. Since industries are collections of organisations that are supplying goods or services, by measuring those organisations' output, it is possible to understand the size and observe the trends of industries. This cannot be done with tourism, however. Referring to tourism as an 'industry' infers 'that the tourism industry provides all the facilities, services and goods consumed by all tourists' (Leiper *et al.*, 2008: 209). This would assume that tourism is wholly industrialised: that is, the services and goods that industries produce are consumed only by tourists. However, examples such as retailers, restaurants, cafes and petrol stations challenge this assumption. It is important to be clear on this aspect, especially concerning the discussions in the next chapter about employment law and casualisation in industries that are partially industrialised in tourism. Such businesses may have tourists as part of their customer base but they are also likely to deal with customers who are not tourists. Therefore, such examples are not fully industrialised in tourism but are only partially industrialised in tourism. This is acknowledged by Tremblay, who agreed that tourism is 'partially industrialized – in the sense that many important firms (in terms of expenditures) are only incidentally involved in its strategic organization' (1998: 842).

Examples of the 'factors that directly support tourists' consumption patterns and other experiences' (Leiper *et al.*, 2008: 213), reveal that many of the factors that support tourists are not fully industrialised in tourism. These seven factors, which were derived from the work by Stear (2002), include:

- Natural and built attractions that are free.
- Public goods (e.g. roads, parks).
- Transportation, accommodation, entertainment and other trip-related aspects that are provided by tourists themselves.
- Transportation, accommodation, entertainment and other trip-related aspects that are provided by friends and relatives.
- Information and other resources supplied by other tourists.
- Goods and services supplied by organisations that do not have deliberate strategies aimed at tourists, and for which 'tourists are merely an incidental – not strategic – subset among their customers' (Leiper *et al.*, 2008: 213). Examples may be, in some (but not all) cases: retail shops, cafes and restaurants.

- Goods and services supplied by organisations that have business strategies aimed at tourists. Some examples are commercial accommodation, travel agencies and theme parks.

Leiper *et al.* (2008: 213) note that the first six of these factors are 'non-industrial factors' with respect to tourism, and only the last factor comprises tourism industries. However, there may be limitations on some of those 'tourism industries' as well. For example, some theme parks (also referred to as visitor attractions and tourism attractions) may have some business strategies aimed at tourists, and other strategies aimed at other segments. This point was made by Swarbrooke (2002: 9), who states that 'the term "tourist attraction" is actually a misnomer since most visitors to attractions are not tourists in the accepted sense of the word'. Swarbrooke (2002) identifies some exceptions, such as Disney World in Florida and Legoland in Denmark. He makes an important point because many visitors to attractions might be day visitors who are not staying within that region (i.e. not tourists). An example of this is Australia Zoo, one of the major attractions on the Sunshine Coast, Queensland, Australia. While located within the Sunshine Coast, the operation draws heavily from the Brisbane and Gold Coast regions (both regions are south of the Sunshine Coast within the state of Queensland). There are daily train and coach services taking visitors to Australia Zoo for one full day. The importance of these destinations is evident from a daily coach operation on the Gold Coast that includes picking up passengers from all major hotels. A similar but separate service is provided for Brisbane passengers, which also includes daily pickups from major hotels.

A further illustration of the point made by Swarbrooke (2002) can be seen at Sovereign Hill, Ballarat, in the state of Victoria, Australia. Sovereign Hill was opened in November 1970 and is a recreated goldfields township situated on a 15-hectare site in Ballarat that is linked with the richest alluvial gold rush in the world (Sovereign Hill, 2022). While Sovereign Hill is regarded as a 'tourism icon in Australia and a winner of major tourism awards' (Sovereign Hill, 2022), and was judged Victoria's Best Major Tourism Attraction at the 2003 and 2004 Victoria Tourism Awards, tourists are only one of its market segments. Day visitors from Melbourne and local residents are also part of its visitor mix, and education is a critical market for this major attraction and deliberate business strategies are focusing on that segment. Around 20% of Sovereign Hill's market is derived from students, most of whom come from Melbourne and greater Melbourne. Interestingly, through a discussion on partial industrialisation in tourism over a decade ago with Sovereign Hill's then Deputy CEO, Tim Sullivan, the response was: 'the propensity to have Sovereign Hill described purely in terms of tourism has been one of my absolute bug-bears in trying to raise awareness of the significance of what we do' (T. Sullivan, personal communication, 10 October 2009).

This response links with a suggestion made by Leiper *et al.* (2008: 211) that 'private-sector associations purporting to represent "the industry" rely on the conventional concept to exaggerate the scale of their contribution to tourism's economic impacts'. So, from an 'industry' perspective, it can be desirable to include all activities from businesses linked with tourism. However, the case in point with Sovereign Hill highlights that this may be in conflict with what the individual operator believes and desires.

Interest in PIIT has historically been limited. There was an attempt to advance PIIT's theoretical underpinnings through a diagrammatical model (Leiper *et al.*, 2008) to provide a clearer insight into this area (Figure 4.2). The authors explain through their model that tourism is an activity in which only some industries have business strategies aimed at targeting tourists. Other businesses may have tourists as part of their customer base but do not actively set out to attract tourists and do not see themselves as being involved in tourism (Leiper *et al.*, 2008). Therefore, tourism is partially industrialised.

Some forms of tourism that comprise a large percentage of organised package trips and a high use of businesses specifically targeting tourists are considered highly industrialised (Leiper *et al.*, 2008). In such a

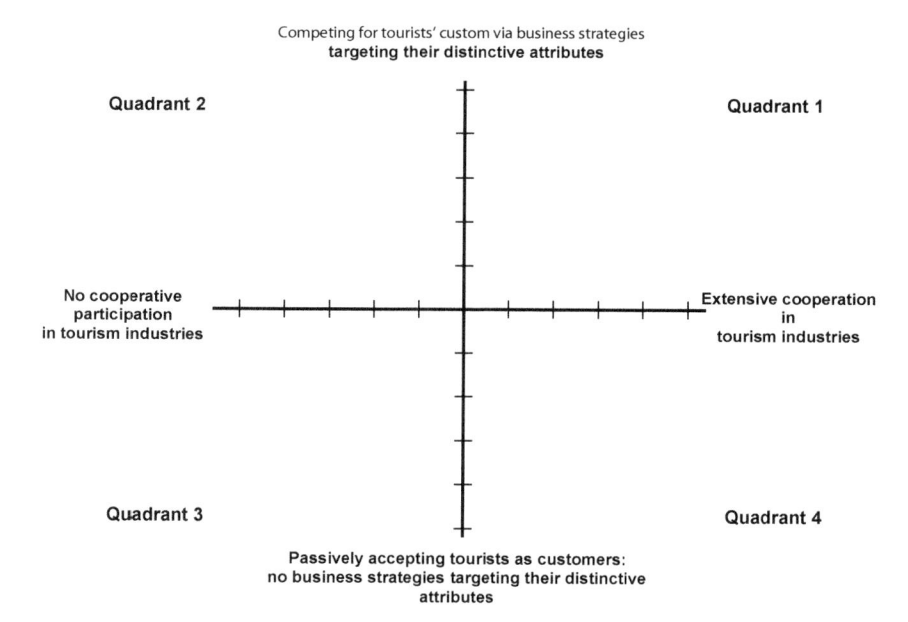

Figure 4.2 Partial Industrialisation in Tourism Model
Source: adapted from Leiper *et al.* (2008: 215).

case, most of the businesses the tourist deals with (e.g. travel agencies, tour operators, souvenir stores and accommodation) have extensive cooperation with tourism industries and have clear business strategies targeting tourists and would be established in the top right-hand area of Quadrant 1 in Figure 4.2 (Leiper *et al.*, 2008). However, these same tourists will also utilise other businesses that are located in the other three quadrants. For example, businesses such as grocery stores, petrol stations, newsagencies and retail outlets may have tourists as part of their customer base but generally do not have any specific business strategies that target the distinctive attributes of tourists. Such businesses are passively accepting tourists and are not participating in tourism industries in any cooperative way (Leiper *et al.*, 2008).

In contrast, a high level of domestic travel in Australia involves independently arranged trips, and participation in non-industrialised activities and, as such, is industrialised to a lesser extent (Leiper *et al.*, 2008). In examples of low-level industrialised tourism, the location and concentration of most of the organisations are in Quadrant 3 in Figure 4.2, with small clusters in the other quadrants. A trip to a destination, taken by driving a private motor vehicle, staying and eating in the home of a relative and going to the beach, has a low level of industrialisation. This simple example serves as an important consideration in understanding the complexities involved in the tourism system (which is discussed in Chapter 2) with regards to industrialisation and the implications of the level of industrialisation of any tourism system.

This is a useful consideration, particularly where visiting friends and relatives (VFR) travel is concerned. There is a perception that VFR travellers 'come naturally' to a particular destination (Morrison *et al.*, 2000: 110). As such, VFR travel is rarely considered worthy of an individualised marketing approach (Morrison *et al.*, 2000: 115). It is also considered, in economic terms, to hold less status than other forms of tourism (Lehto *et al.*, 2001). However, it is not known how industrialised VFR travel is in an absolute sense and it is also not known how industrialised it is relative to non-VFR travellers. Levels of industrialisation of both VFR and non-VFR travel will also vary by destination. It may well be that, in a popular tourist region, VFR travel is just as industrialised as non-VFR travel in that area because VFR travellers undertake similar activities as non-VFR travellers. This concept of relative partial industrialisation (PI) is therefore important to an understanding of the industrialisation issue of VFR travellers. VFR travel may not be a highly industrialised form of travel. However, the question is important in respect of how industrialised it is relative to other forms of travel because it is only through a comparative analysis of VFR and non-VFR travel that this can be fully understood (Morrison *et al.*, 2000). VFR travel is discussed in Chapter 13 of this book.

Conclusion

This chapter has explained the concept of an industry and provided a detailed explanation of why tourism comprises multiple industries and is not one giant industry. This chapter has also taken the reader through an introduction to the concept of partial industrialisation in tourism (PIIT). The chapter presents key foundational aspects relating to the complex nature of tourism that will help the reader better understand the industrial aspects discussed in the next chapter.

5 Employment Law Impacts on Tourism Industries

'A trap is only a trap if you don't know about it.
If you know about it, it's a challenge.'

China Mieville, *King Rat,* p. 254

Introduction

This chapter introduces the reader to key problematic employment issues found in some businesses in the tourism system. There are aspects relating to processes in organisations that can give rise to control and abuse. Some of these aspects are especially prevalent in a number of industries relevant to tourism. Noting the point raised in the previous chapter – that tourism is partially industrialised – this chapter discusses various employment matters that are particularly prevalent in industries such as hospitality, retail and fast food (remembering that those industries also serve tourists). The focus of this chapter is on the disadvantages that occur due to employment structures. Behavioural aspects such as bullying are discussed in the next chapter. This chapter is concerned with the structures in the workplace that create disadvantages.

Some of the employment legislation may create an opportunity for a power imbalance and for control and abuse, and even subtleties of bullying may result. Heavy casualisation of staff in businesses can also exacerbate the power imbalance. This chapter may serve as useful reading for those interested in improving their understanding of workplace agreements and the areas in which tensions may arise in businesses that serve tourists. In addition, this chapter outlines how broad the impact of problematic behaviour is when discussed in a tourism framework.

The chapter begins by providing the reader with a broad understanding of employment laws and outlining in what ways certain countries are ranked higher than others for the conditions under which employees operate. It then details the legislative framework in Australia and explains Awards and Enterprise Agreements. An understanding of these at a basic level is very important for anyone. They map out the conditions under which someone 'agrees' to operate. Many organisations that serve tourists (e.g. retail, hospitality and fast food) recruit young vulnerable people on a casual basis. Many such businesses also employ tourists. For example, it is not uncommon for young people to travel and have temporary longer stays in various destinations where they find employment (typically in bars and hotels). Where conditions are not fair and reasonable, it creates an unfair situation for the employees and can result in a high turnover of staff. Such matters may have a negative impact on those businesses that serve tourists (and that also serve non-tourists).

A poorly known but important component discussed in this chapter is zombie agreements. Zombie agreements are enterprise agreements that have passed their nominal expiry date but are allowed to continue operating (i.e. living dead agreements) due to a loophole in the employment legislation. Some particular cases are highlighted in this chapter to dispel the myth that working for a well-known brand does not guarantee appropriate modern conditions. After reading this chapter it is hoped that readers will be more aware of workplace conditions, will ask about the employment conditions before agreeing to accept a job and read the paperwork before signing it.

The Fast-Food Industry

Fast-food restaurants are known for having a consistent menu across locations so that meals are recognisable and familiar with a predictable level of quality. There is no table service, meals are inexpensive, and service focuses on being very fast. A newer segment is the fast-casual segment, which is the fastest-growing segment of the restaurant industry. The fast-food industry is a heavy employer of casual employees, many of whom are teenagers. As an industry, it generates more than US$570 billion in revenue (Sena, 2022). Fast-food restaurants are a significant proportion of the restaurant sector; together with fast-casual restaurants they are jointly known as Quick Service Restaurants (QSR) and account for more than half the restaurant sector's sales (Sena, 2022).

As fast-food restaurants provide a consistent and recognisable menu, they are often a popular choice for tourists who may want a quick and relatively inexpensive meal that they know what to expect. Some particular elements from a workplace perspective can occur, however.

At many fast-food restaurants, store managers are employed who are teenagers. Problems can arise from this because teenagers are unlikely to have been through adequate training on some of the complex matters in today's workplaces. A particular example is assault claims.

Assault claims are serious matters. They are also complex matters and require a solid understanding of the internal processes for handling these issues as well as external processes. This section will not endeavour to detail these but will highlight a number of key points:

- Organisations will have policies and procedures for handling various issues, but assault is a criminal offence.
- Organisations should not be playing judge and jury to events that should be investigated externally.
- If an alleged event occurred externally to the organisation (i.e. not on workplace grounds, not a workplace event held elsewhere, not an event supervised/managed by workplace management) then it should be referred to the appropriate external agency.
- Those who are accused are not to be assumed to be guilty because an allegation against them was made.

This chapter will not drill into detailed legislative aspects; however, the matter of procedural fairness (sometimes called natural justice) is touched upon. Two cases are provided below. I stress once again that assault claims are serious matters, but there are times when allegations are not factually based. Because assaults are so dreadful, reactions in workplaces can be unbalanced, and this can be especially dreadful if the allegation was not true and was fabricated out of spite. As awful as that sounds, this can and does happen and I will now share an example of this.

Example One: False allegation of physical assault

In late 2021, an 18-year-old male who worked for a fast-food restaurant store as a trainee manager was rung up and told not to go to work that day for his scheduled shift because of a 'workplace complaint'. Initially, he was not told what that complaint was. He was suspended. As it unfolded, he was made aware that a colleague had lodged a formal complaint against him for 'physical assault'. Naturally, this is an extremely serious allegation and dismissal is a likely outcome. He was advised that the complainant had supplied a photo of her bruised wrist, which she alleged had been caused as a result of the physical assault. The reason I am intimately familiar with this case is that the 18-year-old was my eldest son.

As his support person, I requested a copy of the allegation statement, a copy of the photo with the bruised wrist, and the CCTV footage of the area in the store in which the alleged incident took place. The photo of the alleged bruised wrist was of the wrist from the right hand. The CCTV footage showed the complainant dropping a bag of cooked food on the floor, picking it up from the floor, and then adding additional food from the warmer into that same dropped bag. The male respondent (i.e. my son) could be seen grabbing the bag of food being re-filled (that was held in the complainant's left hand). In slow-motion, it was clear that there was no contact whatsoever with any part of the complainant.

Contact was only made with the bottom of the bag, which was then thrown into the bin by my son (which is a workplace requirement as anything dropped on the floor must be treated as potentially contaminated and must be disposed of).

In summary – the bag of food was held in the complainant's *left* hand. No contact was made with anything else apart from the bag. The alleged bruise was on the wrist of the *right* hand. It was revealed through the investigation that the allegation was false. The point that needs to be made clearly here is the vulnerability of teenagers without experience and with a power imbalance. Without a support person requesting materials to enable an investigation on behalf of the accused, the ending to this may have been very different. In many cases, stores are managed by teenagers without an understanding of such complex matters. It can be easy to assume an allegation is true. Accused people may feel powerless, overwhelmed and confused. They may resign or may be asked to find another job.

The key message in stories such as this example is for people to get support, ask for evidence, and ensure they are provided with procedural fairness. Procedural fairness is a key aspect in any proceeding but is also embedded in organisations. Procedural fairness, in simplistic terms, means having the opportunity to be heard (and heard by someone without bias) before a decision is made. This example is but one example – there are others, especially in other domains such as coaches of female rowing and other sports.

Example Two: Employing one gender to avoid allegations of physical and sexual assault

There is a hot chicken store in Melbourne, Australia, that is in many ways similar to a KFC-type offering. It is a fast-food restaurant but it is independent and not part of a major chain. A friend of mine who lives in Melbourne has frequented this store for more than 10 years. He observed that the restaurant only employed teenage males, which struck him as unusual. Observing the staffing at other similar dining venues showed a high presence of females. My friend, curious, recently asked the owner why he only employed males. The owner told him that he used to have so much trouble with allegations of physical and/or sexual assault when he employed both genders. The allegations took up a lot of time and energy and created a terrible workplace culture. He decided to employ males only and has had no trouble since.

Casual Employment

This section discusses casual employment. It focuses on conditions in Australia; readers from other countries should note that the particular details such as hours and loadings may not apply in their regions.

However, the general points about rights and reasonings are important universally, and interested readers can find some general pointers for raising specific questions for other countries if needed.

Casual employment has become a growing 'concern' in Australia, which has one of the highest rates of casual workers out of the 34 countries within the membership of the Organisation for Economic Co-operation and Development (OECD) (Khadem, 2019). Indeed, the proportion of casual employees is one of the highest in the world, with around one-quarter of Australian employees having no leave entitlements (Peetz, 2020). One problem with casual employment is that the lack of rights and the constant threat of having reduced working hours or of being dismissed creates a significant power imbalance where employers have enhanced power (Peetz, 2020). As of August 2016, there were almost 2.5 million casual employees in Australia, compared to approximately 7.4 million permanent employees (Gilfillan, 2018).

Casual work can be defined as 'employment without the leave benefits provided by the National Employment Standards' (Markey & McIvor, 2018: 593). That is, permanent employees have access to paid leave entitlements such as sick leave, family violence leave and annual leave, while casual employees have no access to paid leave entitlements. Casual employees are also far less likely to have on-the-job training opportunities compared to permanent employees (Gilfillan, 2018).

The lack of training opportunities can also create risk. For example, the state of Victoria's *COVID-19 Hotel Quarantine Inquiry Final Report* revealed that the 'casually employed security guards were particularly vulnerable because of their lack of job security, lack of appropriate training and knowledge in safety and workplace rights, and their susceptibility to an imbalance of power resulting from the need to source and maintain work' (ACTU, 2020: 9). It was also found that 'significant outbreaks of COVID-19 occurred within industries such as aged care and meat processing – both of which have highly casualised workforces' (ACTU, 2020: 10).

Casual employees are generally deployed on an ad hoc basis, without any guarantee of future work, without paid annual/sick leave, and daily work shifts may be shorter. Because there is a lack of security and an absence of standard benefits, casual employees in Australia are compensated in all modern awards (which outline the minimum conditions and wages) through a casual employment 'loading', which is 25% on top of the base wage (Markey & McIvor, 2018).

This is where high caution is needed. While this loading is indeed in all modern awards, some clusters of businesses within an industry may have an enterprise agreement rather than refer to the award. In addition, not all employees who are casuals are paid the casual loading rate. In some cases, this is because the employee is paid an undifferentiated 'all up' rate, which does not specifically mention a casual loading because it is built into the rate. In other cases, however, employees may be underpaid. Specifically, retail and hospitality have been found to fail to comply with awards based on numerous audits that have taken place, and it is thought that around one-third of employees in retail and hospitality did not receive the penalty rates to which they were entitled (Peetz, 2020). Retail and hospitality industries have been found to be 'among the worst for award breaches' (Peetz, 2020: 10). Modern awards are standardised and are not negotiable. An enterprise agreement may apply to the employees of a particular organisation, tailored for that organisation. The details are negotiated within the organisation and then approved by the Fair Work Commission.

On the surface, this all seems quite reasonable, but there are areas where such arrangements can create unfair situations for employees. Some examples could include a case where a cluster of businesses of a franchise nature set up an enterprise agreement but there is no clear presence of a union that represents those employees. If in addition, such a cluster of businesses primarily employs teenagers on a casual basis, this makes those employees especially vulnerable.

Employees aged between 15 and 24 years of age are significantly more likely to be employed on a casual basis compared with those who are aged 25 and above (Gilfillan, 2018). Significantly, around 76% of employees aged between 15 and 19 years of age were identified as being casual employees (Gilfillan, 2018). Hospitality and retail industries, which also serve tourists, have very high proportions of casual workers (Gilfillan, 2018). Specifically, 65% of employees in the Australian Bureau of Statistics (ABS) 'accommodation and food services' industry group were casually employed in 2016, with hospitality workers ranked as the occupation with the highest share of casual employees, at 79% (Gilfillan, 2018).

In such situations, those employed teenagers will generally lack education in industrial relations and management areas. In addition, it may be their first job, in which case they have little if anything to compare their present conditions and salary to. Turnover may be high, which may result if employees realise they will receive better conditions and pay if they work for a competitor business.

Enterprise agreements are made and approved under the Fair Work Act (2009) (Cth) in Australia. When these agreements expire, employees are left to work under conditions and pay that could be unsuitable. Management may not be motivated to terminate and update the agreement, as they are financially advantaged by the expired agreement. Employees are unlikely to realise this. The situation that results in employees being inadequately compensated for their work continues, perhaps for years. After all, management is unlikely to be motivated to make it fair, and teenagers are unlikely to understand and request that the agreement be updated.

An example: McDonald's

At the time of writing, a matter is live involving 72 McDonald's-owned sites across Australia. McDonald's is a significant employer of young people in Australia (Puddy, 2022). The case involves seeking $100 million from McDonald's for what was alleged to be a failure to provide employees with their 10-minute breaks that employees are entitled to under the Fast Food Industry Award. Under the award, employees must receive a paid 10-minute break if they work for 4 hours or more, and two lots of 10-minute paid breaks if the employee works for more than 9 hours. According to one employee's statement, 'McDonald's inconsistently applied break rules in the three years he worked for the company and at times denied him 10-minute breaks' (Puddy, 2022).

Employment Laws

Employment laws vary across countries. These employment laws relate to tourism and hospitality industries as well as to other industries. Due to the high level of casualisation that can occur in tourism and hospitality industries, it is important for those working in tourism and hospitality to have an understanding of the minimum conditions and rights they have as a worker. The next section focuses on the key piece of legislation for employment in Australia – the Fair Work Act (2009). However, for readers outside of Australia, this section presents a generic introduction to employment law.

Workers have different rights depending on industry type, trade unions and country. Employment legislation in countries covers key employment issues such as working hours, pay, entitlements (e.g. sick leave, annual leave, maternity/paternity/adoption leave), redundancy and retirement. Protection, such as occupational health and safety, bullying and harassment, unfair dismissal, anti-discrimination laws and whistleblowing protections may also feature in the employment legislation.

Employment laws in different countries vary, and some countries are regarded as having more generous worker rights than others. Five countries that are regarded as having good employment laws, from the perspective of the employee are (Global People Strategist, 2019):

- Austria – employees are paid for 43 days leave each year from work (not including parental leave). Disabled workers comprise 4% of their employees.
- Belgium – has the highest wages among European countries.
- Denmark – employees have 25 days of paid annual leave each year.
- Finland – employees are entitled to 105 days of paid maternity leave, and 54 days of paid paternity leave. Parents can transfer up to 69 days

from their quota to the other parent. Employees are encouraged to develop their own agreements in their sector.

- Germany – employees are entitled to a minimum of 20 days of paid leave each year. Women are entitled to 13 weeks of paid maternity leave. Fathers can share a 3-year leave arrangement with their partner to enable a system where, jointly, parents can be with their child until their child turns 3 years old.

European countries are generally acknowledged as looking after employees. In terms of women's rights, gender pay gap, satisfaction scores, and work–life balance, the top-ranking countries are Norway, Denmark, the Netherlands and Sweden (Human Resources Director, 2019).

The gender pay gap metric, along with the inclusion of women in the boardroom and parliament, reveals the top five countries (in order) as: Norway, Denmark, Belgium, Luxembourg and New Zealand (Small Business Prices, 2022). In that same list, Australia ranks 20th, the United Kingdom ranks 27th, and the United States ranks 28th (Small Business Prices, 2022).

Working hours are fewest for Germany (1,371 work hours per person per year), followed by the Netherlands (1,420), Norway (1,427), Denmark (1,438) and France (1,473) (Small Business Prices, 2022). The United Kingdom ranks in 13th place (1,675), while New Zealand sits in 18th place (1,762), the United States in 20th place (1,765) and Australia in 22nd place (1,803) (Small Business Prices, 2022). Countries with more than 2,000 working hours per person each year include Poland (2,039), Greece (2,042), South Korea (2,124) and Mexico (2,137) (Small Business Prices, 2022).

Another assessment of workers' rights is through the ranking for violation of rights. The International Trade Union Confederation (ITUC), which is the largest trade union federation in the world, ranks 139 countries based on 97 indicators to determine these rankings (Fast Company, 2014). Countries rank well if employees have rights such as being able to form unions, engage in collective bargaining, and have the freedom to strike without penalty. Where employees are repressed when they attempt to request better working conditions, this limits employee rights and contributes to worse scores. Countries are scored based on whether there are only sporadic violations of employee rights (the best score: − 1) right through to where there is no guarantee of rights (the worst score: − 5). Again, European countries do well with liberties, with Austria, Belgium, Denmark, Finland and Germany among the 12 countries that score a 1 (Small Business Prices, 2022). Among those countries earning a 3 (which means there are regular violations of rights) are Australia and the United Kingdom (Small Business Prices, 2022). The United States earns a score of 4, which means there is systematic violation of rights (Small Business Prices, 2022). The complete definition of a score of 4 is: 'Workers in countries with the rating of 4 have reported systematic violations. The government and/or companies are engaged in serious efforts to crush the collective voice of workers putting fundamental rights under continuous threat' (Fast Company, 2014).

While these are general measures, these broader frameworks and cultures do tend to have a wide impact within sectors in each country. It is also worth noting that tourism and hospitality tend to have a lot of factors that can make employees in tourism and hospitality industries especially vulnerable.

For example, flight attendants and pilots who work for US airlines are not paid for the 30–50 minutes that they are working when the passengers are boarding the plane. The flight attendants only get paid from the time the cabin doors close until the plane lands and the doors open. While pilots are not required to be onboard during the boarding process, the flight attendants are. This is the case in the United States. Salary arrangements can vary across countries and even between different airlines. A comparison of these is unnecessary for the scope of this book and the example given is simply to highlight that in many industries that are partially in tourism, conditions may not be what is viewed as fair by comparison with other industries. Many industries that are partially in tourism are also ones that pay poorly or have high rates of casualisation and other issues. Notably, Delta Airlines has announced that it will begin paying its flight attendants during boarding, although the pay rate will be half their usual hourly rate (Kelleher, 2022).

The Fair Work Act (2009)

This section briefly discusses key components of the Fair Work Act (2009) that can result in a power imbalance. A key loophole in the act will be outlined, which can create abuse of employee rights. The Fair Work Act (2009) is a key piece of legislation in Australia relating to employment. Readers from other countries will have legislation in place for employment, which in some cases may be similar. This section focuses on conditions in Australia, however, and specifics will be peculiar to Australia. Readers from other countries should note that particular details, such as hours and loadings, may not apply. However, the general points about rights and reasonings are important universally, and interested readers can find some general pointers for raising specific questions for other countries if needed.

Awards and Enterprise Agreements

Industry employment awards exist in Australia to provide information to employers and employees on key workplace information such as rights, responsibilities, pay rates, benefits and protections. Awards are particular for each industry (e.g. the fast-food industry award is different to the hospitality award).

In some cases, an enterprise agreement may be considered more appropriate for a business. This is an agreement between employers and employees, where they agree to apply to the Fair Work Commission to vary the terms of the relevant industry award. There are three types of enterprise agreements:

- Single enterprise agreements – are created by an employer, or at least two employers who share a single interest (e.g. franchisees), with the employees.
- Multiple enterprise agreements – created by at least two employers together with the employees of those different enterprises. Employers do not need to prove that they are a single interest. This may relate to organisations involved in projects (e.g. construction).
- Greenfields agreements – available to a new enterprise such as a new business or new project where employees have not yet been employed. The employer will need to make the agreement with a specific union.

BOOT: Better Off Overall Test

A key criterion for consideration when approving an enterprise agreement is what is known as the BOOT: the Better Off Overall Test. The Fair Work Commission will not approve an application for an enterprise agreement unless it is satisfied that employees will be better off overall compared to the relevant award. At first blush, this sounds like a superior deal for employees. However, the danger is that better off overall, when it is approved, does not mean better off overall after some time has passed. As is discussed later, it is not uncommon for enterprise agreements to continue to operate for many years (even after they have expired), in which case employees might be worse off.

In addition to outlining the working conditions and salaries, there are four compulsory inclusions in any enterprise agreement:

- A *dispute resolution process* – so that the Fair Work Commission or an independent third party can settle disputes that may arise relating to the National Employment Standards (NES) or the terms of a modern award.
- A *consultation provision* – so that employers can consult their employees if there are major workplace changes, and so that employees have representation during *consultation processes.*
- An *individual flexibility agreement* (IFA) – so that any individual employee can vary the terms that are in the enterprise agreement for that individual's particular needs.

- A *nominal expiry date* for the enterprise agreement, which will be no longer than 4 years after the date the agreement was approved by the Fair Work Commission.

The Fair Work Act (2009) Section 186 states:

(5) The FWC must be satisfied that:
   (a) the agreement specifies a date as its nominal expiry date; and
   (b) the date will not be more than 4 years after the day on which the FWC approves the agreement.

It is important to note that expired does not translate to expired in the manner in which the word is generally understood. For example, an expired driver's licence means that it has passed the period of being valid. The critical word in (a) is 'nominal'. Nominal means 'existing as something in name only: not actual or real' (Mirriam-Webster, 2022). Accordingly, the expiry date is *nominal* only. It is an indicator that parties should be putting together an updated agreement. Expired does not mean terminated, and an agreement that is past its nominal expiry date will continue operating until it is terminated.

Terminating Enterprise Agreements

Under the Fair Work Act (2009), an application for termination can be made to the Fair Work Commission. The relevant section is Section 225:

If an enterprise agreement has passed its nominal expiry date, any of the following may apply to the FWC for the termination of the agreement:

(a) one or more of the employers covered by the agreement;
(b) an employee covered by the agreement;
(c) an employee organisation covered by the agreement.

Expired enterprise agreements continue until they are terminated and, as outlined in Section 225 of the Fair Work Act (2009), the application for termination either comes from at least one of the employers listed in the agreement, at least one of the employees who is covered by the expired agreement, or an employee organisation (i.e. a union) that is covered by the agreement.

There have been cases where an employee discovers that the conditions they are working under are not competitive and they leave, and after they resign they then try to apply to terminate the expired agreement. However, once they are no longer employed, they are ineligible to apply for termination. Similarly, there is not always an employee organisation (i.e. a union) that is covered by the agreement. As such, a union cannot apply for termination unless they are acting on behalf of an employee, who is then the applicant.

This can make the situation difficult to have these expired agreements terminated. Financially, employers are advantaged by paying lower wages, so in many cases are not motivated to apply to terminate the agreement. The employees, who are often working for organisations that serve tourists, may be unwilling to apply as they may be afraid of repercussions. The balance of control sits with the employer because the employee, who is often casually employed in tourism and hospitality industries, is dependent on the employer for work and income. Often, employees have no idea how to go about the process. Expired agreements can continue being operationalised for many years after they pass their nominal expiry date. This is discussed in more detail in the next section on zombie agreements (i.e. expired enterprise agreements).

As employers may not be motivated to terminate an agreement that has passed its nominal expiry date, it will continue unless an employee (or union, where one is covered by the agreement) is willing to apply to terminate it. As is evident in the next section (see Table 5.1), the four applications for termination of expired agreements came from employees, with assistance from their relevant union. That is, the employee was the applicant in the matter.

Employees can undertake the application process without assistance from a union. However, the process is resource-intensive, complex and time-consuming. While information including relevant forms can be easily sourced from the Fair Work Commission website and looks relatively straightforward, matters can quickly become involved through the process. There is a form to file, called Form F24B. The form is not complicated to fill out – the challenge is in providing the details for the employers and then serving them. On the surface, this sounds quite simple but, for agreements that involve many employers, and where the agreement was made a long time ago, locating those companies, some of which could be deregistered, is complex. As outlined in Table 5.1 in the next section, some agreements involve large numbers of employer firms (e.g. 61, 84).

The company structures are often complicated. Some agreements list the company name and the store location, making it more straightforward to determine whether all employers covered in the agreement are still operating. Others, however, only list the company name. The company name is not the store name. Also, the Australian Business Number (ABN) and company name on an employee's payslip may be different to the company name and ABN of the owner of the business covered by the enterprise agreements. Some of the companies operate as trusts, which can be configured in various ways. Untangling these details to piece together the link between the expired agreement and the payer can be very time-consuming and complex. In short, it is little wonder that agreements that pass their nominal expiry date continue for many years: the process is not easy.

The relevant section from the Fair Work Act (2009) for assessing the application for termination is Section 226:

Section 226: When the FWC must terminate an enterprise agreement

If an application for the termination of an enterprise agreement is made under section 225, the FWC must terminate the agreement if:

(a) the FWC is satisfied that it is not contrary to the public interest to do so; and
(b) the FWC considers that it is appropriate to terminate the agreement taking into account all the circumstances including:
   (i) the views of the employees, each employer, and each employee organisation (if any), covered by the agreement; and
   (ii) the circumstances of those employees, employers and organisations including the likely effect that the termination will have on each of them.

As provided in Section 226 of the Fair Work Act (2009), the views of termination are sought from employees and employers. Therefore, every employer needs to be served the relevant papers that go to the Fair Work Commission so that they have the opportunity to outline their views. Similarly, all employees must be made aware of the application for termination. Again, termination of an expired agreement is not a simple process. Disadvantaged people are often those who work in firms that serve tourists and who are expected to be positive.

The Fair Work Commission

The decision and process of a Directions Hearing (a brief hearing to set the directions for the case and give a sense of timeliness) for termination of an expired agreement are in some ways like decisions in the Family Law Court (which is discussed in Chapter 9). The outcome is not predictable and there is a discretionary component to it. There is guiding legislation, but how the hearings are run, and what the decision may be, is not a precise science (like family law).

Who the deputy president or commissioner is on the day at the time can make a difference. As was told to me by a person who has attended many Fair Work Hearings: 'if I know who the Commissioner is for the case, I can just about predict the outcome' In other words, each deputy president or commissioner will go about things in their own style, often based at least in part on their backgrounds and values. It may or may not be as expected.

It is perhaps also relevant to understand that appointments to the Fair Work Commission are by the Governor-General of Australia on the recommendation of the Australian government. Therefore politics and political values are involved. Such a process may result in appointments being from strong employer backgrounds, which unions and employees may feel presents a bias against them.

In late 2018, the then Labor party leader, Bill Shorten, accused the government of the day of 'stacking' the Fair Work Commission with people from strong employer backgrounds, after 6 new appointments to senior positions were made, bringing the number of employer appointments to 20 in a row (Karp, 2018). The most recent appointments made at the time of writing were Mr Michael Easton, a deputy president, and four commissioners (commencing between April 2021 and July 2021) (Attorney-General's Department, 2021).

Zombie Agreements

At first blush, the term 'zombie agreement' may sound peculiar. After all, zombies are fictitious, they are known as dead people reanimated, who have no ability to speak or move easily. In other words, zombies are 'walking dead'.

A zombie agreement is a 'dead' (i.e. expired) enterprise agreement that continues to have 'life' despite the expiry date having been passed. The term was originally coined by the Australian Council of Trade Unions (ACTU). The ACTU was formed in 1927 and is Australia's leading trade union organisation. Despite such enterprise agreements having passed their nominal expiry date, they can live on unless an application is made to the Fair Work Commission to terminate the expired agreement. The Fair Work Act allows for expired agreements to continue operating until they are terminated. An employer or an employee can apply to the Fair Work Commission to have the zombie agreement terminated.

Zombie agreements are common in hospitality industries, and also in retail and fast-food industries (Fair Work Claims, 2019). More than 4,000 zombie agreements dated between 2006 and 2009 across hotels, fast food and retail were identified in 2021 (The Fair List, 2021). A recent application to terminate a zombie agreement in the hospitality industry, *Application by Henry Thom* [2022] FWCA 1543, was successful, with termination to take effect on 9 June 2022, four weeks after the hearing. The application to terminate the zombie agreement was made by one of the casual employees of the 'prominent hospitality employer'(Employer Services, 2022). The commissioner was scathing:

[34] It is difficult to understand how an employer could have, for so many years, knowingly deprived a large number of employees of penalty rates, to which they would have otherwise been entitled under the relevant award, simply because it lawfully could do so.

[42] What I have to say in this part of the decision is clearly obiter, however I consider it necessary to say. The effect of this Employer having the benefit of an agreement made in 1999, without the payment to employees of

penalty rates, at least in the last decade, is a disgrace. It has resulted in this Employer having an enormous competitive advantage over other employers who pay to employees penalty rates in accordance with the relevant awards or their own agreements which satisfy the better off overall test.

[43] I consider it necessary for a light to be shone on these kinds of archaic arrangements. Presently, it is incumbent upon employees, often casual employees, to make an application to the Commission, to request termination of an agreement where an employer does not have the intestinal fortitude to recognise what a significant benefit it has had for a substantial period of time and make its own application. The result of an employer making its own application is that it would signal to its employees that it recognises the inferior entitlements owed to its employees, and that it wishes to meet and rise to community standards contained within awards. At the very least, it would demonstrate that it accepts that it should pay to employees the same rates that a new business would be required to pay to its employees.

[2022] FWCA 1543

The Merivale Group

A particular example of a zombie agreement is The Merivale Group, which is a private company that has property assets predominately in Sydney, New South Wales, across the hospitality and entertainment industries. Merivale employees were paid under an enterprise agreement that was signed in 2007 and that expired in 2012. Staff were not receiving penalty rates on weekends and public holidays, which they would have been under the hospitality industry award. On 2 November 2018, two casual Merivale employees applied to the Fair Work Commission to terminate the 2007 Merivale zombie agreement (Farrell & McDonald, 2018).

The differences between the expired agreement pay rates and the relevant award for casual employees were significant. While rates vary based on age, one employee was paid $6 an hour less than the hospitality award for Saturday shifts, $10 an hour less for shifts on Sundays, and $25 an hour less on public holidays (House, 2019). At the time of termination, 71% of Merivale's employees were casuals, and 48% worked on a visa (House, 2019). This highlights an incredibly critical point as to how these expired agreements continue for so long.

Hospitality and fast-food industries employ a large number of casual staff, many of whom are teenagers and/or migrants. Teenagers, university students and migrants are vulnerable groups who can easily be taken advantage of. They may be unfamiliar with the comparison (i.e. award) rate, desperate for employment, and unaware that they are employed under an expired agreement.

The Fair Work Commission terminated the expired Merivale enterprise agreement, requiring Merivale to apply the relevant award from March 2019.

Subway

Another example of a zombie agreement can be found in Subway. This is a different example from the Merivale Group example and far more complex. While Merivale had a zombie agreement that related across its portfolio, Subway is a different and more complicated structure. The work conditions at one store can vary from another store because the stores are on different agreements.

Before outlining the zombie agreements that exist for many of the Subway stores, it is useful first to present an overview of the company. The history of Subway commenced in 1965, when Fred DeLuca, at the age of 17, and his business partner Dr Peter Buck, opened their first store (Hanson et al., 2014). Subway is privately owned and has expanded rapidly due to its franchising. The company is owned and operated by Doctors' Associates Incorporated (which is a private company). The parent company name was created because Dr Peter Buck has a PhD in physics, and Fred's goal was to go to medical school (Myers, 2017).

Subway has more stores than any other fast-food restaurant (Hanson et al., 2014; Khoema, 2020). While Subway has more locations than McDonald's, McDonald's has a presence in more countries (Khoema, 2020) and also has a higher revenue (John, 2020). While both McDonald's and Subway operate on a franchise model, McDonald's owns around 20% of its restaurants, while all Subway stores are franchised. There are significant cost differences in setting up a store, with Subway being much cheaper. However, the manner in which Subway operates its franchising is recognised as a significant problem (Hanson et al., 2014). Franchise owners have been known to build a store up but not to be entitled to benefit financially from building up its value.

From a strategic management perspective, Subway is regarded as having core competencies of: superior locations, a quality product and excellent customer service (Hanson et al., 2014). The 'Eat Fresh' slogan is supported by Subway baking its own bread (Hanson et al., 2014), although all stores use the same bread, which franchises receive as frozen dough to thaw out before baking it (Myers, 2017).

One aspect of Subway's financial success is the employment conditions. The agreements for many of the stores have been set up by a company called Independent Purchasing Company Australia Ltd (IPCA). IPCA operates in 13 countries, and supports more than 3,000 Subway restaurants through its mission: 'Our mission is to help Subway franchisees across Asia Pacific be more profitable and competitive – today and in the future' (IPCA, 2020). That mission statement is worth a second read; the company is completely upfront that its goal is for Subway to make more money. While some of those ways are through purchasing power, one of the ways in which money might be saved for some franchise owners is through establishing enterprise agreements (in

Australia, and the equivalent in other countries) that end up operating well past their nominal expiry date, resulting in employees operating under out-of-date conditions.

By way of example, Figure 5.1 is a screenshot of a search undertaken on the Fair Work Commission website. From inputting the company 'IPCA' a list of 13 different enterprise agreements is generated. The date each agreement was created is listed, and the agreement can be opened

Document	Agreement Title	Publication Type	Matter Number	Member Name	Date Created	Details
PDF 1.04 MB	IPCA Enterprise Agreement 2014	Single-enterprise agreement Agreements	AG2015/1970	Gregory - Commissioner	07 May 2015	⌄
PDF 1.16 MB	IPCA Enterprise Agreement 2013	Single-enterprise agreement Agreements	AG2013/11487	Bull - Commissioner	21 November 2013	⌄
PDF 1.25 MB	IPCA (NSW) Enterprise Agreement 2011	Single-enterprise agreement Agreements	AG2011/7126	Kaufman - Senior Deputy President	19 July 2011	⌄
PDF 832 KB	IPCA (VIC) Enterprise Agreement 2012	Single-enterprise agreement, Agreements	AG2012/4224	Kaufman - Senior Deputy President	23 April 2012	⌄
PDF 835.8 4 KB	IPCA (WA) Enterprise Agreement 2012	Single-enterprise agreement Agreements	AG2012/4220	Kaufman - Senior Deputy President	23 April 2012	⌄
PDF 1008 3 KB	IPCA (QLD) Enterprise Agreement 2012	Single-enterprise agreement Agreements	AG2012/4275	Kaufman - Senior Deputy President	23 April 2012	⌄
PDF 1005 68 KB	IPCA (TAS) Enterprise Agreement 2011	Single-enterprise agreement Agreements	AG2011/7100	Kaufman - Senior Deputy President	19 July 2011	⌄
PDF 1.14 MB	IPCA (SA) Enterprise Agreement 2011	Single-enterprise agreement Agreements	AG2011/7133	Kaufman - Senior Deputy President	20 July 2011	⌄
PDF 2.09 MB	IPCA (WA) Enterprise Agreement 2011	Single-enterprise agreement Agreements	AG2011/7091	Kaufman - Senior Deputy President	20 July 2011	⌄
PDF 1015. 23 KB	IPCA (QLD) Enterprise Agreement 2011	Single-enterprise agreement Agreements	AG2011/7265	Kaufman - Senior Deputy President	19 July 2011	⌄
PDF 843.8 9 KB	IPCA (NSW) Enterprise Agreement 2012	Single-enterprise agreement Agreements	AG2012/4260	Kaufman - Senior Deputy President	23 April 2012	⌄
PDF 1.25 MB	IPCA (VIC, ACT & NT) Enterprise Agreement 2011	Single-enterprise agreement, Agreements	AG2011/7098	Kaufman - Senior Deputy President	19 July 2011	⌄
PDF 2.16 MB	IPCA (Western Australia) Enterprise Agreement 2010	Single-enterprise agreement Agreements	AG2010/11678	Kaufman - Senior Deputy President	23 November 2010	⌄

Figure 5.1 List of IPCA enterprise agreements on the Fair Work Commission website
Source: Fair Work Commission (2022b).

and read. The list in the screenshot is for those clusters of Subway stores under enterprise agreements developed by IPCA. There is a longer list of agreements for other Subway stores. Searching for 'Subway' agreements is easier as many are named in a more obvious way (e.g. Subway Kawana, created 26 August 2010; D & R Subway Pty Ltd, created 15 December 2011 with a nominal expiry date of 15 December 2012). Others are less obvious (e.g. Wilkus Pty Ltd enterprise agreement 2015, with Wilkus Pty Ltd as the trustee for Subway Trust T/A Subway Colannades). However, a search of the Fair Work Commission website for 'Subway' will bring up those. The less transparent ones are the cluster of Subway stores under the name 'IPCA', because someone would need to know to search for 'IPCA' to find them. Those agreements also tend to be more complex due to the larger number of employers covered.

As of the time of writing, 4 of the 13 enterprise agreements had been terminated, requested by a Subway employee. Nine of the enterprise agreements still operate, despite having expired many years ago and the pay being below the current award rate. The list provided in Table 5.1 is

Table 5.1 List of enterprise agreements for IPCA on behalf of Subway employers

Name of Enterprise Agreement	Number of employers covered	Date approved	Expiry date	Terminated or operating
IPCA (WA) Enterprise Agreement 2010	39	23/11/2010	24/11/2014	Operating
IPCA (VIC, ACT & NT) Enterprise Agreement 2011	60	19/7/2011	20/7/2015	Operating
IPCA (QLD) Enterprise Agreement 2011	55	19/7/2011	20/7/2015	Operating
IPCA (TAS) Enterprise Agreement 2011	3	19/7/2011	20/7/2015	Operating
IPCA (NSW) Enterprise Agreement 2011	84	19/7/2011	20/7/2015	Terminated 19/10/2020
IPCA (WA) Enterprise Agreement 2011	10	20/7/2011	21/7/2015	Operating
IPCA (SA) Enterprise Agreement 2011	18	20/7/2011	21/7/2015	Terminated 12/5/2020
IPCA (NSW) Enterprise Agreement 2012	22	23/4/2012	24/4/2016	Operating
IPCA (QLD) Enterprise Agreement 2012	15	23/4/2012	24/4/2016	Operating
IPCA (WA) Enterprise Agreement 2012	4	23/4/2012	24/4/2016	Operating
IPCA (VIC) Enterprise Agreement 2012	14	23/4/2012	24/4/2016	Operating
IPCA Enterprise Agreement 2013	47	21/11/2013	22/11/2017	Terminated 12/5/2020
IPCA Enterprise Agreement 2014	40	7/5/2015	8/5/2019	Terminated 26/8/2021

ordered from the oldest to the most current agreement. As can be seen in Table 5.1, many of these were done at the same time; essentially the same agreement that has been adjusted to account for state/territory requirements and labelled accordingly.

The agreements are typically a little over 50 pages in length. Understandably, they are often not read by the employees, who are typically casually employed teenagers with little or no employment experience. As 18-year-old Caitlin Lindon from a Melbourne Subway stated, she was given 'a contract, which had a few things outlined in it, but it all seemed pretty normal to me, because I didn't know any better' (McPherson, 2020). When employed, Caitlin Lindon had 'no idea' that the enterprise agreement that she was operating under 'had been negotiated more than 10 years ago' (McPherson, 2020).

There are thousands of others of a similar age to Caitlin Lindon who are employed by Subway, many of whom may be unaware they are operating under zombie agreements. Teenagers are provided with a bundle of documents and asked to sign and return them. Understandably, they assume everything is in order. Legally, there is nothing wrong with operating under an expired agreement with salary conditions that are below the relevant award. However, just because it is not illegal does not make it right. McPherson (2020) states that 'it is estimated thousands of Australian employees working in a range of fields are employed under these "zombie agreements" – which are perfectly legal because of a loophole in industrial relations law'. I would argue that the number is well and truly far above 'thousands'. Take the second listed agreement in Table 5.1 as an example: IPCA (VIC, ACT & NT) Enterprise Agreement 2011 which has 60 employers covered in it. Some of those employers have multiple stores. Each of those stores is likely to employ around 20 people on average (larger stores will employ around 30 people). Accordingly, such agreements could potentially cover around 2,400 employees (assuming 60 employers having on average 2 stores with each store having on average 20 employees) who are impacted just by one of those enterprise agreements that have expired. Extrapolate that across all industries (hospitality, fast food and retail are the most common industries for zombie agreements), and this is likely to mean tens of thousands of impacted employees. Sadly, as outlined in the next section on casual employment, many of these impacted employees are teenagers. That job may be their first work experience, which does not present a positive imprint of what working life is like.

An example: Application to terminate a Subway (IPCA) enterprise agreement

This example was current at the time of writing, and one of the more involved cases as it involved a request to terminate a non-union agreement that covered 60 employer firms across three states/territories.

This particular case involved a cluster of Subway stores (as discussed in the previous section, there are many cases just like this one relating to Subway) and involved an application to terminate an enterprise agreement, (listed second in Table 5.1). At the time of application, the enterprise agreement had the largest number of employers of all the active expired Subway enterprise agreements.

Another important aspect of this case is that the applicant was a 17-year-old. This point will be highlighted later in this book when family law matters are discussed, whereby a child of 17 is not allowed in family law courts for matters that involve them. Yet, a 17-year-old can be the applicant against a global company.

I am intimately familiar with this particular case because the 17-year-old applicant was my daughter. This provided me with a closer, inside view of this particular case than would be possible from the outside. It presented insights into 'the underbelly' of tourism. Some of what I present in this case is more than operational: I outline aspects as I perceived them from being a part of the inside. The particulars of the case are publicly available online through the Fair Work Commission's website (Fair Work Commission, 2022a).

As many tourists dine out at fast-food restaurants, and it is also common for tourists, as working tourists, to work at fast-food chains, understanding the steps involved in a case may be useful. Since tourism is a system, experiences for the tourist through each element will impact their overall travel experience.

The steps in this case were as follows:

- January 2022 – application to FWC. Form F24B and Form F24C. After application, company searches commence. Every one of the 60 employers had an Australian Securities & Investments Commission (ASIC) search undertaken. At the time of writing each search cost AU\$9.95.
- 1 February 2022 – Directions – set up timelines and steps to be taken over a 2-month process
- Step 1 – search the 60 employers (by 15 February 2022). Each employer had to be sent the forms submitted (i.e. F24B and F24C) plus a copy of the Directions. These had to be sent by registered post for proof of service. Proof of service had to be supplied to the FWC.
- 16 February 2022 – procedural mention (to get a better feel for the case). This was a conference call with audio only; no visual. I was present as a silent attendee. My daughter, as the applicant, was present, but the paperwork submitted had made it clear that she was a member of the SDA Union and they were representing her. Similar to a lawyer's role – they were to do the representing and the talking. Also present were members of the other side. This was IPCA as the respondent, as well as Subway. These were two global companies with

a lot of resources at their disposal ... and a 17-year-old applicant was up against those resources.

What struck me immediately (again, remembering that these are only my perceptions), was the tone of the deputy president. I felt like I was back in the family court again. It was that same crisp tone, a tone that did not invite negotiation. It felt to me that there wasn't much opportunity to do anything but follow the steps she wanted to be taken.

While it was made clear from the beginning of the mentioned hearing that the applicant was a minor and that the union was representing her, a request from the other side was put forward by the deputy president to the applicant. The union lawyer tried to answer on her behalf but he was cut off and the deputy president said, crisply: 'I want to hear from the applicant.' In my view this was unfair. She was 17 and unaware of the implications of what was being sought. The default position would typically be to say that sounded fine because it seemed from the tone of the deputy president that to say otherwise would displease her. The applicant was silent. The question was asked again. The tone was one of displeasure. Again, the applicant was silent. The union lawyer again spoke to answer for her and this time he was not cut off. There was no option but to let him speak. The silence from the applicant was the smartest response. It was, as I said, in my view unfair. Again, this is part of the underbelly.

Because of the complexity of this particular case, and how old the agreement was, it was not possible to know whether every employer had been located and served. Franchises can change hands or be de-registered. For this particular agreement it was difficult to locate businesses due to how the employers had been listed in it. Some agreements list the location of the store, which makes it much easier to check and serve the business owner, but was not the case in this particular agreement. Because of this, the deputy president decided to vacate the previous Directions, and issue new ones (dated 23 February 2022). This was very unfortunate. It meant that one month was lost in one fell swoop. It also meant that all the employers had to be served yet again. Aside from the potential confusion, this was also expensive – remembering that every employer served had to be served by registered post so that there was evidence of them being served. At the time of writing, a letter by registered post costs AU\$4.30. As there were 60 employers and this then had to be done twice, and the ASIC searches previously done cost \$9.95 each, it is easy to see how these complex agreements can be costly as well as confusing to try to terminate.

Keep in mind that most employees in these organisations are casual, and they are teenagers. Many are still at school. It is not uncommon for the employees to be 15 years of age. These processes and expenses are not feasible. The system is, in my view, not geared towards facilitating termination. While technically it can be done, it is so difficult and so resource-intensive, that an employee would need to subscribe to their union to act on their behalf.

The Directions provided a series of steps of what needed to happen, by whom, and by when. There were two key components of the Directions that revealed, in my view, a bias against employees. Below is an extract from the Directions, showing steps 15 and 16. Also, the error in the Directions should be noted. IPCA is referred to as a company trading as Subway in the Directions. This is not correct. They are separate companies.

[15] **By close of business Wednesday, 6 April 2022**, the Applicant is to file in the Commission, and serve on all Employers and the Independent Purchasing Company (Australasia) Limited T/A Subway, any further material in support of her application to terminate the Agreement, including material outlining her views, circumstances, and the likely effect the termination of the Agreement will have on her. Each Employer must then provide to all of its employees covered by the Agreement via email, any material upon which the applicant relies.

[16] **By close of business Wednesday, 20 April 2022**, any employee who wishes to do so, is directed to file in the Commission, to serve on the Applicant, their Employer, and the Independent Purchasing Company (Australasia) Limited T/A Subway any material and witness statements upon which they rely, including:

- Material which addresses whether it is or is not contrary to the public interest for the Commission to terminate the Agreement (s.226(a) of the Act);
- Material which expresses the views of the employee regarding the application to terminate the Agreement (s.226(b)(i) of the Act); and
- Material which describes the circumstances of the employee, including the likely effect that the termination of the Agreement would have on them. This may include submissions on the impact of the Agreement no longer applying to them and the *Fast Food Industry Award 2010* instead setting the terms and conditions of employment (s.226(b)(ii) of the Act).

At first blush, these steps may appear fine. Looking at step 15, here is the problem I see with it. The applicant files material by close of business Wednesday 6 April 2022 and serves that material on all employers and the respondent company. Each employer must then provide that material to its employees. But, by when? There is no deadline. The next step in the Directions, step 16, has a due date of Wednesday 20 April 2022. Technically, the employers could provide their employees with the material by that same deadline. Or after that deadline. It doesn't say when the deadline is. That material could potentially be informative for employees to then present to the commission on how the current agreement impacts them.

Step 16 provides employees with an opportunity to contribute their views on the termination. This is appropriate. This is expected to be enabled. But look closer at how those employees must do that. They must serve the applicant, their employer, and the IPCA (i.e. the respondent) with their submission. So, first, they need to work out how to serve the applicant and where the applicant is. They also need to do that for IPCA. And they have to serve their employer. Identification could result in reprisal.

Potentially, a lack of submissions from employees could be argued by the other side as a lack of interest in termination. However, when the steps in the Directions are read closely, it is clear that commenting as an employee is complicated and risky. I mentioned the failure to provide a deadline for providing employees with materials from the applicant from step 15 in the Directions. I am aware that at least some employees covered by the outdated agreement did not receive the material.

- 18 May 2022 – hearing (forthcoming at the time of writing).

While on the surface there are processes for termination, these are not simple, not necessarily fair, and there is a discretionary component as to how the Directions are played out, which will depend on the Deputy Commissioner appointed. Similar to family law, where there is a discretionary component this underbelly impacts tourism. In this particular case, employees who work for organisations such as fast food, retail or hospitality which are partially in tourism, impact tourism employees. The conditions can also impact working tourists, who are often attracted to those same industries for their employment during working holidays. Thus, this underbelly impacts tourism employees and tourists.

Employer/Employee or Principal/Contractor

This chapter has highlighted various aspects related to the employer/employee relationship, and outlined the Fair Work Commission processes. So, what happens if it isn't an employer/employee relationship but is instead one of principal/contractor? Independent contracting follows different processes to that of recruiting employees, and the Fair Work Commission has no jurisdiction over independent contracting.

At the time of writing, the Fair Work Commission had numerous cases waiting to proceed – on pause, waiting for judgements from the High Court of Australia on two key cases. What was referred to as 'the long awaited decisions' (HWL Ebsworth Lawyers, 2022) of those two key cases had judgements for both determined on 9 February 2022. Those two cases were: *Construction, Forestry, Maritime, Mining And Energy Union & Anor v Personnel Contracting Pty Ltd* [2022] HCA 1 (Personnel

Contracting), and *ZG Operations & Anor V Jamsek & Ors* [2022] HCA 2 (Jamsek).

Both cases examined whether the relationship between the parties was one of employer/employee or whether the relationship was one of independent contractor. The case *Construction, Forestry, Maritime, Mining And Energy Union & Anor v Personnel Contracting Pty Ltd* [2022] HCA 1 examined whether a British backpacker (Mr McCourt) who travelled to Australia on a working holiday visa was an employee or an independent contractor. Mr McCourt had signed an Administrative Services Agreement with a labour-hire company that traded as 'Construct'. Mr McCourt commenced proceedings against Construct to seek compensation, as well as penalties, that he argued were owed to him under the Fair Work Act 2009 (Cth), while Construct argued that Mr McCourt was a 'self-employed contractor' (High Court of Australia, 2022a). The High Court of Australia determined that the terms used in contracts were not the guiding principles but, instead, that the nature and intent of the contract were critical. Since Construct determined who Mr McCourt undertook work for, this was determined to constitute an employer/employee relationship (High Court of Australia, 2022a).

The case *ZG Operations & Anor V Jamsek & Ors* [2022] HCA 2 (Jamsek) concerned two men who were initially employed to drive trucks for a company and who drove that company's trucks (not their own trucks). After around eight years of working as employees, the company invited the respondents to 'become contractors' and buy their own trucks to drive. The two truck drivers agreed and established partnerships (with each respective wife) and executed written contracts with the company. Income was declared as partnership income. The respondents sought entitlements they declared as being owed to them pursuant to the Fair Work Act 2009 (Cth) such as long-service leave and superannuation. The primary judge determined that the respondents were independent contractors. The Full Court overturned that original judgement and determined that the relationship in 'substance and reality' was that of employer/employees (High Court of Australia, 2022b). However, the High Court of Australia unanimously held that the respondents were not employees of the company and that 'the only relationship between the drivers and the company be a contract for the carriage of goods' (High Court of Australia, 2022b: 1).

The key point in both these cases is that the terms used in the contract are not as important as the contractual terms applied (HWL Ebsworth Lawyers, 2022). In other words, how the parties describe their relationship with each other through the contract will not be 'determinative of what is their actual legal relationship' (Gilbert and Tobin Law, 2022) and the 'ultimate characterisation of the relationship is focused on rights and duties established by the written contract' (Holding Redlich, 2022).

The case of *Construction, Forestry, Maritime, Mining And Energy Union & Anor v Personnel Contracting Pty Ltd* [2022] HCA 1 highlights the risks to vulnerable groups such as tourists who may be travelling on working holiday visas. As was highlighted earlier in this chapter, loopholes in the legislation can leave vulnerable groups such as teenagers, migrants, and tourists in a scenario of a power imbalance where they are open to being in a situation that abuses their vulnerability. Tourists, such as the British backpacker in the case of *Construction, Forestry, Maritime, Mining And Energy Union & Anor v Personnel Contracting Pty Ltd* [2022] HCA 1, can be vulnerable to abuse in the form of unjust practices through 'sham contracting arrangements' (HWL Ebsworth Lawyers, 2022). Such unjust practices are part of the underbelly of tourism – affecting tourists as well as industries that serve tourists.

Conclusion

The importance of taking care of employees should not be under-estimated. This chapter has outlined the various opportunities for control and abuse through unjust practices that can occur in industries that serve tourists; and, in some instances, it is tourists who are employed. Such scenarios affect the tourists being served and can also impact tourists because such firms often employ tourists who travel around their own country or who travel internationally on working holiday visas. Some employers may seek to find loopholes and take advantage of employees. The sham contracting arrangement discussed in the last section is a key example. Noting the issues for the employees raised in this chapter, it is also worth noting that there can be multiple adverse aspects for employers as well. Firstly, employers may find themselves in a constant cycle of re-advertising, re-training and re-hiring. Secondly, they may lose credibility and customers may avoid that business. Thirdly, good employees are incredibly important, especially in service industries such as hospitality. In fact, employees often deliver a key part of the tourism experience through the relationship those employees have with guests/customers and other staff (Harkison, 2022). The next chapter examines abuse and bullying in tourism industries to further our understanding of the tourism system element 'industries'.

6 Abuse and Bullying in Tourism Industries

'If you alter your behaviour because you are frightened of how your partner will react, you are being abused.'

– Sandra Horley

Introduction

Tourism industries are varied. They include smaller workplaces with highly casualised staff as well as large bureaucratic organisations. Problem behaviour may be particularly compounded in regional areas during times of staff shortages. These may have been exaggerated as a result of COVID where international travellers could not enter countries, which may normally be an important component of some tourism industries (e.g. hospitality). Accordingly, some problematic behaviour among staff may be overlooked or diminished during difficult times as managers may be unwilling to lose staff, even staff who might be a bully, due to the difficulty to source replacement staff. In addition, during difficult times, family-run tourism businesses may face financial pressures that can contribute to family violence. Larger organisations can sometimes be an environment for bullying. This can occur in different organisations and can also be prevalent in places of education. Education (mainly secondary and tertiary) is relevant to tourism, attracting students from outside of the region including international students. It also generates VFR travel through the student becoming a host to VFRs. However, education is also an important component of family violence because children exposed to family violence may exhibit behavioural problems at school. Lack of awareness of family violence can result in a type of secondary victimisation for school-aged children who live with family violence.

This chapter is the third to discusses the tourism system element of 'industries'. While many aspects could be discussed concerning problematic behaviour in tourism industries, this chapter will focus on two components. First, it will first focus on workplace bullying and abuse and outline the type of abuse and bullying that occurs in industries relevant to serving tourists. It will then discuss primary/secondary education concerning how family violence impacts children at school.

An introduction to tourism industries was presented earlier in this book. However, this book is designed to be read in segments that can stand alone. The chapters can be read in any order. This is to accommodate busy readers who may want to consume only a particular segment of this book that is relevant at a particular time. Accordingly, for those readers who may not have read previous chapters, a small number of important aspects will be highlighted to provide context for this chapter.

Firstly, tourism comprises multiple industries: it is not one giant industry. Secondly, tourism is partially industrialised. That is, tourism comprises firms that may belong to their own industry but may also serve tourists despite having no distinct strategies aimed at tourists. Therefore, tourism is partially industrialised with firms that belong to a particular industry as well as partially in tourism. Examples include fast-food, hospitality and retail. Those particular industries were discussed in detail regarding employment issues previously.

Workplace Abuse and Bullying

In many ways, being abused or bullied in the workplace may feel similar to the behaviour experienced in the home environment for those living with family violence. Feelings such as repeated hurtful remarks, psychological abuse, intimidation, threatening behaviour, verbal attacks, and playing mind games, can be experienced through family violence as well as through bullying in the workplace. Bullying in the workplace may include (Australian Human Rights Commission, 2011):

- Repeated hurtful remarks or attacks.
- Making fun of your work or you as a person.
- Sexual harassment.
- Excluding you.
- Playing mind games.
- Ganging up on you.
- Psychological harassment.
- Intimidation.
- Giving you pointless tasks unrelated to your job.
- Giving you impossible tasks that cannot be done within the timeframe or with resources provided.
- Deliberately altering your work hours or schedule to make it difficult for you.
- Deliberately withholding information relevant to doing your job properly.
- Pushing, shoving, tripping or grabbing you in the workplace.

- Physically attacking you or threatening you.
- Initiating or hazing (where you are made to do things to be 'accepted' as part of the team that might be uncomfortable, humiliating or inappropriate).

Workplace bullying can have significant impacts on a person's well-being. It can result in anxiety, depression, inability to sleep, and departure from the workplace. It is worth keeping in mind that some people living with family violence in their home environment may also be facing bullying in their workplace environment. This can be additionally damaging as there becomes no safety zone to escape the psychological abuse, with no opportunity to feel safe and to have a chance to feel relaxed and be calm. Just as bullying is described as being in a violent environment (Zhou *et al.*, 2021), family violence is also a violent environment. Neither is healthy and neither is safe.

Workplace Abuse and Bullying in Tourism

Earlier in this book, the concept of partial industrialisation in tourism was explained and it was shown how industries such as fast food, retail and hospitality are partially in tourism. These industries were presented as having particular structural problems with regard to employment. These industries are also ones in which problematic behaviour can occur. These types of businesses can be highly stressful due to the focus on customer service and the high level of customer interaction, and it has been 'reported that 87% of frontline employees working in the fast-food industry in Australia repeatedly experienced uncivil behavior during work' (Zhou *et al.*, 2021: 309). Incivility makes employees less efficient, de-motivates, and compromises the quality of work (Sarwar & Muhammad, 2020). Employee emotional well-being is a strategic human resource management factor (Ariza-Montes *et al.*, 2017) and, accordingly, low employee well-being will also impact the firm's competitive advantage. As such, aside from a duty of care, management should be concerned with employee well-being.

Some types of abuse have included employees having hot coffee thrown at them by an irritated customer followed by being threatened with rape or physical harm (Marsh, 2018). According to one employee, who was involved in the survey of fast-food workers, a customer threatened to 'slit their throat because they didn't have a flavour of a particular item in stock' (Marsh, 2018). Of the 1,000 employees who were respondents in the study, 71% were female and 41% were under the age of 17 years. Accordingly, what the study indicated was an abuse of female teenagers.

Anything that suggests a perceived injustice or discrimination will have negative consequences (Sarwar & Muhammad, 2020). While a failure in procedural fairness will result in employees believing that procedures employed by their employer for determining outcomes are unfair, if employees perceive that they are being rewarded unfairly (e.g. underpaid) they will tend to develop negative feelings (Sarwar & Muhammad, 2020).

Sadly, bullying is not necessarily addressed by legislation in all countries (Ram, 2018). Sweden was the first country to enact anti-bullying legislation, in 1993. Other Scandinavian countries then followed. Australia's legislation was quite recent – in 2014 – while some countries (e.g. Germany, the US and the UK) do not have specific national laws that oppose bullying in the workplace (Ram, 2018).

Education

> 'Past my bedtime
> Blue and red lights
> Come take you away'
>
> (Benson *et al.*, 2016)
> From 'DNA' by Lia Marie Johnson

Readers may wonder why I am starting this section about education by quoting from a song called 'DNA' by Lia Maria Johnson. By the end of this section, the reasoning will be clear. For anyone unfamiliar with the song, I highly recommend listening to it and watching the video clip, which is available on YouTube (Johnson, 2016).

Imagine being that child, and it is past your bedtime. The police come to the house and the 'blue and red lights' take away your father, who was violent and abusive towards your mother. The next day you go to school. You have hardly slept. Your mind is racing. A parent – a person you are supposed to trust and who is supposed to keep you and your loved ones safe – was hurting your mother. He was yelling at her. He was banging his fist on things in the house. He was intimidating. Your mother was scared and crying. You don't know what it all means. You are tired and scared and confused. You are unable to concentrate in class. You are exhausted. You fall asleep at the desk, with your head resting on your arm. Minutes later you are being yelled at by the teacher, who sends you to the principal's office and issues you with a detention note that has to be signed by your parents.

Where I am heading, with the above hypothetical scenario, is that education can be an environment for secondary victimisation of victims (children) of family violence. Just as the courts can be an avenue for secondary victimisation for victims, so too can schools. We know family violence is common. We also know that a 'substantial amount of domestic violence is witnessed by children' (Richards, 2011: 1). Children exposed to family violence can be impacted in various ways, such as (Richards, 2011: 3):

• Depression
• Anxiety
• Trauma symptoms
• Increased aggression

- Antisocial behaviour
- Lower social competence
- Temperament problems
- Low self-esteem
- The presence of pervasive fear
- Mood problems
- Loneliness
- School difficulties
- Peer conflict
- Impaired cognitive functioning
- Increased likelihood of substance abuse

If we look carefully through the above list of behaviours that could potentially be displayed, many of them could trigger a behavioural management process in a school. In other words, the victim's behaviour at school, caused by living with family violence, is misunderstood and the child is assumed to be 'naughty'. Their behaviour may trigger various punitive approaches embedded in the school's policies. If that number increases, it could even give rise to the child being expelled from the school. I wrote on this topic for a newspaper article, where I argued: 'If schools have no design for the aspect of family violence impacts, then I wonder how we are really helping the next generation' (Zentveld, 2021). Further, I argued:

> Do we really think that children exposed to family violence will operate the same as if they were not exposed to it? If school behavioural processes have nothing built-in to account for family violence, then this in itself suggests we are obtuse to the impact on children. (Zentveld, 2021)

The Department of Education in Victoria (Australia) identifies various behavioural indicators relating to family violence (Department of Education and Training, 2018), recognising that schools may be well-placed to detect that family violence is occurring. However, since some of those indicators are the same as those that trigger a school's punitive behavioural procedure, it seems that the child may be more likely to receive detention or suspension than help. How are we protecting children if we are focused on punishing them?

Once the punitive system has geared up, it only gets worse. Once caught up in it, it is useful to know a few basic rights. I will now introduce procedural fairness – one of the most important but misunderstood concepts I think I have come across. While procedural fairness is embedded in Australia, there may be similar or the same concepts in other countries. It is worth checking.

In Australia, Chief Justice Robert S. French said: 'procedural fairness is part of our cultural heritage' (French, 2010: 1). He argued that it is 'instrumental' in 'good decision-making'(French, 2010: 1) as well as giving dignity to individuals. Procedural fairness involves the fair hearing rule as well as the rule against bias. This means that the following must apply:

- Giving the person prior notice about an allegation and how it may impact them.
- Disclosing to them the critical issues to be addressed in the hearing.
- Conducting a hearing where the accused has a reasonable opportunity to present their case.
- The decision-maker must not be biased. They must be able to make an objective and impartial decision.

In other words, you cannot just receive an allegation against someone and decide the person is guilty. I wonder how many school students are alleged to have done something and been 'sentenced' without procedural fairness.

Again, this is Australia-centric and may or may not be generalisable to other countries, but schools (and many other organisations) must have policies in which procedural fairness is identified as embedded in how behavioural management procedures will operate. This is mandatory. While I have not trawled through every state act, by way of example the Education and Training Reform Act 2006 states in Part 4.3.1 that a requirement for the registration of a school is that 'the school policies relating to the discipline of students are based on principles of procedural fairness and do not permit corporal punishment'.

So, let us assume for a moment that procedural fairness is implemented. And let us assume a teacher alleges something that the student denies. Let us assume there are no witnesses, no CCTV footage, nothing. It is one person's word against the other's. That's all there is. Who is going to be believed? The student or the teacher? I think we all know the answer. So, does that mean there is a natural bias to believe the teacher and assume the student is lying? If so, why? Is that a reasonable bias?

Research suggests that 'as children get older, their understanding of deception improves and they become increasingly able to deceive others' (Goodman *et al.*, 2006: 2). In a study where adult participants observed videotaped interviews of children as well as adults either lying or telling the truth, observers were able to detect the children's lies more accurately than lies by adults (Goodman *et al.*, 2006). Further, the research also revealed that observers in the study were biased toward judging adults' statements as truthful. The study also revealed that some individuals are particularly skilled at detecting lies. The key point from this is that children who are exposed to family violence, and exhibit behavioural problems, may find themselves in an endless downward spiral where home is unsafe and school represents punishment. Their statements, should they be afforded procedural fairness as is the legal requirement, are less likely to be received as credible even if they tell the truth.

Similar to the need to address the legal system handling family violence, we also need to address the education system. We wonder why we have generational abuse, yet we teach children they will be punished for being a victim. I don't think we are looking at the problem through the right lens. Perhaps, if we kept in the forefront of our minds to 'be kind, for everyone you meet is fighting a hard battle' (quote by theologian, Ian McLaren, in his 1894 book *Beside the Bonnie Brier Bush*), we may be more likely to pause and assess the situation instead of adopting a 'tick and flick' punitive approach.

Conclusion

This chapter has discussed behavioural problems in tourism industries, with a specific focus on bullying in the workplace, and the education environment. It outlined what workplace bullying is, how it impacts people, and the ways in which it is prevalent in tourism industries. Education with respect to primary and secondary schooling was then discussed, and the ways in which power imbalances can impact children were outlined. The next chapter continues the discussion on the tourism element, tourism industries, with a focus on events.

7 Family Violence Spikes around Major Events

'It is fine to commiserate with a man about his bad experience with a previous partner, but the instant he uses her as an excuse to mistreat you, stop believing anything he tells you about that relationship and instead recognise it as a sign that he has problems with relating to women.'

– Lundy Bancroft, *Why Does He Do That? Inside the Minds of Angry and Controlling Men*

Introduction

This chapter is the final 'industries' chapter and outlines the correlation between events and family violence. Family violence can increase during celebratory family events (e.g. weddings) and at Christmas. It also can increase during significant sporting events, where reported incidents of family violence rise dramatically. With regard to the connection between family violence and family events such as Christmas, there is some overlap between this chapter's focus on events, and Chapter 13, which discusses Visiting Friends and Relatives (VFR) travel. It is only a slight overlap and the focus of the discussion relating to events such as Christmas is in this chapter.

Events

The field of events is closely intertwined with tourism. With VFR travel, key events such as weddings, funerals, milestone birthdays and graduations will hold great importance and be a motivator for travel. Events for VFR travel can be of three main types:

- Social catch-up travel events.
- Significant family/friends events (e.g. graduation, christening, funeral, significant birthday, wedding).
- Community/sporting/tourism events that are attended.

These events may result in a spike in family violence. A combination of stress and alcohol can add to the foundation of family violence and result in more episodes. Christmas is a time that is consistently associated with an increase in family violence. Because of the unique situation of VFR travel, astute friends/family can carefully support their victim friend/family member if they are aware of the signs of family violence.

As outlined earlier in the Power and Control Wheel (Figure 3.4), isolation is a key component of family violence. However, despite the strategies employed by perpetrators, there are still 'open doors' for victims of family violence through VFR travel. Social catch-up events can create an opportunity for friends and family to connect with the victim in person. However, care will need to be taken to ensure the victim knows that they are supported but without their being an attempt to interfere – or the well-meaning friend/family member may find themselves pushed away, a psychological coping mechanism of the victim in the abusive relationship (Carver, 2019). Significant family/friends events are also opportunities for connecting more broadly with family and friends and widening support circles through connections.

It needs to be recognised that there is a strong correlation between festive events and family violence. Family violence incidents increase during Christmas and the New Year period (Collard, 2018; Gilmore, 2018; Perkins & Butt, 2018). There is also a strong correlation between sporting events and family violence (Boutilier *et al.*, 2017; Gallant & Humphreys, 2019; Pescud, 2018). Research undertaken in Canada in Calgary, Alberta, revealed a significantly higher rate of family violence during key sporting days, with some sporting events reporting a 15% increase and key cup games revealing a 40% increase in reports of family violence (Boutilier *et al.*, 2017). Research in Australia has revealed a similar pattern with State of Origin game nights (see next section).

Results in other countries reveal the same pattern. A key example is the World Cup, where reports of family violence increase markedly (Dearden, 2018). Such problems resulted in the creation of a poster campaign to highlight the relationship between family violence and football matches (Figure 7.1).

Tourism and events carry risks regarding family violence and, as such, it is critical for family violence to be discussed within the tourism/events discipline. Such discussion is new to tourism/events. Events hold significant risks of family violence, with spikes in incidents of family violence at family event times such as Christmas as well as sporting events such as football.

State of Origin: Australia

A key sporting event in Australia is the 'State of Origin Series', which is an annual rugby league event. Each year two Australian states, Queensland (Maroons) and New South Wales (Blues), hold three

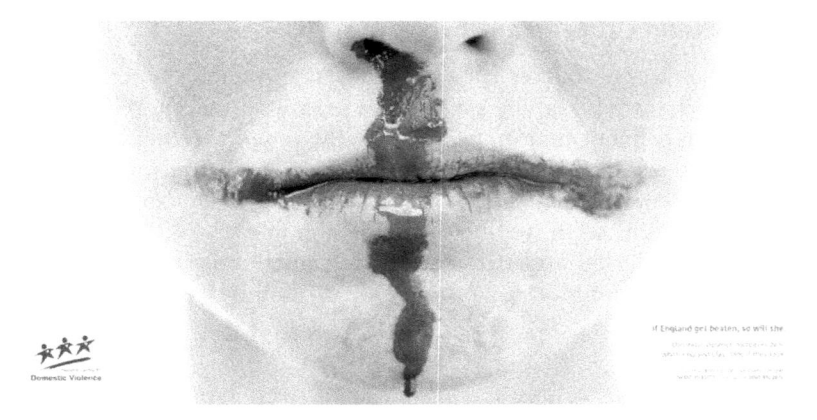

Figure 7.1 Poster campaign highlighting the relationship between football matches and family violence
Source: Deighton (2018).

games and the team that wins the most games is declared the winner. It is considered to be one of Australia's premier sporting events and the stadiums in which the games are played tend to sell out; the television audience is also substantial.

However, there is a relationship between this major sporting event and family violence. Data from the New South Wales Bureau of Crime Statistics and Research across six years (2012–2017) revealed a 40.7% average increase in family violence linked to the event (Foundation for Alcohol Research & Education, 2018). In the study, family violence phone calls were monitored between 6pm Wednesday and 6am Thursday for the weeks around the three State of Origin games. During that 12-hour period on State of Origin game nights, 'women and children in New South Wales are 40 per cent more likely to become victims of domestic violence. This is a significant and consistent spike across the three-game series in each and every one of the years examined' (Foundation for Alcohol Research & Education, 2018). Whether the teams won or lost did not alter the statistics: either way the family violence rates were approximately the same (Pescud, 2018).

Football/Soccer: England

While research in Australia revealed little difference in the family violence rates for whether a team lost or won, research in England highlighted differences, where rates were highest if the team lost. According to research undertaken at Lancaster University, family violence reports to police rose by 38% after matches in which the English national football team lost (Truong, 2018). If the English national football team won, family violence rates still increased but by 26% (Truong, 2018).

Birthdays and Other Family Events

When married couples separate, they may or may not think about how to work through family events once separated. Often, parents have a parenting agreement that maps out how the separated couple deals with school holidays, the birthdays of the parents, Christmas, the birthdays of the children, Mother's Day, Father's Day and other family events. At the time, it might seem well planned and suitable. However, these events can result in friction and stress and can trigger abusive and controlling behaviour. It is common for problems with family violence to occur at Christmas time.

Christmas Time

Christmas can be a wonderful time, where families reconnect and there are festivities and celebrations. People may travel significant distances to reconnect with family and sometimes stay for weeks at the destination. However, Christmas can also be a time when family violence spikes:

> Most of us, when we think of the festive season, think of a time of joy, celebration, and family togetherness. Unfortunately, for victims of family violence it can be a time of increased fear and distress. The statistics show that incidents of family violence increase significantly during the Christmas to New Year holiday period, compared to the rest of the year. (Tonkin Legal Group, 2020)

Similar to the discussion earlier in this chapter about family violence spiking around major sporting events, an increase in family violence can also be associated with major family events. Alcohol consumption is a contributing factor in many cases of family violence. Of course, alcohol is not the cause of family violence: if it was, everyone who drank too much alcohol would be a perpetrator of family violence. There are men who do not drink alcohol who are perpetrators of family violence and most people who drink alcohol, even too much alcohol, are not violent people (Wilson & Taft, 2015). Instead, alcohol may exacerbate other components and certainly the risk increases once alcohol is involved. It is estimated that alcohol is involved in up to 50% of partner violence in Australia and 73% of physical assaults against partners (Wilson & Taft, 2015).

Other factors than alcohol consumption may contribute to family violence spiking at Christmas. There can be financial stress as Christmas can be expensive with buying gifts, nice food and wines; and, if travel costs are involved, this adds to the cost. The children are on school holidays and require more time and attention, which again can add to the stress. In addition, spending time with extended family members can result in tensions and arguments. Each of these factors, and the combination of some of these factors, can create additional stresses that can increase the potential for episodes of family violence, with people with volatile personalities aggravated. There is also greater opportunity for abuse as increased time together presents more opportunities.

Conclusion

Major community events and sporting events are promoted by destination marketing organisations because major events can encourage people to travel to that destination. Events are usually associated with increased use of commercial accommodation as well as an injection of funds through other areas of the local economy such as retail, hospitality, fast food, fuel and groceries, as well as local attractions and activities. Major events, including sporting events, as well as family events such as Christmas and weddings, can be times in which family violence increases. People need to be aware of the risks and try to look at strategies to mitigate risks where possible. For sporting events, if possible, it might be helpful to try to stay away from a partner who may be violent.

8 Family Violence at the Tourism Destination

'People think being alone makes you lonely, but I don't think that's true. Being surrounded by the wrong people is the loneliest thing in the world.'

– Kim Culbertson, *The Liberation of Max McTrue*

Introduction

As was introduced earlier, tourism is an open system. Tourism is impacted by externalities such as law, politics, and the environment. There are five elements in the tourism system – a tourist, a generating region (where the tourist usually resides), industries that provide products and services for the tourism experience, a transit route (how the person travels from their generating region to their destination), and a destination. This book presents the case that family violence impacts every one of these five tourism elements. There are subsidiary components within these elements as well as external to them. The conceptual framework for this book, the adapted Whole Tourism System Model, is presented again below, to assist the reader with visualising which part of the framework is being discussed in this chapter without having to refer back.

This chapter focuses on the tourism element of 'destination', represented in Figure 8.1 by the ellipse at the far right. This chapter, together with Chapter 9, focuses on aspects of the destination that impact the tourist from the perspective of control, bullying, abuse and family violence. The central discussion is controlling and abusive behaviour in the form of family violence; specifically, controlling and abusive behaviour within the family. The underbelly is in the stories, and even one story can be impactful. Sometimes hearing just one story that someone can relate to or that gives someone hope is impactful. It may resonate with an individual more than something based on a sample size of hundreds or thousands. However, in terms of our understanding of tourism motivation, have we got it right or is it idealistic?

= tourism industries

Figure 8.1 Whole Tourism System Model
Source: adapted from Leiper (2004).

Push and Pull Theory

There is significant tourism literature on destinations. Taking time to go on a holiday away from home is considered to involve several 'push' aspects – things that 'push' a person to want to go away on a holiday. There are also 'pull' components – things that 'pull' a person to choose one destination over others. Accordingly, destination attributes are important.

But who chooses the destination? Children's preferences for tourism choices are said to be 'highly taken into account by parents' (Curtale, 2018: 172). It would be extremely reasonable for parents to want to make choices that appeal to their children. Ideally, the choice of destination would be a whole-of-the-family affair. However, in abusive and controlling environments, the destination choice may be made by a perpetrator of family violence who may feel entitled to choose on behalf of the family. It may not always happen that way of course. However, it is important to understand that family holidays may not always involve families organising and agreeing on a destination. A holiday with a perpetrator of family violence may involve greater emotional labour and be somewhere removed from places of security. And a holiday away from a perpetrator of family violence, once separated from them, can be a mixture of feeling free but feeling afraid. These emotions are captured in some of the stories within this chapter.

Destination attributes are considered to be central pull factors in the travel decision-making process. Note that I mention the travel decision-making process. Tourism literature is filled with information about the travel decision-making process. The literature will tell us that a potential tourist chooses the destination that responds best to their needs and will have the best potential to meet their expectations.

Looking at the social psychology theory of tourism motivation, again there is an assumed undercurrent that everyone travelling has the same motivation. Motivation to travel may be considered to involve two forces: '(1) the desire to leave the everyday environment behind oneself, *and* (2) the desire to obtain psychological (intrinsic) rewards through travel in a contrasting (new or old) environment' (Iso-Ahola, 1982: 259). In explaining this theory, Iso-Ahola states that the tourist:

> may escape the personal world (i.e. personal troubles, problems, difficulties and failures), and/or the interpersonal world (i.e. co-workers, family members, relatives, friends and neighbors) and he may seek personal rewards (e.g. feelings of mastery, learning about other cultures, rest and relaxation, recharge and getting renewed, ego-enhancement and prestige) and/or interpersonal rewards (e.g. varies and increased social interaction, interacting with friendly natives or members of the travel group, interacting with old friends in a new place or with new friends in an old place). (1982: 260)

The point I make in this chapter is: Who? *Who* is in our mind when we read these tourism theories? *Whose* decision is the destination? *Who* is escaping difficulties? *Who* is resting and relaxing? Like all theories, assumptions are made. Tourism theories have relied on assuming that tourists are not living with family violence. Is selecting a destination a whole-of-the-family decision? Is the victim of family violence escaping personal troubles and difficulties? In family violence, the decision-making may rest centrally, or even entirely, with the perpetrator. In family violence, the victim is taking their difficulties on holiday with them.

Maslow's Hierarchy of Needs

Probably many readers are familiar with Maslow's Hierarchy of Needs. Abraham Maslow's 1943 paper titled 'A theory of human motivation' (Maslow, 1943) is still heavily referred to. Both my older children (aged 19 and 17 at the time of writing) are familiar with it as they studied it in year 12 psychology and business management. Many people may not have read Maslow's 1943 paper but they may have heard of his work, or come across the well-known pyramid that depicts human motivation based on his paper. While the pyramids that describe the order of human motivations are well known, none of these pyramids was developed by Maslow, whose paper contains no figures or tables.

Maslow's theory of human motivation can help us to understand why many victims of family violence may be unable to experience tourism in the way that others might. The reason is that safety is a foundational, primary need, and a person cannot work properly towards the higher needs while lower foundational needs are unsatisfied. Maslow stated:

> Human needs arrange themselves in heirarchies of prepotency. That is to say, the appearance of one need usually rests on the prior satisfaction of another, more pre-potent need. Man is a perpetually wanting animal. Also no need or drive can be treated as if it were isolated or discrete; every drive is related to the state of satisfaction or dissatisfaction of other drives. (Maslow, 1943: 370)

Maslow (1943) proposed that the most foundational needs are 'the basic needs', which are physiological needs such as food and water. He suggests that the need for food and water if hungry and thirsty will be a stronger motivation than anything else such as love and esteem. Maslow (1943: 374) states that if a person is 'dangerously hungry' then they will have no interest in things such as writing poetry, buying a car or buying a new pair of shoes.

The next need identified by Maslow is safety, which, 'if it is extreme enough and chronic enough, may be characterized as living almost for safety alone' (1943: 376). Maslow goes on to highlight that an understanding of safety is best viewed by observing children and infants, because they do not inhibit their reaction, while adults have been taught to inhibit their reaction and 'we may not be able to see this on the surface' (1943: 376). Concerning the reaction of children, Maslow states:

> Another indication of the child's need for safety is his preference for some kind of undisrupted routine or rhythm. He seems to want a predictable, orderly world. For instance, injustice, unfairness, or inconsistency in the parents seems to make a child feel anxious and unsafe. This attitude may be not so much because of the injustice per se or any particular pains involved, but rather because this treatment threatens to make the world look unreliable, or unsafe, or unpredictable. Young children seem to thrive better under a system which has at least a skeletal outline of rigidity, in which there is a schedule of a kind, some sort of routine, something that can be counted upon, not only for the present but also far into the future. Perhaps one could express this more accurately by saying that the child needs an organized world rather than an unorganized or unstructured one.
>
> The central role of the parents and the normal family setup are indisputable. Quarrelling, physical assault, separation, divorce or death within the family may be particularly terrifying. Also parental outbursts of rage or threats of punishment directed to the child, calling him names, speaking to him harshly, shaking him, handling him roughly, or actual physical punishment sometimes elicit such total panic and terror in the child that we must assume more is involved than the physical pain alone. While it is true that in some children this terror may represent also a fear of loss of parental love, it can also occur in completely rejected children, who seem to cling to the hating parents more for sheer safety and protection than because of hope of love. (1943: 377–378)

Maslow's hierarchy of needs is often shown diagrammatically, as in Figure 8.2, although, as mentioned previously, Maslow did not present his theory as a pyramid or indeed as any diagram. The needs are typically presented as a pyramid, where the largest foundational items are at the base of the pyramid because those elements need to be satisfied first. A person is not motivated for higher-order elements unless the foundational elements are satisfied.

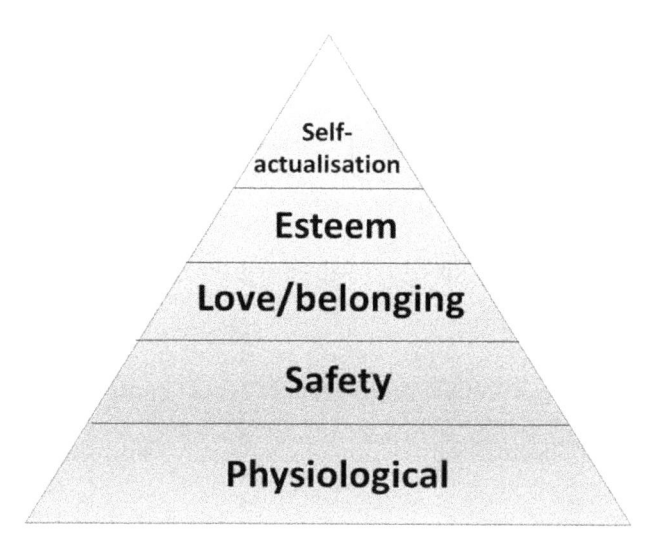

Figure 8.2 Maslow's Hierarchy of Needs

The reason I present Maslow's hierarchy of needs is that it high-lights extremely well that a person who fears for their safety cannot be motivated by higher-order elements. It is in many ways fascinating that, as far back as 1943, Maslow wrote about the importance of stability and predictability for children and the impact on them if they did not feel safe. Yet strangely, 80 years later, we are still questioning why family violence is a problem and why children living with family violence may exhibit behavioural oddities. Indeed, I argue that a person living with family violence (victims and children) cannot achieve the same levels of enjoyment (or any enjoyment in some cases) of a holiday to a destination that may be possible by others. I further argue that tourism theories are flawed, as they assume tourists are all willingly and cooperatively choosing to engage in touristic activities. I propose that the theories are deficient and do not speak for travellers who live with family violence. I remind readers of Maslow's (1943: 376) words, mentioned earlier: 'if it is extreme enough and chronic enough, [the person] may be characterized as living almost for safety alone'. A person preoccupied with safety cannot possibly appreciate the views and the activities at the destination.

Case Example

The city of Albuquerque is in the US state of New Mexico. It was the night before Thanksgiving, a major national holiday and time of celebration in the US. The emergency dispatchers (911 in the US) received a phone call about an unresponsive woman. The ambulance arrived and the emergency workers found Nicole to be dead with suspicious marks on her face and her neck that suggested strangulation. Nicole's boyfriend, Francisco, who had called 911, was arrested for murder as well as for tampering with the evidence (Women Against Crime, 2022).

This story is true. Sadly, it is not an isolated case. Women are often subjected to family violence around major holidays. Holidays such as Thanksgiving, Christmas, major sporting events and New Year are times of heightened risk. Times of family reunions and connections are times of increased risk for many victims of family violence. A holiday is supposed to be fun and relaxing and a time for getting away to enjoy touristic experiences. In all the tourism literature – the incredible volume of books, book chapters, journal articles, doctoral theses, reports and other documents – tourism material tells us that tourism is positive. Holidays are good for us. Nowhere does the tourism literature spotlight the underbelly of tourism – that holidays come with greater risk for those who live with family violence. Family violence does not take a holiday. In fact, family violence often flourishes at times of holidays.

The Post-Separation Family Tourism Experience

Alannah & Madeline Foundation ambassador Ashton Kline and his brother Grant outlined the holiday they had once their mother had managed to separate from their abusive father (Alannah & Madeline Foundation, 2014). They described it as a time when they felt safe and could be themselves. This family holiday (under the new family structure without the abusive father) was described in the following way in a video:

> Ashton: We were lucky enough to get a couple of weeks away on the Murray River on a houseboat: Mum, Grant and myself. It was the first time that Mum felt really safe. She was actually able to be herself as well without feeling threatened or as if she had to protect us.

> Grant: I just remember Mum hating the water and we were all so excited to go but she was so nervous. Every time the boat would rock she'd come with her suitcases packed and ready to abandon the boat.

> Ashton: It was the first time we were able to be together as a family unit and just be ourselves.

There are several key points in the story. Firstly, both children report the holiday in a positive light. The holiday is described as a 'family unit' without the abusive father. The absence of the father does not impact the assessment of the 'family unit'. The mother is described as being able to 'be herself' and not having to focus on protecting the children or feeling threatened. The holiday was described as a time that they could 'be ourselves'.

Is Travel with a Perpetrator of Family Violence a Holiday?

If a victim of family violence is holidaying with their 'threat' and needing to be on guard for the children and themselves, is it really a holiday? Are they able to rest and relax? Does it improve their well-being? Does it improve their stress levels? Are there any restorative benefits at all?

The notion of a holiday spent travelling to a destination away from home is very different when someone is holidaying with a perpetrator of family violence. As outlined in the next chapter, there can be limitations on destination choice even after separating from a perpetrator of family violence.

I sometimes think about whether scholars who write about tourism, and in particular family tourism, have wondered whether the theories hold when a family is living with family violence? Often, holidays are defined around push motivations (i.e. what aspects 'pushed' someone to want to take a holiday away from home). Holidays are also considered to be an escape (Iso-Ahola, 1982) and a break from routine (Crompton, 1979). Family holiday experiences are seen to be 'the family doing fun activities that are different to normal and which create positive memories' (Schänzel & Yeoman, 2015: 143). The same authors also argue that 'holidays can play an important role in strengthening family relationships and building of social and family capital within the immediate and extended family' (Schänzel & Yeoman, 2015: 145).

It would seem that, when such definitions and thoughts were developed, it was with an idealist ideal of family in mind. Such definitions do not capture the underbelly of tourism. Such definitions do not speak to the people having to endure holidays with a perpetrator of family violence. Such holidays do not strengthen or build. They often involve abuse.

A different definition of 'family holiday' put forward is this: 'a purposive time spent together as a family group (which may include extended family) doing activities different from normal activities that are fun but may involve compromise and conflict at times' (Schänzel et al., 2012: 3). On the surface, it may seem that the concept of conflict was to be inclusive of all families including those involved in family violence. However, in the same book, it is said that 'it is not a holiday if it is not fun. If it is fun then it is a holiday' (Schänzel et al., 2012: 3). Given the controlling nature of family violence, the holiday destination could be chosen by the perpetrator of family violence. If things do not go as desired in the eyes of the perpetrator, abuse may be released.

My Tourism Experiences with a Perpetrator of Family Violence

In the Overture, I mention that, as someone whose expertise was in tourism, people thought it odd that I wasn't fond of travel. For me, going away with a perpetrator of family violence was not fun and relaxing; nor was it getting away from anything I wanted to get away from. What I wanted to get away from I was taking with me. Even worse, I was away from places of familiarity, comfort and support lines and was somewhere unfamiliar in cramped conditions. The flights were terrible. Driving was terrible. Travel will be discussed in Chapter 10 about 'transit routes'. But in terms of the destination, things were only good if things went the way they needed to for Mr Ex. For him, trips away were a time of relaxing. The children would often want to go to the beach and play in the water. Supervising young children near the water was not relaxing and enjoyable for Mr Ex so, generally, he would relax and I would take the children to the beach to supervise. The advantage of this was that he was doing what we wanted and not being bothered, which could keep him in a better mood.

One time we were holidaying on the Gold Coast (Queensland, Australia) with family. We had one unit in an apartment, my brother and his family had another unit in the same apartment block, and my parents had a different unit. Each family had their own unit but we would come together for meals and various activities. One time, my mother commented that everything was left for me and why didn't Mr Ex spend time doing things with the children. It must have seemed puzzling. But when you understand family violence, and that perpetrators have a sense of entitlement and so only want to do things that go their way, then it makes complete sense. For me, it wasn't so much the destination that was terrible when travelling: it was the trip there. I share a few aspects of this in the next chapter. Travel for me was a terrible experience. I would say the experiences were bad enough for it to create what I call an 'imprint'. I use the word imprint whenever something that may be quite trivial for some is especially memorable for a person. It becomes an imprint. Imprints are possible for people even from a young age.

For example, I have clear memories of travelling as a 4-year-old on a plane, alone, to visit my grandparents because my parents wanted to go to the US with my older brother and go to Disneyland. I was a bit young for such a trip, so I was put on a plane to stay with my grandparents. I was 4 years old. I was bought a 'Golden Book' (books for young children, with a golden binding – www.penguin.com.au/books/brands/little-golden-books) and was seated next to an elderly lady. I asked her on the journey if she would read the book to me, please. She ignored me. I imagine she was not too pleased with being put in the position of some sort of babysitter for someone else's child. Her reaction of ignoring me confused me and crushed me. I still remember it. When I arrived I was greeted by my grandparents with a giant teddy bear. I named him 'Golden Teddy'. I still have him. This is an imprint. I do believe that it is possible to recall things that are, as I call them, imprints.

Having said that, there are a great many things that happened to me when travelling as a tourist that I do not remember. This may be because they were not significant enough for me to bother remembering them. Or perhaps I didn't want to hold on to the memory. Perhaps I did not see things because my focus was on safety. I sometimes would not see the beautiful view or the stunning sunset. I looked but I did not see. Sometimes, when your world is filled with fear and you live on guard, you cannot see and enjoy the beauty that you travelled to see.

My First Tourism Experience after Separating from a Perpetrator of Family Violence

The first time I travelled to a destination after separation was in July 2018. It was to celebrate my mother's 80th birthday and many relatives and friends of theirs were travelling to be there, in some cases thousands of kilometres. I remember my mother inviting us to stay with her and my brother, which would have meant my family would have been split with me and two children staying with my mother and whoever else was staying there, and the other two children staying with my brother and his family. At this stage, it was about nine months after separation, and Mr Ex and I had still not settled on the parenting and financial situation.

In Australia, and perhaps in other countries, everything you own and earn after separation and prior to settlement is considered a joint asset. I was quite aware of that and wasn't feeling very motivated to save money that would only be shared with Mr Ex. In addition, I wasn't feeling like compromising my concept of family at a time when I was still trying to discover what the new family structure was.

I declined the split family offer and searched for a property in the vicinity. I found the most amazing place. It had a private pool, was walking distance from the beach, had a bedroom for each of my children, had numerous loungerooms, board games, and had a separate villa just for me with its own bathroom, bedroom, kitchen and lounge. It was divine. At that stage I was still dealing with the legal aspects regarding parental and financial agreements so did need to have a space to set up my laptop and work. I also selected a BMW car. It was outrageous. I figured that there was no point in saving my income because I only was going to have to give some of it to Mr Ex. But, most centrally, after 17 years of horror where I felt I could choose nothing, I chose outrageous options. It felt silly and wonderful and it was the most wonderful tourism experience I can remember. I loved that holiday. I am glad I chose what I chose. I chose every outrageous part of it on my own, although I did show the property to the children before ordering it, to ensure they were also happy.

I am glad I was outrageous because there was no point in saving money that I had to give away to Mr Ex, and also I wanted to be with all my children and have no stress (such as shared bedrooms can create).

I did not want to split the children between two separate households. I did not want to have to compromise or share or be anything but me. It was wonderful. I will remember it fondly for ever as it was a beautiful holiday but it was also made more beautiful because Mr Ex had not been in contact so I had no idea where he was living and I did not have to seek his permission for the children to travel.

Solo Travel to a Destination While Living with Family Violence

When I was married and trapped in a controlling and abusive marriage, I did have some escape moments, which were for work. As an academic, I was expected to share my research with a broad, ideally international audience. When the children were young, I happily and ignorantly went to an annual conference to present my research. While I did not enjoy holidays per se (i.e. holidaying with Mr Ex), I did enjoy the work conferences. Some nights I would order from the hotel menu and sit in my room alone and have dinner delivered and watch a movie. Others considered this odd because they were enjoying late nights and parties every night. I revelled in the silence and the peace. I also found this easier to report on because I was always asked whom I ate dinner with, and how old they were, and had to show photos of them so Mr Ex could be satisfied there was no threat. While away on these trips, I would also walk from my accommodation to the centre of the city we were staying at for the conference and just soak up the atmosphere. I loved each day so much.

As the children became older, I started to realise that things did not go well for them when I was away. When they were young they said little and had no means of communicating with me. Oblivious, I thought they were in good care and I enjoyed my time away; time away, where I did not have to share a bed or anything with a person I could not respect.

The children began to find means of informing me that they did not want me to go and that things were worse when I was not home. I would receive text messages to say that they were abused, there was yelling, and they were punished for laughing.

My last trip away from the children while living with family violence was in April 2016. I still have the text messages from the children from that last trip. I sent a text message to my daughter Chantelle:

Me: 'Has the week been okay for you?'

Chantelle: 'Yeah. Just yelling'

Me: 'Much?'

Chantelle: 'Yes. And lots of beer. When I was doing the cat job [jobs relating to caring for the cat – feeding, changing water, doing litter box] he tried to hide his beer bottles from me.'

And from that same trip away, text messages from one of my younger boys, Jonathan:

> Jonathan: 'I got no one to put me to bed. And no sweet kisses and hugs I love you and reply about how it has been when possible. We are not aloud (sic) to message you for more than three mins sorry can't talk for long.'

Four days later:

> Jonathan: 'Seb made a fart noise then dad smacked him he isn't aloud (sic) to go to basketball and got marks and got choked and he is yelling and screaming at us now and yeah. Hope you have had a good day.'

And so, the trips away were no longer an option. The trips that gave me freedom and joy represented fear and punishment for the children. Ironically, in my job I was meant to go on these research trips, and promotion for academics is at least in part linked with sharing one's research at a major conference. I realised I was trapped. Not to go was to miss my trip away from Mr Ex and miss the opportunity to be promoted. To go was to fail my children. No promotion pathway accommodates this conundrum adequately. And so, I stopped travelling. My last trip away from the children was in April 2016.

Holiday Stories from Others

Holidaying with a perpetrator of family violence is not something you find in tourism literature. Or at least, if it is there, I have not stumbled upon it. I think it fair to say that it isn't the type of tourism topic that boosters would like to see. Tourism is about rest and relaxation. It is about escape. It is about good times. Holidaying with a perpetrator of family violence may not involve good times. Having said that, everyone's story is different and some people living with family violence may find that holidays bring out a better side of the perpetrator because they might be doing things they like or spending time doing activities that reduce time with the victim.

However, some stories I have heard from those I have communicated with have had themes of being trapped and unhappy. One woman told me that her partner (who went on to be her husband) spent most of the time sleeping when they were on any type of holiday together and she wasn't quite sure what she was meant to do with her time. She said that on the first holiday she had with him (before she married him) she spent hours in the dark in a motel bathroom sobbing. She said that she had no money to leave and didn't know how to get out. When they did marry several years later, he told her that this holiday they had together had been their honeymoon so they didn't need to have another one.

She told me that during any type of holiday together, because he would spend most of the day sleeping, she would walk around the hotel alone. Making things worse, she did not have a driving licence, which added to her feeling of isolation. She also chose not to get on a plane because she didn't want to upset him and 'he had convinced me I was hopeless'.

In other words, being on a holiday when someone is holidaying with a perpetrator of family violence can feel like being trapped – but at another location. It is not relaxing. It is not an escape.

Experiences of a Woman from Europe

This story was told to me by a woman from Europe. It is presented largely verbatim with a few minor edits for readability/grammatical purposes only:

> Holidays are supposed to be a time of fun, relaxation and joy. Of course, there is a bit of stress related to the preparations and the travelling time but in cases of abuse this goes to a totally different level, to the point that I have heard friends experiencing this and saying things like: 'I dread the holidays period because of all the abuse that I know I'll have to endure from my ex!'

> The most extreme incidents of abuse in our case came at the brink of and after separation. Most examples of how this impacted our holidays also relate to this time. The mess started with any attempts to agree on the holiday period. My ex often uses communication about the children as one of his ways to exert control, and he'd often harass me with unnecessary communication requesting me to engage in extensive communication (e.g. demanding pictures of what we do when the children are with me or asking for explanations of what we do during our time together); or instead, he'd simply stop replying to very important information, such as emails where I ask him to address safety concerns, like car seats not attached to the car, or windows being left wide open next to our very young children at times when they were closely supervised.

> And holidays have a broader meaning for me than others. I am not a national in the country we reside in, so to be able to see my family, I need to travel. And of course, it's important that the children come as well, as this is their only chance to connect to this part of their heritage, to practice the language, and of course very importantly, to see their maternal grandparents. My ex knows this very well, so he often uses this as a way to exert his control.

> Before we had the final court order establishing what happens during holidays, my ex would simply refuse to let me travel home, so I would have to request specific hearings for this, as if I simply took the children with me I could be accused of abduction. The court would always grant me permission but did nothing to ensure that I didn't have to keep coming back to court. Can you imagine if you have to go to court every

time you'd like to travel?! And the same would happen even for simpler things like going camping. While our court order already established that the children lived with me, my ex's contact with the children was so regular that it would prevent us from going away for more than two nights, and this was only during school holidays, as he had a few hours of contact during every weekend. This was happening in the eyes of the court, but for two years, the court failed to address it.

While on holidays, my ex would request to talk to the children every day, meaning that instead of being able to go out and get on with our day, we'd be held back in the house until the call had finished. When I communicated to him that this was excessive and getting in the way of our holidays, so I'd be reducing this to twice a week, he'd start a campaign of harassment through numerous text messages and emails demanding to talk to the children every day. Even after our court order clearly stated that only two calls a week were to be organised, he'd continue harassing us to try to get more.

Once, I tested positive for Covid as soon as I arrived at my parent's home abroad. It was Christmas. I obviously had caught the virus while still in the country where we reside but was asymptomatic and tested negative. Hence why I could travel. As a result of testing positive, I was held back for one extra week as a result of having to self-isolate. I had the results of the test in writing and a letter from the GP stating the period that by law I was required to self-isolate and I provided my ex with a copy of the letter. These were indeed not the type of holidays that I had hoped for. The children were with my parents, and I was self-isolating in one room on my own, at Christmas. The number and nature of messages that I received from my ex demanding that I brought the kids back to our country of residence (while I was ill and upset about not being able to spend time with the kids and my family) was horrendous. He even got to demand that my parents (both vulnerable) had to take a plane to bring our children back.

Our court order establishes that we have to provide each other with details of where we take the children when taking them abroad. While it would normally be desirable to do the same when travelling nationally, I explicitly asked the court not to order this, as I would be very worried about my ex turning up during any of our trips to cause us upset. This was as a result of him once turning up at my home just when we were getting ready to go camping. He came with his mum. They rang the bell and when I opened the door, his mum took out her phone and pointed it out at me, as if she was recording me. I asked her to put the phone down but she didn't. Eventually, they left after I told them that if they didn't leave, I'd call the police. Once they left, I carried on loading the car to get ready. The kids got very confused and stressed about the possibility that their trip with me could be cancelled because of finally having to go with their dad. It was very stressful for us all.

The final court order makes provisions for the holidays. These are 50/50. Since the children are still young and there are concerns about my ex's ability to look after them and the children need time to adjust, it established that this year they would not go with him for longer than seven days. And to make it fairer for my ex (yes, to make it fairer to the abuser, you got it right…) they decided that the same would apply to me. This was despite my solicitor pointing out that I am not a national citizen, and the summer holidays are one of the few occasions when we can visit the maternal grandparents and that the children had always gone for three weeks at a time, even during the previous two years of the proceedings. However, the courts wanted to favour the proven abuser instead.

Conclusion

A key point to take away from this chapter is that tourism motivation theories are based on an assumption that everyone in the travel party has agreed and negotiated the destination. It is assumed that the destination has been considered by all members of the travel party and that all members of that same travel party obtain the benefits of rest, relaxation, escape and well-being.

Boosters of tourism are interested in furthering this idea that tourism is all-positive. It would be convenient to think that tourism has no downside. It would be convenient to pretend that family violence is not happening. However, these tourism motivation theories are based on an invalid and deeply flawed assumption. Like the non-existent can opener that the economist holds in the Introduction to this book, these tourism motivational theories are based on a false can opener that does not exist. To reveal the real truth would spoil the 'all-positive' mirage that tourism relies upon. The reality is that tourism is not always positive. Tourism has an underbelly. For some people, going on holiday is worse than being at home.

The next chapter continues the discussion of the destination but focuses on equal shared parental responsibilities. While this component is relevant to the Family Law Act in Australia, sadly there are similar processes in place in other countries and, accordingly, the key messages are worthy of note globally.

9 Equal Shared Parental Responsibility

'We, the human race, don't value children, we say we do but we don't. If we did, the legal system could be completely different globally.'

– Efrat Cybulkiewicz,

Introduction

This is the second chapter that focuses on the tourism system element 'destination'. This topic could sit across a range of elements from the whole tourism system but I positioned it within destination so that the impact of mobility due to equal shared parental responsibilities could be highlighted. As the focus is on family law in an Australian context, readers outside Australia need to be aware that components of family law in Australia may not be generalisable to other countries. Such readers interested in the detail of the equivalent family law act will need to undertake some reading of relevant documents to ascertain whether equal shared parental responsibility, or an equivalent, exists in their country.

This chapter outlines how the Family Law Act 1975 provides for the default position of 'equal shared parental responsibility' and what it means. This chapter will also discuss how this default position can impact separated people. Potential impacts can include separated people who have children by the ex-partner being unable to relocate, or having limitations placed on travel outside the region.

A poorly understood outcome of the Family Law Act, which particularly impacts victims of family violence and their children, is that any travel out of the area must be agreed upon by the ex-partner. Controlling individuals may choose to be disagreeable with approving travel for the ex-partner when that ex-partner has their allocated time with the children. There might also be specific court orders in place limiting the time period each parent can holiday outside the region with the children. Some court orders place limitations on the amount of time the abusive ex-partner can travel with the children, and, 'to be fair', will place the same limitation on the victim parent. Thus, post-separation, tourism opportunities can be thwarted for victims of family violence.

When there are children involved, particularly younger children, separation can be complex. Courts will want to ensure in almost all cases, that both parents have access to the children. Time with a parent who is a perpetrator of family violence may not be in the child's best interests, and may not be what the child wants. Younger children have little, if any, voice. Decisions made by courts may be disheartening for victims and their children. There is also a difference between 'time with' a parent and 'equal shared parental responsibilities'. It is possible for an abusive parent not to have the power to make decisions about the child (e.g. where they go to school, their religion) by the victim being awarded 'sole parental responsibilities' to make the major long-term decisions on their own, but the abusive parent can still have 'time with' the child.

Custody

A film called *Custody*, directed by Xavier Legrand, was released in 2017. Being in French but with English subtitles may have limited its international audience. The film came to Australia in 2018 through the boutique cinema chain Palace Films. Therefore, it was only available in major cities. My friend David, who is a lawyer and lives in Melbourne, rang me to tell me I simply must watch the film, which was by then at the end of its screening and appearing in a small number of Melbourne suburbs. It seemed a bit of a bother to work out the transport to get to Melbourne City and then to the suburb where the film was screening. David insisted. He said that all the magistrates he knows and talks to were talking about the film and he would map out exactly the transport process and order the tickets and pick me up from the train station. I had to see it he explained. He told me that the film was exactly what I had been talking about that happens. I am glad David made me watch the film. I have never had such an emotional impact from a film in all my life. David and I even talked about the perfect characters – the mother being so exhausted that she sat in court without emotion or energy. She looked frail and tired. The father was a large-framed man. His physical bulk adds impact and power. He is physically imposing.

The film director did extensive research for making the film. He spoke to judges, lawyers, police who attend family violence incidents, victims and perpetrators. He observed court proceedings as part of his learning for making the film. The film opens with a custody court hearing where the mother is seeking sole custody of her 11-year-old son,

Julien. Her daughter is almost 18 years of age. The mother provides a letter from Julien as evidence that he doesn't want to see his father.

> Judge: 'Julien is 11. He's in 6th grade at Monod Junior High. He said:
>
> "My parents separated a year ago. I live with mum and my sister. There's a party for my sister's 18th birthday. We live with Papy and Nana, except my father. I can't play outside. We're scared that man will come. Papy screams. It's not good for him. When he comes, I worry about mum. All he wants is to hurt her. He's no father. I'm glad they're divorcing.
>
> Josephine dislikes him but she's old enough to not see him. I won't see him either or be forced to every other week or weekend. I won't see him again. That's all."'
>
> Judge says to the two parents: 'Which of you is the bigger liar?'
>
> Mother: 'We just want peace.'
>
> Father: 'I just want to talk to my kids.'
>
> Judge: 'Your children have turned against you.'
>
> Father: 'Because of what their mother says.'
>
> Lawyer: 'We ask for your ruling your Honour.'
>
> Judge: 'Nothing here is black and white.'

Allegations of violence are presented in court, but the mother has no evidence. It is her word against the father's word. The judge grants shared custody and orders Julien to spend alternate weekends with his father.

Should the Voice of Children be Stronger?

In an opinion piece I wrote, published in *The Courier* in 2020 (Zentveld, 2020), I asked whether the voice of children should be stronger in family law matters. I include the article in this book:

> The underlying foundation of the Family Law Act is to act in the best interests of the child. Can that realistically be achieved without the voice of the child? Family violence is a particular situation in which the voice of the child tends to be absent from decisions that are made on their behalf. A violent parent may be fined, made to pay court costs, and made to pay for the damage done to property. I wonder about the damage done to the child's brain though. Who pays for that?
>
> Research shows that exposure to familiar violence interferes with the receptors of the brain, which can be particularly damaging in children. Wouldn't it be a powerful message if perpetrators of family violence were made to pay for the child's therapy needed as a consequence of being exposed to family violence.
>
> Therapy, if needed and wanted by a child who has been exposed to family violence, could be needed for years – perhaps even the rest of

the child's life. Children who have witnessed or experienced traumatic violent episodes sadly often relive them in their minds. For some children, the episodes replay in their minds in their dreams; or something triggers their mind to go back to that episode. Even writing the surname that belongs to the abusive parent can trigger the flashbacks. Not enough is known about this, and sadly, there is inadequate flow of this knowledge into the legal system where decisions get made about penalties, intervention orders, and parenting order matters.

On Thursday 23rd July 2020 I attended a meeting with other representatives from Victoria's universities and peak organisations that work in the family violence space. There was strong acknowledgement that the voice of the children is largely missing. Practitioners are greatly aware of the issues; university researchers are limited in their research in this space due to strong ethics boundaries and limitations. It makes it harder to have this information available.

Courts do not make it easy for children's voices to be heard. Children are not allowed in court and their affidavits are likely to be struck out. Older children can hold down jobs, drive a car, have full control over their bank account and be responsible for their health record and have a Medicare card. But they are not permitted to tell a judge that they do not want to spend time with a parent who they are fearful of and who they do not trust their behaviour. In Victoria, children as young as 10 can be arrested and charged for criminal matters. Yet older teenagers cannot attend court to state whether they want contact with an abusive parent.

Imagine being regularly verbally or physically abused by a colleague and then told you should share an office with them. It would never happen. So why would we have a child who has been tormented by a parent told they have to communicate or spend time with them? What does that do to their brain? Where is the voice of the children in court? An independent children's lawyer is not the answer in all cases. Not all matters have lawyers. Not all parents can afford them. Some family law matters involved self-represented litigants. And a children's lawyer is still not the voice of the child.

Sadly parents sometimes get lost in a focus on their rights and children can be a type of commodity that can be used as a tool for vindictive measures aimed at the other parent. Children get caught in between; and may be quite lost inside as they are compelled to communicate with a parent they cannot trust the behaviour of and who does not take responsibility for their abusive and controlling behaviour. This is not healthy for children. Arguments between parents about their own rights are missing the point completely about parenting. They do not have rights. They have responsibilities. And the underlying foundation of the Family Law Act is to act in the best interests of the child. While time with both parents should be regarded as best in normal situations, there is enough evidence to show the trauma to a child's brain from being exposed to family violence. Being forced to spend time with or communicate with an abusive and controlling person may in some cases not be in the best interests of the child. Just as being forced to share an office with a colleague who is abusive would hardly be expected to maximise productivity.

Research has shown that witnessing family violence is a significant predictor of post-traumatic stress disorder in children. Imagine being in the wilderness in a flimsy 2-man tent with a large grizzly bear circling the tent. You do not know what the bear will do. It may do nothing. But it may hurt you. You do not know what the bear will do next. That is what living with an abusive and controlling person is like. You are forever on edge. As a society, we need to understand the impact better – in our schools, in our workplaces, and in our court systems. Those children are part of society's future and we need to do better by them.

The Voice of a Child

As presented in the previous section, the voice of the child is largely absent from court. Independent children's lawyers may be appointed. They may not necessarily represent the child's wishes. An example of that was presented under the pseudonyms Zac and Carly, who were ordered by court to live with their violent father, despite him holding a knife to their mother's throat, throwing Zac across the room, and putting the cat in the clothes dryer and turning it on (Hill, 2019). A protest letter written by 15-year-old Carly said:

> My name is Carly and I am scared of my dad. I have seen him in a rage throw my brother across the room. He has held a knife to my mother's throat telling her how easy it would be to cut it … and the court has given me to him.
>
> I have tried to tell all the legal people involved how scared he makes me but I am too young for anyone to listen. Why am I not allowed to help decide what happens to me? I feel like I'm screaming in a sound-proof room because my voice has been stolen from me… . At what point do I become old enough to have a voice? At what point will those with the power choose to let me be heard?
>
> I need someone to hear my voice and understand that all I want is a life without fear. The only person to listen to me is my mum. She believes me when I tell her I am scared and keeps me safe but they will jail her for listening to me … I need your help. (Hill, 2019: 162)

What is Equal Shared Parental Responsibility?

Custody is discussed as parental responsibility in Australia. Parental responsibility in many countries essentially means the rights and responsibilities a parent has for a child. In Australia, and many other countries, there is legislation that guides parents who separate towards the legalities of those responsibilities. It is often a situation where both parents, regardless of who has the most time with the child, equally and jointly make the major decisions about the child.

Parental responsibilities in Australia

Equal shared parental responsibility is the default legal position in Australia, meaning that both parents of children under the age of 18 will be responsible for the major decisions for long-term issues. These long-term issues are things such as religion, medical matters, the child's name, and where the child goes to school. Another example is a passport: a parent cannot apply for a passport for a child to travel overseas without the consent of the other parent.

The default position is that separated parents will need to discuss the long-term major issues for the child and agree on them. This can be complex, of course, because there might be differing views on which school is best, or what sort of health treatment the child should receive.

Equal shared parental responsibility should not be confused with time. One parent may have the child most of the time or even all of the time. In fact, it is usual that a child does spend unequal time with each parent, because it might be more practical for the child to have one main household. It is exceptionally rare for there to be no provision for access to the children by the father, with only 3% of fathers refused access to their children by the courts (Hall, 2019).

Parental responsibility is about the capacity to make decisions about the child; it is not measured by time with the child. However, this does not change the legalities in decision-making. If a parent wants to change the school the child attends, or relocate to a different city, this can be challenged by the other parent.

The alternative position, which is very rare, is sole parental responsibility. This is where one parent is given the parental responsibilities on their own and the other parent has no legal input into the decision-making. It is difficult to know exactly what proportion of people have sole parental responsibilities because not all cases go to court. Some parents when they separate might agree on how they share the assets and how they manage the parenting responsibilities. For parents who make their own arrangements, the default position of equal shared parental responsibilities will apply. Some parents may also create a parenting plan and, in some of those cases, the parents may apply to the Family Court of Australia for a consent order to make that agreement legally binding. In those cases that do go to the Family Court, the majority of cases are for equal shared parental responsibilities. In an article by Unified Lawyers (Reardon, 2021), it was stated: 'It is extremely rare for the Court to award sole parental responsibility and operates under the presumption that equal shared parental responsibility will be best for the child.'

For the Family Court to award sole parental responsibility to one parent, they will require evidence such as:

- police statements proving physical violence or sexual assault.
- proof of an Intervention Order, if you have one, against the other parent.
- documents showing that the other parent has mental health issues which inhibit their ability to make sound decisions on the child's behalf.
- proof that the relationship between both of the child's parents has broken down meaning the parents can't discuss and agree on decisions on behalf of the child.
- information showing that one parent is making decisions that contradict the child's best interests. (Reardon, 2021)

Parental responsibilities in England

There are similarities between the English judicial system and the judicial system in Australia. As outlined in the Children Act 1989, Section 3, parental responsibility is defined as 'all the rights, duties, powers, responsibilities and authority which by law a parent of a child has in relation to the child and his property'. Both parents share parental responsibilities, but Section 1 of the Children Act is concerned with the welfare of the child and orders may vary if there is reason to believe the welfare may be compromised.

Parental responsibilities in Scotland

Parental responsibilities in Scotland are managed through the Children (Scotland) Act 1995. Matters relating to custody (i.e. residence), access (i.e. contact), and other specific orders, operate through this act. The act refers to parental responsibilities in Section 1 and captures that 'if the child is not living with the parent, to maintain personal relations and direct contact with the child on a regular basis'. The act also mentions the rules in the context of being 'practicable and in the interests of the child'.

Parental responsibilities in the United States

In the United States the default position is for parental responsibilities to be handled by both parents. This seems to be considered a parental right rather than a parental responsibility. The underlying assumption is that parents act in the best interests of their child/children. A case worth reading concerning this assumption is *Parham v. J. R.*, 442 U. S. 584, 602. It is also seen almost as a constitutional right of parents to raise their children as they see fit, as was discussed in the case *Troxel v. Granville*, 530 U.S. 57 (2000) before the US Supreme Court. In that case, it was held that 'the interest of parents in the care, custody and control of their children is perhaps the oldest of the fundamental liberty interests recognized by this Court'. Further, it was said that 'it cannot now be doubted that the Due Process Clause of the Fourteenth Amendment protects the fundamental right of parents to make decisions concerning the care, custody, and control of their children'.

Family Law Act 1975 – Section 61DA

A poorly understood outcome of the Family Law Act 1975, which particularly impacts victims of family violence and their children, is that any travel out of the area, and passport applications, must be agreed upon by the ex-partner. Controlling individuals may choose to be disagreeable in approving travel for the ex-partner when that ex-partner has their allocated time with the children. Thus, tourism opportunities can be thwarted for victims of family violence, particularly post-separation.

The keys parts of the Family Law Act 1975 are:

(1) When making a parenting order in relation to a child, the court must apply a presumption that it is in the best interests of the child for the child's parents to have equal shared parental responsibility for the child.

Note: The presumption provided for in this subsection is a presumption that relates solely to the allocation of parental responsibility for a child as defined in section 61B. It does not provide for a presumption about the amount of time the child spends with each of the parents (this issue is dealt with in section 65DAA).

(2) The presumption does not apply if there are reasonable grounds to believe that a parent of the child (or a person who lives with a parent of the child) has engaged in:
   (a) abuse of the child or another child who, at the time, was a member of the parent's family (or that other person's family); or
   (b) family violence.
(3) When the court is making an interim order, the presumption applies unless the court considers that it would not be appropriate in the circumstances for the presumption to be applied when making that order.
(4) The presumption may be rebutted by evidence that satisfies the court that it would not be in the best interests of the child for the child's parents to have equal shared parental responsibility for the child.

(Family Law Act 1975, Section 61DA)

Family Courts 'Silence' Family Violence Victims

Women, both from Australia as well as overseas, have told me that they have felt victimised by the Family Law Court. They have felt silenced, abused and misunderstood. There is a major problem in my view with the system. Section 121 of the Family Law Act in Australia essentially limits the opportunity to disclose what happens in cases. This is mainly so that journalists who are court observers do not present details in the story that might enable a reader to identify the people involved in the case and disclose matters such as home address, occupation or religious affiliation. This is indeed most appropriate. However, it also has a silencing impact that is broader: it limits people from revealing problems. When cases are not fair, how does society know about it? There are some stories available, written under pseudonyms, or anonymous. This limits impact and credibility, however, as a result. There are similar legislative frameworks in at least some other countries.

People can report things going wrong in an organisation in the public sector and be protected under the whistleblowers act, but the courts seem to be an engineered system that is impenetrable to scrutiny. Although in Australia the Family Law Act does permit the publication of court proceedings in some instances, such as where the audience is primarily members of any profession of a publication of a technical character. It is also allowed if the 'account of proceedings or any part of proceedings' is by 'a person who is a member of a profession, in connection with the practice by that person of that profession or in the course of any form of professional training in which that person is involved' (Family Law Act Section 121 f1). Accordingly, an educational book, such as this one, allows for knowledge sharing but, of course, this is limiting and a very small number of people fit into these provisions.

An article from *The Independent* in 2021 stated: 'domestic abuse victims are routinely "silenced" by the family courts and forced into letting dangerous ex-partners see their children' (Oppenheim, 2021). Further, the article states:

> In a letter, shared exclusively with *The Independent*, over 40 experts in the family law and violence against women and girls sectors urged the government to take urgent action to protect domestic abuse victims. The experts warned the Ministry of Justice released a report around a year ago stating the family courts are putting domestic abuse victims and their children at risk of additional harm, yet the system remains wholly unchanged since the research was published. (Oppenheim, 2021)

The article also includes comments from Dr Adrienne Barnett, who was a barrister for more than 30 years where she specialised in family law, who said:

> Some women are afraid to even raise the abuse because they risk being accused of parental alienation and feel powerless to protect their children. Survivors have said that if they knew how bad the family court proceedings would be they would have stayed with their abusers. They and their children cannot wait for change. (Oppenheim, 2021)

I want to stress that statement from the above quote: *survivors have said that if they knew how bad the family court proceedings would be they would have stayed with their abusers.* I repeat it and italicise it deliberately, as this is a crucial point. And for those who have read the Overture at the beginning of this book, you will be aware that this was part of why I stayed living with family violence for so long. I knew what the system was. I knew what I would be facing. I knew what I was up against. I stayed because of the risks in the system. Family law courts are not family-friendly. I stayed in an abusive marriage until the youngest of my children was almost 12 years of age so that they had some opportunities of saying that they did not want to spend time with the other parent. Where they would be old enough to understand and make choices that I could not be blamed for. Even then, a judge tried to force contact against their will, so I had to fight yet again (Journey Three from the Overture). People may struggle to accept that the court systems are that bad. My Journey Three is an example of what can go wrong. Honestly, if I had not been through it and had been told the story, I might struggle to believe it. It seems absurd. Yet it happened to me. It happens to others.

The next section presents an example of dealing with the family court. It comes from another person, who shared her story with me and allowed me to include it in this book. She told me that once the risk of litigation was behind her, she may try to tell her story more openly so that perhaps she can help spread the word and lobby for change.

Experiences of Dealing with the Family Courts – from a European Woman

This experience of separation, and dealing with the family law courts, was shared with me by a woman from Europe. This story is presented virtually verbatim, with only a small number of minor grammatical/typing edits undertaken:

> Abuse often gets worse at the brink of or even after separation. When my ex and I were together, there was gaslighting, manipulation and physical intimidation, but I always thought that there was a line that he'd never cross. I always thought he'd never lay a hand on me. However, when I said that I wanted to get divorced, he crossed that line I thought he would never cross. He grabbed me by my jaw and pushed me.
>
> He also did other things that I could have never imagined, such as taking my car away to prevent me from going to work, and breaking into the house (when he had already moved out) to steal my personal documents such as university degrees. He also sent a false tip to the local council to prevent me from getting the single person council tax discount, simply to cause me difficulty. He used our children extensively to manipulate

me and caused me such unhappiness. He sent me frequent text messages that promised that he would never stop until he destroyed me.

Health professionals (i.e. health visitor, GP and counsellor) were all very concerned about his behaviour, not only about its impact on me as the kids' primary carer but also on the children directly. Those professionals kept encouraging me to seek support from the police and court.

The domestic abuse charity advisors were very aware of the situation, and they had warned me to be careful when raising my concerns in court. They'd explained that most of the abuse my ex committed would bear limited consequences, both in terms of child contact, as well as in terms of pursuing a non-molestation order. They agreed that it was abuse but they explained that the reality of court and the police was very far apart from legislation and from understanding the dynamics of abuse.

What really struck me was one particular incident with a board member of a local domestic abuse charity. This related to the Vice-president of such charity who happened to be my ex's parents' neighbour. Given her important roles in the community, including her role in these and other key volunteering associations and as an ex-magistrate, she wrote a letter of support for my ex to court during our proceedings. She may have well done this without any knowledge of our case. However, I would expect that given her role in the local domestic abuse charity, she would be well aware that abuse underlies many cases of divorce. She mentioned as one of the reasons to support my ex's case, that it was beautiful to hear the children playing in the garden next to her house while visiting the paternal grandparents. She was tipped about ours being a case of domestic abuse and pressurised by common contacts (including the local press) to remove her support. I was later informed that she had decided to do so due to the pressure. Nevertheless, my ex sent, once again, her letter of support to court, so I contacted her to get clarity on whether she had actually withdrawn her letter. She confirmed that she had, but asked me, in a very cold response, to never contact her again. That was the reply that I (a victim of domestic abuse as proven in court) received from the Vice-chair of one of our local domestic abuse charities, who I contacted because she had written a letter of support for my abuser in our court case.

This incident in my view captures the problems that we face addressing domestic abuse. Firstly, it shows how little understanding and awareness there is about abuse. Even those in positions specifically designed to support victims of abuse, may not necessarily understand that a person who seems on the outside to be a nice guy can be an abuser at home and that abuse is horrendously common, especially during divorce proceedings. Secondly, those personal connections become more important than standing up to abusers, which is another reason why abusers continue thriving in our society. And thirdly, these dynamics, the ones that perpetuate domestic abuse, are also present in domestic abuse charities. This is how intrinsic abuse is to our society. It is in front of our eyes and we still cannot see it.

Those with enforcing powers (i.e. police and the court) were also incredibly unsupportive. The police didn't do anything and even destroyed my video statement about the physical assault incident without letting me know. Social services took on our case on several occasions due to concerns about safety and emotional abuse, but then they'd mysteriously drop it months later without even letting us know. I find it shocking how you are encouraged to leave, and even questioned by society if you don't (i.e. how often we hear questions like 'Why didn't she leave?'!) and then when you do, you are left to hang out to dry. Even if the abuse is proven, it'll make little difference, as abusers hardly ever face consequences and there is no real protection for the victims. And these allegations of abuse may turn against you. Victims of abuse are systematically failed and betrayed.

I managed to prove in court that I had been subjected to abuse. I wasn't able to prove coercive control, but this was only because I wasn't even given the opportunity. The judge didn't even let me talk about it and said twice that if I brought it up once again, we'd move on with the hearing and wouldn't let me talk. But I did manage to prove that my ex had verbally abused me in front of the children, that he withheld the children beyond the agreed time on purpose and caused one of our children to miss a dose of antibiotics, and the incident of physical assault. I did this without legal representation, despite the lack of support by the police who had deleted my video statement without warning, and during a three-day court hearing against my ex, his barrister and solicitor. Nevertheless, as often happens in court, this got whitewashed and, in a later hearing, the judge even got to say that my ex was abusive but I was overprotective, as if this was in any way comparable or as if it balanced things out!

The courts are, in my view, highly responsible for the continuous perpetuation of domestic abuse. Even when abuse is proven, it is often not taken seriously and it makes a very limited difference to the outcome. And I am not just talking about the level of contact, which from what I've seen is hardly affected, but in terms of the level of protection that the resulting order gives to the victims. Besides, by minimising the abuse, the court adds to the trauma of the victim and encourages the continued abuse by perpetrators. I accept that the system expects me to facilitate contact between my children and their father but, if the system expects me to do so, I would hope that they'd have the obligation to ensure that it is safe for me, physically and mentally.

During my experience of the court proceedings, I shockingly learned that many judges are not even trained in domestic abuse. This is despite being such an endemic problem in our society and underlying such a high percentage of family dynamics and divorce cases. It was made law in the latest domestic abuse bill that all family court judges have to go through this training. However, the government decided to dismiss this aspect of the law due to a lack of funding. The government is not only breaking the law but also failing victims of domestic abuse, as a result.

Experiences of Dealing with the Family Courts – from a UK Woman

This story was published in *The Independent*, revealing the experiences of a woman who escaped an abusive marriage, only to face further abuse from the judicial system (Anonymous, 2021):

> Years after I escaped a marriage where I was emotionally, physically and financially abused, my ex-husband tried to control me by forcing me back to court to fight for my child.
>
> This week a report found 9 out of 10 women get no support through the family courts, that the experience risks re-traumatising them and many abusers use the justice system as a form of coercive control. I am one of those women.
>
> I have never willingly chosen to go to court. Writing about it now, I feel triggered by how horrendous each of the half-dozen occasions were.
>
> I arrived early, hid in a corner of the open-plan area, trying to shrink into furniture fixed to the floor. Waiting to be called, I'd feel the urge to empty my bowels, as sweat dripped down my back. I work in communication. But in hearings, I became almost incoherent with stress and fear, as my abuser literally held court.
>
> For years he refused to mediate, broke court orders, frequently failed to provide for our child. Sometimes his behaviour left me no choice but to make a court application for her welfare. When I took him to court, it was my fault. So too when he filed the application. He wielded the threat of court like a stick.
>
> My father accompanied me to most hearings. I could feel his pain as a parent unable to protect his own child. My new husband came once too, but it was stressful for both of them. I welcomed their support, but they couldn't protect me from my past or from facing that man in the tiny courtroom.
>
> After one hearing, my ex became aggressive. A court attendant hurried me into a waiting room, offered my dad and me an alternative exit. I do not count this as support because what I needed – a legal system that understands abusers use courts to control and retraumatise their 'victims' – would have prevented this situation in the first place. Early on, I spent the equivalent of almost a year's salary on legal fees, borrowed money from friends and family, accruing debt that took years to repay. He accused me of squandering my child's future, despite failing to provide for her financially. Not even some of the UK's best legal minds saw the hold this man had over me.
>
> He represented himself, playing the penniless, persecuted parent in court. A mate of his sat alongside him as a 'McKenzie Friend' – a person attending court in support of someone who does not have legal representation. I was intimidated because this was the same person whose home I had fled to years earlier, after my ex-husband had assaulted me. The judge took pity on my ex, awarded him more contact. He refused

to move closer to us. My daughter struggled with the long round trips, so I moved back to the area where her father had once isolated me from friends and family.

Throughout her primary school years, we were in and out of court. The visits would often coincide with something significant in my life: a new job, a new relationship. My ex tried to hit me where it hurt. Later he refused my request to move with her closer to my family. He accused me of abuse, reported me to the NSPCC, police, her school. They found nothing to support his claims. The judge politely rebuked him for wrongly accusing me of child abuse, but my ex still told me I would lose my daughter, and I was scared to speak out.

By the time she reached adolescence, it was obvious he was gaslighting her. He refused to admit he could no longer provide for her. Her school got involved because they were worried about her welfare.

Terrified of what he might do to her, I gave a statement to the police, detailing his behaviour across the years. I was asked if I wanted to press charges, warned about the challenge of proving coercive control. I chose not to, fearful of his reaction. I was given security alarms for my home, told I would merit a 'blue light' response if I called 999. I was allocated an independent domestic violence advocate because the abuse had been so serious, advised the physical violence would have been punishable, but too much time had passed since he shoved me and said nobody would believe me if I reported it.

We went back to court when my ex refused to mediate about my desired move. My independent domestic violence advisor was unable to attend. My ex shared with our daughter my court application in which I accused him of abuse against me and her. He told her I was lying, that I was mentally ill. She was devastated, unsure of who to trust.

A social worker told me just before the hearing date that he had agreed to the move. The judge applauded his gesture, gently rebuked him for breaking another court order.

Days later, my daughter learned her father was moving far away. It was something he had not told the judge. Recently she asked how her father had been allowed to lie in court. Don't they make you swear to tell the truth, she said. If only it was that easy. As long as abusers are able to use the courts to further intimidate those they seek to control, justice will only be on their terms. The legal system needs to wake up to how horrific family court can be for those who suffer coercive control, and needs to recognise the power that some people hold that ends up further hurting those most at risk.

Harm Panel Report

The story above shares experiences with the family law system in the UK. The woman is far from alone in her experiences, which are echoed throughout a report known as The Harm Report. On 25 June 2019 the UK Ministry of Justice published a final report 'Assessing Risk of Harm to

Children and Parents in Private Law Children Cases'. The 216-page Harm Panel Report was released after public consultation and was considered a 'much anticipated panel report assessing the risk of harm to children and parents in private law cases' (Kivela, 2020). The report had been commissioned due to widespread concern regarding how the family justice system was operating concerning victims of family violence and their children.

In the UK, the court has the power to order child arrangements that govern whom a child should live with, spend time with, and any other contact. This is similar to other countries, including Australia. The fundamental concern for the court is the welfare of the child, which is called 'the welfare principle', referred to as 'the child's best interests' in Australia.

Earlier in this chapter, it was explained that the default position in the Family Law Act in Australia is for equal shared parental responsibilities. Similarly, in the UK, there is a statutory presumption of parental involvement. It is presumed that the involvement of each parent in the life of their child/children will be best for the child/children. This default position exists unless there is evidence that suggests that there is a risk of harm to the child if there were involvement from a parent.

A key theme from The Harm Report came from the stories of parents, usually but not always the mother. The stories highlighted being 'trapped in an abusive relationship' and that the 'parent puts up with their partner's unacceptable behaviour in an effort to protect their child and until they cannot take it anymore' (Kivela, 2020). When the victim can no longer continue living in the abusive relationship, they take the child/children with them, and then commonly the perpetrator responds by applying to the court for a child arrangements order. The Harm Report reveals that many of the victims who left an abusive relationship experienced 're-traumatisation as a result of having to participate in Court proceedings against their former partner' (Kivela, 2020). The report also highlights:

> an overwhelming 'pro-contact culture' (based on the presumption of parental involvement) which often leads to the Court making orders for face-to-face contact between a child and the perpetrator of abuse that are unsafe and place both child and the other parent at risk of harm. As a result, many victim-survivors regret making the decision to exit the abusive relationship in the first place because they are ultimately left with a Court order that is unsafe and puts them and their child at risk of harm. (Kivela, 2020)

Kivela (2020) reported on a number of key aspects that were concerning:

- Abuse is often minimised and mischaracterised as 'mutual conflict'.
- While coercive control is a criminal offence, the Courts lack the time and resources to give each and every case the time and consideration they deserve. There is a risk that abusive behaviour is left unchecked.

- Actors within the family justice system, while well intentioned, can be part of the pro-contact culture many victim-survivors complained of. The report came across parents being advised by their lawyers not to raise issues of domestic abuse for fear that they would come across as obstructive to contact.
- The more or less total destruction of legal aid is unhelpful, but the problems identified in the report existed in the family justice system before.
- Parental alienation is commonly used as a counter-allegation by a parent who is being accused of abusive behaviour by the other. The impact of this counter-allegation is that it switches the emphasis from the perpetrator of abuse to the victim-survivor.
- The trauma victim-survivor's experience as a result of going through the Court system – including giving evidence – undermines their ability to present and articulate themselves. The victim-survivor's energy is focused on remembering details about their case and they lose focus of the basic coping mechanisms they need to practice in order to simply get through the traumatic experience of being in Court and giving evidence. As a result, the perpetrator of domestic abuse will often appear cool, calm and collected by comparison.
- Children's voices were often not being heard, despite this being a factor in the welfare checklist. This was particularly complained of in cases where a child expressed a desire not to spend time with the other parent. The pro-contact culture is partly to blame for this.

These bullet points are incredibly familiar and, while I hesitate to use the term 'universal', I think it is reasonable to say that the problems mentioned in the above list of points are felt across numerous countries. These points were presented as criticisms of the UK family law system. They are the same themes that I have heard from other countries. Family violence is a global issue and, potentially, secondary victimisation in the family legal systems is a global issue. It is certainly beyond one country.

The last bullet point is especially unfortunate. Where are the rights of the child? The film, *Custody*, mentioned previously in this chapter, captures this point. Remember that, while it is a movie, the script was written after extensive research including observations at courts. The film is not one person's story – it is many people's story. Also, those who read Journey Three in the Overture may recall that this happened to me. An order was made for my four children to have forced, court-mandated communication with their father against their wishes. If it had not happened to me, if I had not lived every revolting moment and experienced every hearing myself, I honestly think I could not believe it had happened. All the children had wanted to do was change their surnames.

Changing a Child's Surname

Among the 20 things that are reported about what makes no sense about the movie *Spider-Man: Into the Spider-Verse* is that the parents of Spider-Man have different surnames and that the child has his mother's surname rather than his father's. Apparently, a child having the mother's surname instead of the father's rates as a thing that makes no sense along with spider-hero having nothing to swing from except for the air in the sky. Listed as the tenth item that makes no sense in the movie, the statement is:

> Miles' parents have different surnames, with his father going by Jeff Davis and his mother going by Rio Morales, despite both of them being married to each other. While it's not unheard of for a married couple to keep their original last names, their children almost always end up taking the last name of their father.

> It was never really explained why Miles legally went by the name Morales rather than Davis, with most people just assuming that Marvel made that decision to make his name into an alliteration (like Peter Parker and Bruce Banner). While this isn't a huge issue, it is a bit of a head-scratcher when you think about it. (Norkey, 2018)

Indeed, it is true that a child is normally given the birth father's surname. This seems to be based on habit and tradition rather than logic. It certainly should not be ranked as a thing that makes no sense in a movie. That in itself says a lot about our thinking.

This inequality between men and women is of course hardly new, as women were effectively regarded as the property of men in traditional patriarchy (Stark, 2007). In fact, the history of women changing their surname when getting married stems from the women's ownership passing from father to husband. It is therefore ironic that in today's society where many women on the one hand fight for equality, at the same time they will unquestioningly change their surname when they get married. Despite the complexity and difficulty in changing the child's surname across many agencies, many women change their surname and then become, based on tradition, the property of the husband. The children, too, will generally hold the father's surname. It can be complicated for children who have either witnessed or experienced abuse at the hands of their father to have to 'keep' his name throughout their childhood, and the psychological impact of that process is an area worthy of examination in the future through other research.

Perhaps after reading my journey into changing a child's surname, readers may be deterred from attempting it. It is worth keeping in mind that my experiences were particularly complex because I was dealing with four children, and two had been born in one Australian state, while the other two had been born in a different Australian state. To complicate things, we were living in an Australian state that was different again to both the birth states of the children. Countries other than Australia may have much better processes. Australia has states with their own legislation and then there is federal level legislation as well. This adds to the complexity.

Research would need to be done on the particular country lived in to explore this, and that is not within the scope of this book as it would not be pragmatic to explore that across every country. I think a better place to start for this section is 'Why?' Why change a child's surname? There may not be a reason to change it. The child may have a meaningful relationship with the side of the family to which the surname belongs. I certainly don't think it is appropriate to change it just to be spiteful. In my case, it was not my project. It only arose because my daughter kept asking for it and struggling with the surname which she refused to write or use. Flashbacks about violent episodes in her life sprung to life when she saw the surname. To her the surname was synonymous with abuse. She could not find peace and acceptance with the name. Her psychologist recommended that I change it. There were really solid reasons and the project belonged to my children. I was essentially their conduit to represent them because they could not apply themselves.

There isn't a lot of material to be found on this subject. There are some law firm blogs that make it seem more simple than it is. I have read numerous times in such blogs that parental responsibilities are associated with the child's name, so the other parent only needs to be consulted if there is the default of equal shared parental responsibilities. This was my interpretation of the Family Law Act as well. However, my experience proved that this is no guarantee. Family law cases are someone against someone. The notion of an 'ex parte' application clearly sat awkwardly with the judge appointed for my case.

Literature is scant about children's names. And indeed, 'despite major advances in gender equality, patrilineal naming – children being granted their father's surname – persists as a largely unquestioned norm in those Western countries with predominantly Anglo traditions, even in families where mothers retain their birth names' (Goodall & Spark, 2020: 237). While there has been progress with gender equality in some domains, 'the patriarchal idea that a father asserts "ownership" of a child through bestowing his surname persists' (Goodall & Spark, 2020: 238).

Various studies have looked at women retaining or changing their surname when married. The percentages for women retaining their birth surname are not high – cited as around 23% in the 1990s and 18% in the 2000s (Goodall & Spark, 2020). While I am unaware of research on this specific matter, I would hypothesise that, in general, a woman marrying a man who will end up being an abusive and controlling husband would be unlikely to retain her birth surname. I would expect that a man who feels entitled to make the decisions in the family would be less likely to approve of a wife retaining her surname.

Changing a surname for a child is simple if both parents agree to the change. It is not simple if the parents disagree. In some cases, when parents cannot agree on the surname for their child, the courts are asked to decide for them. An Australian study (Goodall & Spark, 2020) examined five recent cases.

Pave & Hannegan [2018] FCCA 3488 (30 November 2018)
Schafer & Pederson [2018] FCCA 3086 (2 November 2018)
Nasland & Schuster [2019] FCCA 2 (18 January 2019)
Naparus & Frankham (No.3) [2019] FCCA 434 (28 February 2019)
Lac & Yau [2018] FCCA 3851 (21 December 2018)

In these five cases, there was a central dispute over parental responsibility for the child alongside an allegation of family violence. In these five cases there were, also, other pressing aspects relating to custody and visitation rights alongside the surname. Accordingly, the surname change was not the sole focus of the case. This is in marked contrast to the case relating to my application to the courts (outlined in Journey Three). Also, only the initial component of my case was published. The various subsequent hearings through the father appealing the orders made were not published. That aspect is reported only through my own writing in the Overture to this book.

In the Goodall and Spark (2020) article, two of the cases from their selected five cases directly referenced *Chapman & Palmer* [1978], which was one of the cases I had located and was guided by when preparing for my case. The other three cases at least touched on some of the six factors raised in the *Chapman & Palmer* [1978] case. That case is regarded as a seminal case, whereby the remarried mother sought to change the surnames of her children to that of her new husband. This differs markedly from my case, where I had requested to have the children's surnames changed to my birth surname, as well as my eldest son's middle name changed from that of his birth father to that of my birth father. This had been entirely his request. His question to me when discussing the process for the name change, was whether it was possible to request changing his middle name as well as his surname. For him, every time someone said his entire name including his middle name, he heard his birth father's name – first name and last name. He felt that this made him feel aligned and associated not only *with* him but *as* him. Hearing his father's name when hearing his own name was traumatic for him. My case, involved older children whereas the five cases listed above involve younger children.

While my case was markedly different to the case of *Chapman & Palmer* [1978], the key principles from that case listed below were helpful in developing my application. It is worth keeping in mind for any case how a potential application for a change of surname for a child may be mapped against the following six determinants:

- the welfare of the child/children is paramount in the case;
- the short- and long-term effects of any change in the child's surname must be considered;
- any embarrassment likely to be experienced by the child must be considered if the child's name is changed to be different from that of the parent with custody or care and control;
- any confusion of identity that may arise for the child if his or her name is changed or is not changed;
- the impact that any change in surname may have on the relationship between the child and the parent whose name the child bore during the marriage; and
- the impact of frequent or random changes in the child's name.

Even if the case is different in content from *Chapman & Palmer* [1978] (as it was for mine), I found these guiding principles a useful checklist to consider in shaping the narrative for my case. I found it useful to consider these guidelines and it helped me to craft the narrative and try to step back and be objective in my rationale for the request.

The notion of a child's surname is complex. In court, it may be argued that the child's surname is key to a connection with a parent. Children are typically named with their father's surname, and this does not prevent them from having a bond with their mother. However, family violence is a unique situation, and as I saw through the eyes of my daughter, the surname for her was critical and she regarded it as a pathway to personal empowerment and freedom from her abusive past. For her, the birth surname was associated with violence and trauma and she wanted to disconnect those memories.

In two of the cases mentioned above, *Pave & Hannegan* [2018] and *Schafer & Pederson* [2018], both involve a case where the father applies to change the child's surname from the mother's to a hyphenated name that includes his surname. This request was unsuccessful in both cases. In *Pave & Hannegan* [2018] the child was aged 4 years and the father's request was put forward by the mother as being driven by controlling behaviour on the father's part. There did not appear to be any benefit to the child for the name change. In *Schafer & Pederson* [2018], there were two children, who were aged 9 and 10. In this case, the judge stated that 'there is a significant risk that the mother would feel traumatised because it would be a constant reminder of her negative memories of her past relationship with the father'. These two cases highlight a key point that is extremely important in family violence situations: a name can feel like a connection. A connection to a person. If that person was abusive and controlling, then being connected to them could be highly traumatic.

Certainly, as I saw through my daughter, she could not write her birth surname. Traumatic episodes from her past flooded her mind. Dreams plagued her. When she created social media profiles she used her middle name as her surname. On her school test papers, she wrote only her first name. The school kindly enabled her to change her surname informally so that she was known as 'Chantelle Zentveld' on the roll. Of course, as she progressed to higher levels, this became problematic because the official Australian education records are linked to the birth certificate. This is why the older the children became, the more important their name change was. They wanted to disconnect a part of their life that was unhappy and traumatic and be able to establish records for themselves that reflected the person they wanted to be known as and to be freed from the past. Arguing that they can change their own surname when they turn 18 misunderstands the importance of the years (or even one year) that they must endure with the pain of flashbacks and memories. It also misunderstands the importance of entering the next phase of their life after school: they don't want the confusion of records that do not match their name. They want medical records, school records and their driver's licence to reflect the name they want. They want their casual employment records to be in the name they want. Why make things harder for these children if they feel that the change in surname will help free them from their abusive past? Does an abusive and controlling father who has harmed his children deserve to have his surname attached to the child he abused? This should be at the forefront of decision-making.

The fathers' behaviour is considered a reason to not give the children that father's surname. As discussed, naming children after the father's surname is very normal. What the selected cases revealed in the study by Goodall and Spark is that:

> the norm of having the father's name remains largely unchallenged except where there is an exceptional reason to take a different approach to children's surnames. In this way, the supposedly neutral and objective court employs much the same covertly patriarchal logic as do the majority of parents. (Goodall & Spark, 2020: 251–252)

It appears that the law is gendered and that the child having a father's surname was the default preference even in the judicial system. In the cases analysed by Goodall and Spark (2020), it was determined that while the norm was to adopt the father's surname,

> some judges broke with this tradition if the father was perceived as having contravened expectations of 'good fatherhood.' Violence, being absent and/or not paying child support were variously viewed as bad enough to warrant the father's name not being passed on to his children. But this exception only proves the rule, as it suggests breaking with tradition can only be done in exceptional circumstances. By demonstrating

that a father can lose his 'right' to name his child, the normalcy of that 'right' is reinforced. (Goodall & Spark, 2020: 252)

It is important to consider how the child may feel about their surname if they have endured family violence. Sadly, even an older dependent child is unable to contribute in court to the discussions about changing their name. As mentioned earlier in this book, a 17-year-old can be the applicant in a Fair Work Commission case to terminate the enterprise agreement covering potentially thousands of employees who work for an international company, yet a 17-year-old cannot go to the Family Law Court to discuss which parent they wish to spend time with, or to give their opinion on changing their name. The affidavits from my four children (the eldest being 17 at that time) requesting their names be changed and explaining why they wanted that, were struck out at the request of the other side during the appeals component. While the outcome itself was unchanged, it was still unreasonable that their voices on a matter that directly impacted them above anyone else, were disallowed. This is from a court that is founded on acting in the child's best interests.

The surname of a child who has been exposed to family violence could be important to that child and be associated with trauma, and accordingly it could re-traumatise them. The risks to children who witness or are present when family violence occurs are not especially well understood. However, there is growing evidence to suggest that even just being present in the home when family violence occurs, without hearing or seeing anything, impacts children. This is in part because family violence impacts the victim, who in turn is unable to operate as effectively as a result. Fear is very damaging, and inhibits learning, thinking and problem-solving (Edmondson, 2019).

Our understanding of the impacts of family violence on children is improving, and there is some development at court levels. For example, a recent newspaper court report highlighted the following words from a magistrate: 'Courts must send a strong message of denunciation of family violence, particularly when children are involved' (*The Courier*, 2022). The man, who breached an Intervention Order, allegedly to throw metal objects around outside as well as smash a house window, undertook these acts while the children were present. The magistrate, Ron Saines, stated: 'no sentence other than imprisonment was appropriate' (*The Courier*, 2022). However, as has been discussed numerous times in this book, there is a long way to go to improve our understanding and the decisions made in the family legal system.

Conclusion

This chapter is the second and final chapter to discuss the component of the tourism destination with respect to family violence. It has focused on explaining how the position of equal shared parental responsibilities impacts the parents and children after separation. While the matters relating to the connection between the separated parents because of the legal framework are broad and not peculiar to tourism, these matters have distinct impacts on the tourism system. As explained in this chapter, consent may not be provided to take a child on a holiday, or on an international holiday that may require a longer time than usual. Even the process of applying for a passport for a child requires the consent of both parents. This is where the default position of equal shared parental responsibilities can have impacts not considered from the outset. The next chapter focuses on the tourism system element of the transit route.

10 Journeys on Transit Routes with Family Violence

'Abuse and respect are diametric opposites: you do not respect someone whom you abuse, and you do not abuse someone whom you respect.'

– Lundy Bancroft, *Why Does He Do That? Inside the Minds of Angry and Controlling Men*

Introduction

This chapter concentrates on the tourism system element 'transit route' in the Whole Tourism System Model (Figure 10.1). It examines problematic behaviour (bullying, control, abuse, family violence) along the pathway between the tourist generating region (where the tourist resides) and the tourist destination (both from and to). The transit route represents the path that takes the tourist from their generating region to their destination, and the return journey. The transit route may be different or by a different mode of transport on the departing and returning trips.

----- = tourism industries

Figure 10.1 Whole Tourism System Model
Source: adapted from Leiper (2004).

It is important to mention that cruise ships follow a transit route but represent more than simply a pathway between the generating region and a destination. Cruise ships are a journey but also an entire package of a holiday within, and as such are considered outside the scope for the discussion of purely a journey. Cruise ships fit best within 'industries', due to the comprehensive aspect of them. This chapter discusses how problematic behaviour along the journey for the tourist can arise. The impact on those working in these areas is also discussed.

Cancelled Flights and Missing Baggage

In the lead-up to the 2022 Easter long weekend in Australia, a media article outlined that 'Sydney and Melbourne airports were heaving with travellers even before the first flights of the morning, as the Easter long weekend begins' (9 News, 2022). If we imagine ourselves among this chaos, even assuming we are not travelling with a perpetrator of violence, such a situation sounds tense. This is the beginning of a holiday. It is crowded. It is busy. The article continues, outlining that 'tens of thousands of people are expected to take flight today, with one million Australians forecast to get on a plane at some point during the holidays' (9 News, 2022). The same article reported three cancelled Qantas flights in Melbourne in the morning due to shortages of crew, which resulted in more passengers in that terminal from the build-up. Aside from the crowd, there was a shortage of baggage handlers and therefore not only departing travellers were being delayed but also arriving travellers. A flight from Melbourne to Brisbane departed the previous day with no passenger luggage on that flight. Apart from a general inconvenience for travellers, some specific issues reported included not having medication, which was in the suitcase, and not having costumes for a show (9 News, 2022). The star of the Cabaret de Paris, Rhonda Burchmore, was left without any of her clothes, or her show costumes, when she flew from Melbourne to Brisbane for the opening night at the Queensland Performing Arts Centre (Spence & Antrobus, 2022).

Travelling by Airplane with Young Children

Flying can be stressful. Flying with young children can often add additional forms of stress. Sometimes young children are unsettled, will not sleep, are noisy, are bored, and demand attention, which adds to the emotional tax for the parents/guardians. One experience I read was as follows:

> Five years ago my wife and I took our 3 kids (ages 7, 4 and 1 at the time) to visit my sister who lives in Sydney, Australia, for Christmas. Since they didn't sleep much, we spent 16 hours on the plane keeping

them entertained — a lot of walking the aisles, watching movies and playing games. The worst part was our 1-year-old, who was inconsolable at times. Things we let her do included eating patties of butter by themselves and kicking the chair in front of her because we were too exhausted to stop her. It was the plane ride from hell, and I never felt like more of a failure as parent in my life! —Kyle. (Brooks, 2013)

A Recent Flight Experience for My Mother

In February 2022 my mother travelled from Byron Bay, Australia, to Hobart in Tasmania, Australia. After her trip, she emailed me to say that she had a very nice time in Hobart but 'both the flights were just awful'. She explained:

Firstly the flight out from Ballina was cancelled due to water on the tarmac ... they did not tell me. I found out because I couldn't check in. I then was on the phone for 2 hours before hanging up. I had to get a flight out so finally I booked from Coolangatta.

Coming back my flight out was at 12pm from Hobart to Sydney then later on to Ballina. I got to the airport around 10am. Later on there was a notice the flight was delayed. Then at 1pm there was a notice it was cancelled and passengers were told to pick up their bags from the carousel. My bag was missing. After 2 hours found. I had to book another flight but none available for the Monday, wait till the next day flight from Hobart ... Sydney then Ballina. Flight at 6am. Stuck in the Travelodge in the sticks ... No dining room only Subway from a BP station down the track or a fish and chip place 5 k's away. I booked a call for 4am.

Luckily the manager of the motel took pity on me and drove me to the fish and chip place. I couldn't possibly eat at Subway. Arrived at the airport to find my 6am flight cancelled. So I got a seat in the exit row of a flight to Melbourne, then Sydney then Ballina arriving home on Tues at around 3pm. I am lucky I do not look at my phone otherwise I would have discovered my flight at 6am was cancelled, and I would have had to stay another day, but because I did not know I rocked up at the airport and got a seat to Melbourne. So you can imagine I was not feeling all that great after spending (wasting) two days in airports.

The above story is presented verbatim from the contents of the email from my mother. It was not school holiday time. It was not a national holiday such as Easter. It was an off-peak time when travellers might reasonably expect the best chances of avoiding problems. However, as mentioned previously, sometimes things go wrong and it has nothing to do with anything within our control. In my mother's words: 'I was not feeling all that great'. The experience was taxing for her and she felt exhausted for some days later. As mentioned previously, imagine the type of scenarios that do go wrong when travelling, but then add in a person who is abusive and controlling as the travel companion. It is likely to get a whole lot worse. They may feel entitled to blame someone and take it out on someone.

When the Transit Route is Driving

Of course, not all holidays involve a transit route of flying. Many holidays are by driving, or even if they are by plane, a hire car may be arranged to allow for travel around the destination. In one sense, driving can provide more flexibility and avoid some of the issues raised previously in this chapter about flights. However, driving also comes with similar unexpected issues. Here is one story I read:

> One of my most frustrating travel experiences came on a Thanksgiving trip from Santa Barbara to Victorville, California. Traffic was heavy, but moving, until we were just about three miles from Victorville. Then it stopped — for hours. We were trapped in a line of cars that barely moved. There were no roads to either side, nothing but desert. We could have turned around but the only other route would have involved circling back and a 90-mile drive. Since we were only a couple of miles from our destination, we figured this mess was bound to clear up at some point. It finally did — three and a half hours later. Turns out it was a four-way stop that was backing everything up. Because, in spite of the massive housing boom Victorville was experiencing, the city fathers hadn't seen fit to install a traffic light. – Barry. (Brooks, 2013)

Conclusion

The previous sections and stories represent only a small number of stories and problems. Most people would gloss over these stories. The airport stories are not unique. Similar stories happen regularly. Airlines on strike. Crew shortages. Poor weather creating delays or causing flights to be cancelled. If there is a thunderstorm or other severe weather on any flight path, planes may be delayed to avoid that weather, or the flight path might be diverted. If there are weather issues at a connecting airport, the delays at those points may flow on to other airports. Snow. Floods. Storms. Engine trouble with the airplane, so that people sit in the plane, despite having boarded, and wait. And wait. And wait. Busy holiday periods such as Christmas result in more flights, more people, more congestion, more delays. People need to arrive earlier and sit around a crowded airport for hours.

As this book has explained, tourism is an open system and has five elements. It has a generating region (where the tourist starts their journey and usually resides), it has a destination (where they are going to), it has industries that the tourism engages with on their trip, it has at least one tourist, and it has a transit route. This is how we dissect and understand tourism. There are five elements. But they are also connected, because if the journey is a bad experience, it impacts the overall impression of that holiday.

So, these transit issues – the lost baggage, the delayed or cancelled flight, all impact our overall holiday experience. This is a headache for most of us. Now let us imagine, or try to, that instead of us as an individual travelling and enduring this inconvenience, we are travelling with a perpetrator of family violence. That person expects things to go well for them. That person feels entitled. They are not happy. They can't take it out on the pilot or the baggage handler. What do you think might happen? We know that sometimes when we travel, things go wrong. As much as we can be well-prepared and organised, events can occur that cannot be predicted or controlled. Travelling can be stressful. But, when travelling with an abusive person, every little thing that goes wrong blows up, and the person they take it out on isn't responsible. The upcoming chapter discusses the next element in the whole tourism system model – the tourism generating region. This is the departing point for the trip as well as the return point for the trip. It is important to keep this element in mind, since things that go badly on the holiday come back home for the victim. So, if the trip was bad, upon return home can be worse than it was when one left.

11 The Tourism Generating Region: Living with Abuse

'Many neglected and abused children grow up to be adults who are afraid to take risks of striking out on their own. Many will remain dependent on their abusive parents and unable to separate from them. Others leave their abusive parents only to attach themselves to a partner who is controlling.'

– Beverly Engel, *The Nice Girl Syndrome: Stop Being Manipulated and Abused and Start Standing Up for Yourself*

Introduction

This chapter focuses on the tourism system element 'generating region' (depicted in Figure 11.1). In doing so, it focuses on problematic behaviour within the home; in particular, it is concerned with controlling and abusive behaviour. It discusses the tourism generating region, i.e. 'home', where home represents the start of the holiday journey as well as the return from the holiday. While there are many things that could

= tourism industries

Figure 11.1 Whole Tourism System Model
Source: adapted from Leiper (2004).

be discussed with respect to living with abuse, much of that is captured in other chapters. Accordingly, this chapter focuses on an important component related to living with abuse that has not been discussed in other chapters. The chapter discusses gaslighting, kids who side with the abuser, deliberate self-harm, and the impacts on children that parents may choose to deny.

These aspects of living with abuse are relevant to the tourism system in several ways. Firstly, as mentioned in the previous chapter, things can go wrong when travelling home from the holiday. Accordingly, the perpetrator may be additionally irritated and so returning home to the generating region may be returning home to a heightened place of risk and fear. Secondly, some victims work in industries that serve tourists. Those victims live with abuse and if workplaces are wanting to develop improved processes for supporting their workers and improving psychological safety in the workplace, it requires an understanding of what living with abuse can be like. Statistically, there will be plenty of people working in industries that serve tourists that are impacted. The toll of living with abuse, coupled with the emotional labour of service, can be a tipping point and lead to burnout. With the current focus on improving work–life balance, quality of life, psychological safety in the workplace and reducing burnout, we need to look at what stress factors may be impacting workers within and outside the work environment. Living with abuse is part of that.

Gaslighting

Gaslighting is a term that is used to describe a type of behaviour commonly seen in family violence but which can also occur in other settings. Gaslighting is 'a type of psychological abuse aimed at making victims seem or feel "crazy", creating a "surreal" interpersonal environment' (Sweet, 2019: 851). The technique can undermine how a person perceives reality, and they may start to doubt their memories and perceptions. Gaslighting 'should be understood as rooted in social inequalities, including gender, and executed in power-laden intimate relationships' (Sweet, 2019: 851).

The term comes from a 1944 film called *Gaslight*, which was based on a 1938 play called *Gas Light*. In the film, the house in which the main characters Paula and her new husband Gregory live has lights that are fuelled by gas. Gregory wants to make his wife Paula think she is insane, because if she is committed to a mental facility, he will then be able to search for the valuable jewels hidden in the house that belonged to Paula's late aunt. One of the tactics in convincing Paula she is losing her mind is through manipulating the gas lights in their home causing them to flicker and dim while he is in the attic searching for the jewels.

Gaslighting is something that Mr Ex did. I touched on this in Journey Three in the Overture, with respect to the court-mandated phone call. I listed the extraordinary number of times he kept saying

'You are remembering something that didn't happen' or similar statements. A consistent approach with this can make someone doubt their memories and wonder if indeed they are remembering something that didn't happen. Gaslighting can occur during family violence as well as in court when a victim is trying to escape. These are tactics that may arise when a victim is applying for a protective order or is seeking custody of the children. In some cases, where a person is seeking a protective order against the husband, it backfires due to his attempts to gaslight her. In the example I wrote about in Journey Three, there were three key things that prevented Mr Ex from being successful with his gaslighting efforts. Firstly, there are four children, not one. It is much harder to convince all four that they have false memories. Secondly, the children were not drawing on memories as very young children. As older children (the eldest was almost an adult at that time), their thinking is more established and their confidence in themselves is greater than in young children. Thirdly, it was not just their memories. There were so many records of what happened: police reports, school counselling reports, psychologist reports and medical reports. The notion of the children remembering something that didn't happen was pure fantasy and can be considered to be an example of 'magical thinking'.

As gaslighting can have an impact on decisions, judgements and mental health, it is important to be aware of the traits (Gordon, 2022):

- Lying to you – people who engage in gaslighting tend to exhibit narcissistic traits and be 'habitual and pathological liars'. They often say 'You're making things up' and do not change their story or back down even if presented with evidence.
- Discrediting you – they may pretend to be concerned about your mental health as they tell people false stories to make others think you are unstable.
- Distracting you – they change the subject to take away your thinking processes if you call them out on a lie.
- Minimising your thoughts and feelings – telling you to calm down or that you are overreacting.
- Shifting blame – things are twisted so that you are to blame.
- Denying wrongdoing – avoids taking responsibility for their poor behaviour.
- Using compassionate words as weapons – the person might say how much they love you so they would never want to hurt you, to escape responsibility.
- Rewriting history – stories from the past are retold in a way that is favourable to the person who is gaslighting.

This behaviour is not uncommon in family violence. I have often wondered what stories Mr Ex says about me. One woman I spoke to as part of the ethics-approved research project about the relationship between travel and family violence told me that, when she left her husband, he told mutual friends of theirs that she was insane and that she 'was a lesbian drug addict, which is why she left' and that she 'couldn't cope with being a mother'.

This is what people could be living with. Businesses that serve tourists require a high-service mentality. If we don't know what living with abuse might be like it makes it difficult to know what systems to develop to support our employees. We assume they go home and relax at the end of the day and start the day fresh. If we want the tourism system to operate well, we need to understand the underbelly and try to have more support systems and to understand better the signs of abuse.

Children Who Side with the Abuser

In the next chapter, I describe how children might prefer to stay with the non-abusive parent and may spend the bulk of their time there once they are old enough to have input into time with the other parent. However, this does not always happen. In fact, in some cases, the children side with the abusive parent. There are some reasons why this may happen. Abuse creates power for the abuser and therefore siding with the abuser is a link to power (Bancroft, 2022a). If you are not a direct target, but the other parent is, the child might feel safer and protected by being on the side of the abuser (Bancroft, 2022a).

I have heard of this happening in a few cases but, in those cases I have heard of, the child was young at the time of separation. Possibly, there could be an increased risk of children siding with an abuser if separation occurs when they are younger. However, this is just a question I raise as a possibility. It seems plausible that an abuser may have more influence over younger children, and may want to have the children as part of his armoury against the victim.

Deliberate Self-Harm

Deliberate self-harm is a little-understood matter that can arise in children who are exposed to family violence. It can be defined as 'the deliberate, direct destruction or alteration of body tissue, without conscious suicidal intent but resulting in injury severe enough for tissue damage to occur' (Gratz, 2003: 192). Self-harm can take various forms, including:

- Cutting one's own body.
- Overdosing on tablets or other medication.
- Punching one's own body.

- Pulling out hair or eyelashes.
- Burning a part of one's own body.
- Inhaling or sniffing a substance that is harmful.
- Scratching, picking or tearing at the skin on one's own body to the extent that it creates sores and scarring.

The most common form of self-harm is skin cutting (Florida State University, n.d.). Forearm/wrist cutting is a common form of deliberate self-harm among women under emotional stress, which is usually predominately on the left arm since most of the population is right-handed (Leung & Barankin, 2017).

Children who have had exposure to family violence may experience various behavioural traits or have various disturbances or symptoms. One of the consequences of exposure to family violence in children is deliberate self-harm (NSW Government Communities & Justice, 2019). The impact of family violence on children is associated with an increased rate of suicide and deliberate self-harm (Australian Human Rights Commission, 2017).

Deliberate self-harm can be a way for children who have been exposed to family violence to feel a different type of pain. They might cut themselves to feel the pain from the cut so that temporarily they do not feel the pain inside their mind. It may be a coping mechanism for children who are experiencing flashbacks from traumatic violent episodes in their lives. Deliberate self-harm may not be visible. Cutting might be done on the arm but the person always wears long sleeves even if the weather is warm. Other common places for cutting include the thighs and stomach. It can be difficult to notice, but one sign might be the child wears jumpers on hot days, even when doing sport, and may try to find excuses to avoid doing things – e.g. swimming – where the cuts could be visible.

Impacts on Children: Parent Denial

The previous section discussed an example of the impacts on children from family violence that might be hidden. There are other ways in which children might exhibit behaviour that is not rational that can be linked to family violence. Those behaviours might be an expression of their inner pain and might be evident through more discrete behaviours. Sometimes, if later in life a grown child tries to tell their story, the adult might deny it. The example I use to describe this is the book, *Into the Wild* (Krakauer, 1996). Some readers may have watched the 2007 film, based on the book, directed by Sean Penn.

Into the Wild is an expanded version of a 9,000-word article written by the author of the book, Jon Krakauer. It was an international bestseller and has been published in 30 languages. It is based on a true story after Christopher McCandless's body was found on 6 September 1992 in an abandoned rusted bus on the Stampede Trail in Alaska. When the body was found, it was considered mysterious that a young, intelligent, educated 24-year-old man would go on such a mission of self-discovery. The last time Chris had seen his family was 12 May 1990. It is a fascinating story, which raises more questions than it answers. The key part missing from the story in terms of 'Why?' is covered many years later when Chris McCandless's sister, Carine, wrote *The Wild Truth* (McCandless, 2014). As was written by Jon Krakauer in the foreword to the book:

> A lot of people came away from reading *Into the Wild* without grasping why Chris did what he did. Lacking explicit facts, they concluded that he was merely self-absorbed, unforgivably cruel to his parents, mentally ill, suicidal, and/or witless.

> These mistaken assumptions troubled Carine. Two decades after her brother's death, she decided it was time to tell Chris's entire story, plainly and directly, without concealing any of the heartbreaking particulars. She belatedly recognised that even the most toxic secrets could possibly be robbed of their power to hurt by dragging them out of the shadows and exposing them to the light of day. (McCandless, 2014: xiii)

In the book *The Wild Truth*, the reader is introduced to the father, Walt, a violent and aggressive man who beat his wife and children. The father would choke his wife and yell out to the children to watch: 'Kids! Get in here now! Look what your mother is making me do' (McCandless, 2014: 11).

> We were forced to witness, and then wait. We waited in fear of what would happen – not just to ourselves – if we left before being given permission. We learned early on that if you haven't managed to run before the bear smells you, the best course is to just stay really still. Eventually Dad would release Mom, without apology, and she would collapse into the doorway with us. (McCandless, 2014: 11)

Carine also writes of being 'instructed to choose the weapon for our punishment ... hand in hand, we looked through his assortment of belts, trying to remember which ones hurt the least, which buckles lacked sharp edges' (McCandless, 2014: 11–12). The book also highlights how a toxic home life filled with abuse and cruelty can be unknown on the outside, where the perpetrator is regarded with respect by society and presents an image to the public that contrasts steeply with the person indoors. This Dr Jekyll and Mr Hyde contrast was introduced earlier in this book in the 'snakes and ladders' conceptual framework and is discussed further in Chapter 14.

Conclusion

This chapter has discussed the tourism generating region in relation to living with abuse. While various aspects of living with abuse have been discussed in other chapters, this chapter has focused specifically on a number of important aspects not covered elsewhere in the book. To begin with, gaslighting was discussed, which is a common occurrence in family violence. Deliberate self-harm was then discussed, which is not well known but can be a result of children exposed to family violence. In some cases self-harm can result in suicide. Parent denial of the impact of family violence on children is then discussed through the case of Chris McCandless. These aspects impact the tourism system in various ways. For those living with abuse, these circumstances come along on the holiday, too. They don't stay behind. This 'snake pit' existence comes for the journey. Should things go wrong on the holiday (e.g. the flights were delayed, the service was lousy, the accommodation was bad, it was too noisy to sleep, or the baggage got lost), then this cocktail of irritation enters the tourist generating region (i.e. the home) upon the return.

Living with abuse also helps us to understand what complexities victims may face and how we might best create systems to allow employees to reach out for support. Many businesses that are part of the tourism system and serve tourists operate in a fast-paced, high-service environment. Add to that the complexity of living with abuse and not ever being able to rest and relax, and we as a society have a huge problem that we need to accept and try to take steps to improve. The next chapter discusses the final element in the whole tourism system model: the tourist.

12 The Tourist

'Don't light yourself on fire trying to brighten someone else's existence.'

— Unknown

Introduction

This chapter focuses on the final tourism system element – the tourist. The reader is reminded of the Whole Tourism System Model that frames the discussions in these chapters (Figure 12.1). The tourist is one of the five tourism elements, and they can experience the impacts of family violence in their generating region (i.e. where they live), the destination they travel to, and along the transit route from their generating region and on the return journey. They can also experience impacts through the industries that provide them with services and products.

The Separated Person as a Tourist

This book has covered various relevant components of how being a victim of family violence can impact the tourism system. As argued earlier in this book, a victim of family violence may not be able to obtain the type of benefits assumed for tourists. When safety is paramount,

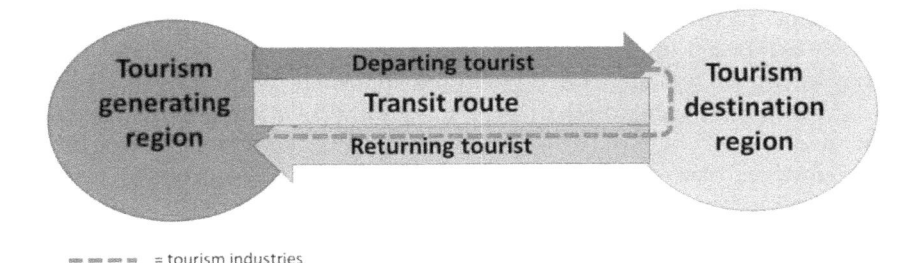

= tourism industries

Figure 12.1 Whole Tourism System Model
Source: adapted from Leiper (2004).

it may leave little room to relax and to enjoy the attributes at that destination. These matters have been discussed. This chapter will focus on a different lens of 'tourist': that is, what opportunities are there to be a tourist if the person has managed to separate from a perpetrator of family violence? Can they finally rest and relax?

This book has previously captured the difficulties of gaining permission to go on holiday. We looked at a case study where a woman was denied permission to go on an international holiday with her children to visit the maternal grandparents because she requested more than seven days for the holiday and because the abusive ex-husband had only been allocated seven days for his holidays with the children. The courts wanted to be 'fair' to the father.

I now want to turn the reader's attention to another factor that might stymie the prospects for a victim of family violence to be a tourist, even if they have managed the great escape (discussed in Chapter 14).

I think by now we appreciate that where there has been family violence, the victim (usually the mother) is focused on protecting her children. Her energies will go on trying to provide them with as much care as possible to ensure their safety. As children grow older and have more rights to state which parent they want to spend time with, it might be that the child/children spends an increasing amount of time with the mother if the father is abusive and controlling. Accordingly, this means that, as children grow older, and grow more expensive, the mother increasingly carries the load. She carries the load disproportionately because the other parent is not considered safe.

Costs of raising children are high. In a report from 2018 citing 2016 costs, it was outlined that the costs of raising two children (a 6-year-old girl and a 10-year-old boy) were AU$340.14 each week (or around AU$17,700 a year) (Saunders & Bedford, 2018). Of course, children become more expensive to raise as they grow older. For example, teenage boys will consume large amounts of food, especially those who are involved in sports. The cost of clothing, footwear and school fees also tends to increase for older children. Older children also cost more with recreation and personal care products and services.

If the majority of the meals are provided at the mother's house, then she is carrying a higher financial load. Other costs, such as school fees, may have been pre-agreed in a parenting agreement so they are shared in a structured way regardless of who has the child for the greater amount of time.

However, once the child turns 18, they are (at least in Australia) to be viewed as independent adults. Any parenting agreement with the sharing of costs is irrelevant, and if there is any child support being paid, it will stop.

The problem is that these days, children are less likely to leave home and be independent adults when they are 18. There is a sustained trend of children staying with a parent/parents longer

(Wilkins & Vera-Toscano, 2019). A recent survey revealed that 'a record number of Americans are back living with their parents', with almost one-third of Americans in the 25 to 29 age group living with a parent/parents (Bove, 2022).

Similarly, young adults returning to their parent's home to live until they are well into their 20s or even 30s is 'a permanent feature of UK society' (Butler, 2020). With high costs of living coupled with low wages, almost two-thirds of single adults without children have either moved back to live with a parent or never left to begin with (Butler, 2020).

In Australia, data collected by the Australian Institute of Family Studies (AIFS) revealed that, in 2016, more than 43% of children aged between 20 and 24 lived with a parent, which was up from 36% in 1981 (ABC News, 2019). Also in 2016, 17% of children aged 25–29 lived with a parent, while 7% of 30–34-year-olds lived with a parent.

In other words, victims who have managed to separate from a perpetrator of family violence might face financial constraints in ways not usually considered. It is not uncommon to think of victims being financially constrained as they may not have been allowed to work, or may have only engaged in casual or part-time employment. They may have fewer prospects. However, I am suggesting that there is another financial trend impacting victims of family violence who separate from their abusive partners: the fact that they protect their children and are the 'safety' house means that they carry the greater load of daily costs of raising a child. Factor in the ongoing time in which children live at home, and the financial drain continues.

Pragmatically, the cost of family violence may continue for a significant number of years. For those victims who raise their children on their own or for the majority of the time, and that time extends into adulthood, they might struggle financially to map out their own future. They may be unable to have savings, buy a house, or go on a holiday. Therefore, the notion of a tourist might be foreign to many victims of family violence. It might be foreign to them while living with family violence because they cannot relax and family violence might escalate when on holiday. Then, if they do manage to escape, they may be so financially drained for so long that they cannot afford to be a tourist anyway. Therefore, family violence impacts the tourism system not only during the stage of living with the perpetrator but also, potentially, after separation as well.

Conclusion

This chapter has outlined the hidden aspect of being a tourist from the perspective of victims of family violence. Those who are living in an abusive and controlling relationship may be unable to obtain the rest and relaxation benefits assumed to be associated with being a tourist. Even after separation, the notion of being a tourist may be problematic due to financial aspects, which may load down the person well after separation. This chapter has covered the final tourism element: the tourist. The next chapter captures a discussion on visiting friends and relatives, which essentially revisits two of the elements of the Whole Tourism System: the generating region as well as the destination.

13 Family Violence and Visiting Friends and Relatives Travel

'The boys had always been her reason to stay, but now
for the first time, they were her reason to leave.'

– Liane Moriarty, *Big Little Lies*

Introduction

This chapter sits across the tourism system elements of destination and generating region (Figure 13.1), depending on whether the tourist plays the role of host in their destination or travels to the destination to visit friends and/or family. This chapter outlines the role that friends and relatives can have in supporting victims of family violence and how Visiting Friends and Relatives (VFR) travel can be an important recovery and support mechanism.

What is VFR Travel?

VFR travel is a substantial form of travel around the world. While VFR travel comprises a significant percentage of visitor movement, it is often not given a lot of attention in Destination Marketing Organisation (DMO)

= tourism industries

Figure 13.1 Whole Tourism System Model
Source: adapted from Leiper (2004).

marketing campaigns and, relative to other forms of tourism, has not been given a great deal of research attention either. Compared to many areas of tourism, the field has attracted a smaller group of researchers, and many of the researchers have not published many VFR publications (Zentveld *et al.*, 2022). Fewer publications by VFR researchers tends to mean that the deeper ongoing research is more limited. When researchers concentrate on a particular field, they often drill deeper and deeper into the layers, which creates greater expertise in that field. However, the number of VFR researchers who have undertaken research to deepen and extend knowledge in the field is relatively small.

Defining VFR Travel

This chapter will explain in what ways VFR travel can connect with family violence. To do that, it is helpful to define VFR travel so that the narrative has context. VFR travel has been defined as 'a form of travel involving a visit whereby either (or both) the purpose of the trip or the type of accommodation involves visiting friends and/or relatives' (Backer, 2007: 369). The definition was later developed into a VFR definitional model to describe it visually (Backer, 2012). The definitional model highlights that there are three different types of VFRs (Figure 13.2). Firstly, there are 'Pure VFRs (PVFRs)', who stay with friends/relatives and who also state that VFR is the main purpose of their visit. The second type is the 'Commercial VFR (CVFR)', who state that VFR is the main purpose of their visit but who choose to stay in commercial accommodation. The third type stays with friends/relatives but does not state that VFR is the main purpose of their visit. They can be viewed potentially as 'Exploiting VFRs (EVFRs)'.

By definition, the understanding of VFR is important in terms of understanding the magnitude and behaviours of VFR travellers. Official data tend to categorise travellers based on the type of accommodation

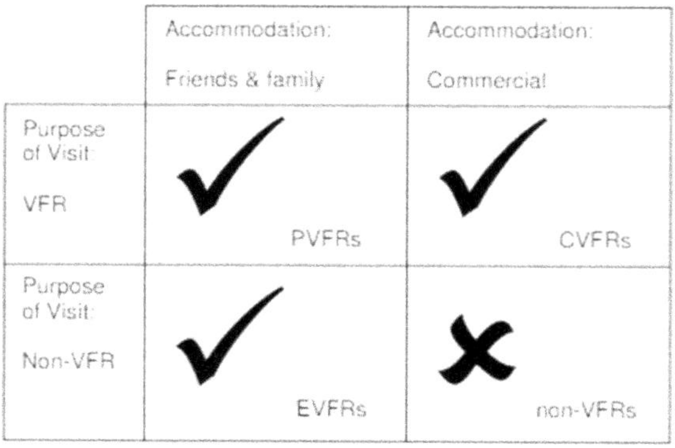

Figure 13.2 VFR definitional model
Source: Backer (2012).

they stay in and the main purpose of visit for the trip. The main purpose of visit may vary for different travellers, with the purpose of the visit being things such as business, medical, leisure, education or VFR. Measuring VFR based on the purpose of visit that the traveller stated could greatly underestimate the proportion of travellers who are in fact VFR travellers. This underestimation can be readily understood because some travellers are VFRs but genuinely identify themselves as being on a leisure holiday (Jackson, 1990). The depiction of the three VFR types, as shown in the VFR definitional model (Figure 13.2), shows that if VFR is measured based only on the type of accommodation or the purpose of visit, one type of VFR will be omitted from the calculation.

The Relationship between VFR Travel and Family Violence

Friends and family can play an important role for victims of family violence. This role can be while victims are living with family violence, when they are trying to escape, or if the victim has separated. The role can be as a VFR traveller to the victim and their family, or as a host to the victim and their family. I will explain these aspects in more detail but will first share some words from others on the connection between friends/family and family violence. These words came from telephone interviews I did with women who had separated from a family violence situation, to explore the role that VFR travel had. This was a specific research project I set out to undertake, which received ethical approval, and has not been published previously. I have not set these out in codings but, rather, present a series of comments from victims (all names are pseudonyms) without grouping them or without assessing unique codes. Only the thoughts and the words matter – not who said them. I want to shine a light on the feelings expressed.

> Victim: 'My father told me that being with Tom had anchored me. Therefore I felt that separating from Tom may not be supported by my parents, and felt a pressure to stay.'

> Victim: 'There was pressure from my friends and family to stay. There was social pressure to stay.'

> Victim: 'Once my friends and family knew my husband was violent, then they supported me leaving.'

> Victim: 'My friends thought he was odd. They thought he was frightening. He made it very difficult for me to see my friends.'

> Victim: 'My friends were scared to ring the home phone in case Albert answered the phone.'

> Victim: 'Mark encouraged me to work night shift, which isolated me from socialising.'

> Victim: 'Having a child made things worse and things blew up after that point. The staff at the hospital could see things.'

Victim: 'My father died when I was 38 weeks pregnant. Because of my stage of pregnancy, I was not allowed to fly. I couldn't drive because I had never got my driver's license. I was always dependent on Lucas. Lucas refused to drive me to my father's funeral.'

Victim: 'friendships made it clearer to see things; to understand what was happening to me.'

Victim: 'One time I lost the car key and so I had to ring Noah and he yelled at me for being lazy and stupid. I felt paralyzed with fear.'

Victim: 'Because of the way Sam behaved, friends and family didn't want to visit me. They said they felt unwelcome. Therefore, it was not possible for me to host friends or family. I would have to visit them.'

Victim: 'Ben was always saying bad things about my parents when they visited. It made me not want them to visit because it always created tension and arguments.'

Victim: 'Increasingly I stopped seeing my friends. If I was with a friend then Oliver would tell the kids I was having an affair. If I said to Oliver I was going to have lunch with a friend, he made such a big deal about it asking why I would need to do that and what a waste of money that was. It wasn't worth the arguments so I just didn't bother after a while.'

Victim: 'My mother would call me on the phone but Tom always complained about how long I was on the phone. I always felt the need to keep phone calls short to reduce the arguments about being on the phone.'

Some key things that can be seen from the above comments are isolation, which is one of the tactics employed by perpetrators of family violence. Friends and family give strength to victims. Perpetrators like to take away strength. Isolation reduces the strength of the connections between the victims and their friends/family and gives the perpetrator a stronger hold on the victim.

The Role of VFR Travel in the Separation Phase

The separation phase is important to examine because often this is when victims of family violence are exposed to the greatest risk. In addition, separation is when VFR travel may provide particular benefits to victims of family violence and their children. While, on the surface, it may seem that separation is the pathway to freedom, if there are children in the relationship, those children connect the parents to each other and this may result in ongoing family violence post-separation. Parents who attempt to provide safety for themselves and their children may find themselves disappointed and perhaps even disadvantaged by the family law court. Unfortunately, laws relating to family violence are implemented by lawyers and judges who often do not understand family violence (Hunter, 2006).

The period of separation is considered to be the riskiest phase for victims of family violence and their children (Australasian Institute of Judicial Administration, 2017; Family Court of Australia, 2018; Meyer, 2015). Accordingly, assessing VFR travel during the separation phase might be important. VFR travel may even provide an important form of support and security to victims of family violence and could assist in improving their quality of life. Such a concept potentially raises important aspects relating to family violence that may even have a transforming role to assist victims in their recovery, in their quest to break free from the hold of coercive control.

The interesting aspect of family violence is that there is more attention paid to the behaviour and the personality of the victim of family violence than to what perpetrators do (Stark, 2007). However, understanding family violence requires consideration of many aspects, and each victim who is freed from an abusive and controlling relationship will require great care – and planning that may take the victim years to put in place. This is where friends and family can assist, and certainly travelling to the victim or getting the victim to travel away geographically may be powerful strategies in the quest for freedom.

Significantly, during the period of separation, where a victim has finally found the strategies and strength to separate but is at great risk of being 'pulled back' by the abuser, and at greater risk of experiencing violence at the hands of the perpetrator, VFR travel can play a vital role. Separation is stressful and exhausting, even for couples who do not have the added layer of family violence. The risks involved in dealing with an abuser make separating far more complicated and draining for a person who is likely to have already been traumatised to the point of having little self-confidence or strength.

What Friends and Relatives Can Do to Assist

It can be challenging for the friends and family of a person in an abusive relationship to know how best to support the victim. Perpetrators of family violence tend to adopt strategies to isolate a victim of family violence because family and friends can offer support, which poses a risk for the perpetrator. Isolating a victim helps perpetrators to maintain control. Women often do not want to leave their abusive partner and may still love them (Hunter, 2006). Instead, what victims of family violence often want is to save the relationship and retain connections with their partner and children, but they simply yearn for safety (Hunter, 2006) and to live without fear. However, abusive men rarely change, as it is in their best interests to behave as they do (Bancroft, 2002).

Isolation is a key tactic employed by perpetrators of family violence, and isolation and family violence are tightly intertwined. Perpetrators of family violence will often tell the victim that the victim's friends and family are trying to ruin their relationship and will often become abusive if the victim wants to spend any time with friends/family away from the perpetrator. Since contact with family/friends can result in abuse from the perpetrator, the victim tends increasingly to withdraw from the friends and family to avoid the abuse from the perpetrator (Carver, 2019). As revealed in the Power and Control Wheel (Figure 3.4), isolation includes controlling who the victim can see, talk to, and where they go.

However, on the positive side, it may be that VFR travel could play an important role for victims of family violence and their children, in aiding recovery after separation. Separating from an abusive partner is considered harder to do than leaving a non-abusive partner and the victim is most at risk during this time (Bancroft, 2002). The man has lost control and often tries multiple tactics to regain it. That control may take the most serious form, such as physically harming the ex-partner, or harming the children as the ultimate form of revenge on the mother. Legal separation can be a form of control, and tactics may be employed to draw out negotiations. Parenting agreements can become complex. The process may be litigated and separation can take years. Women who have been choked by their partners are considered to be at particular risk of life-threatening injury or death during separation (Glass *et al.*, 2008). Thus, the victim might need physical protection and she may need help with caring for the children.

Accordingly, VFR travel (either visits to or from friends/family) may provide critical strength and support at a vulnerable and complex time for the victim. The experiences of how women 'navigate the leaving process and the impact on their safety, health and quality of life' (Broughton & Ford-Gilboe, 2017: 2,469) are acknowledged as being complex and their access to social support and resources are recognised as being important. Thus, family and friends will potentially be helpful at this time. The opportunity to 'escape' geographically through VFR travel may offer numerous benefits. Firstly, time with friends/family may offer important social support. Secondly, being in a different geographic location will make it more difficult for the perpetrator to access the victim or stalk them. And time away may assist in healing and provide an important time for internal healing and strengthening to ensure resilience. The benefits of time away for children were captured by a quote from a respondent in a study by McCabe:

> Caring for my two grandchildren who are currently on the child protection register. They have suffered the effect of domestic violence and physical abuse and neglect. A break from our current area surroundings would be a distraction from above and allow the children to be children for a short time. (McCabe, 2009: 676)

Separation is also a difficult time for victims trying to navigate the legal process to formally separate from their abusive ex-partner and settle property and parenting matters. In Australia, changes to the Family

Law Act in 2006 by the Howard Government resulted in the assumption that equal shared responsibility was in the child's best interests. As was discussed earlier in this book, equal shared parental responsibility means that both parents need to consult each other to make the major long-term decisions that impact their child/children. Such decisions include their name, cultural upbringing, religion, education, health and living arrangements. While Section 61DA of the Family Law Act 1975 allows the presumption to be rebutted if there are reasonable grounds to believe there was child abuse or family violence, proving family violence can be difficult, and abusive and controlling men may recruit lawyers with more aggressive tactics to fight against it. Equal shared parental responsibility may provide some abusive men with the opportunity to continue controlling their previous partner – but from outside instead of inside the house. Abusive and controlling men are often extremely gifted at playing the role of a victim and at making outrageous claims about the victim, which can make it very complex and challenging for the already-weakened victim to fight (Bancroft, 2002). Friends and family can support victims by being aware of these tactics, and helping to ensure the victim is supported and has access to information and resources.

Since 'regular' VFR travel improves the quality of life for most people (Backer, 2018), and social networks and support are beneficial for victims of family violence, it seems axiomatic that VFR travel may hold important links to aiding recovery for victims of family violence and their children. Perhaps packages offering subsidised travel could be provided for particularly needy victims of family violence to encourage VFR travel as part of a rehabilitation programme. Such packages may offer valuable support and important preventative healthcare provisions for victims and their children. While tourism/events are part of the problem of family violence, tourism may also – through VFR travel – be part of the solution.

A pattern of control over the partner is the central behavioural characteristic of a perpetrator of family violence (Bancroft *et al.*, 2011). That control can be exercised through various mechanisms such as criticism, verbal abuse, economic control, isolation and cruelty, among other tactics (Bancroft, 2002). What is perhaps surprising to many people, and makes family violence particularly complex, is that the vast majority of perpetrators of family violence do not tend to have chronic problems with violence outside the relationship with the partner (Bancroft, 2002). This was discussed earlier in the book with the 'snakes and ladders' framework and is also discussed in the next chapter. Perpetrators of family violence can be like a Dr Jekyll and Mr Hyde. This duality can make it more difficult for friends and family to appreciate that what they observe may be entirely different from what occurs behind closed doors for the victim. Understanding this duality is important for friends and relatives. Most perpetrators will restrict their violence to their intimate partner. In fact, most perpetrators of family violence are capable of exceptional self-control, which makes it challenging for police officers to know how to respond if called to an alleged family violence situation (Bancroft, 2002; Bancroft *et al.*, 2011). However, some things that friends and family may notice might be that the person who might be experiencing family violence may be required to 'ask permission' to go out, see or communicate with friends and family. There may also be constant 'checking in' by the partner via text messages or phone calls. The partner may also accompany the victim unnecessarily, to attend the victim's events. There may also be signs of jealousy, accusations of infidelity, or criticism from the victim's partner.

Conclusion

This chapter has explained the relationship between VFR travel and family violence. The connections between friends and family and the victim are important. The more we as a society know about family violence and what to look out for, the better. Watching for signs of possible control and abuse in a relationship that a friend or family member might be in could be extremely helpful. Even keeping a record of possible indicators could be valuable – especially if evidence is required; lack of evidence is often a factor in reducing the chances of obtaining protective orders or other components relevant to family violence. Such aspects could assist that friend or family member if they do feel they are ready to try separating from an abusive relationship. The great escape is discussed in the next chapter.

14 The Great Escape

'If you walked away from a toxic, negative, abusive, one-sided, dead-end low vibrational relationship or friendship – you won.'

– Lalah Delia

Introduction

This chapter outlines why 'just leaving' is not so simple. Family and friends of victims can assist by understanding the complex components of human behaviour and the risks of leaving. As outlined earlier in this book, escaping family violence is not simple, and can be thought of as 'snakes and ladders' where there are ladders out of the 'snake pit' as well as 'snakes' that pull you back down. The conceptual framework is presented again in this chapter (Figure 14.1) to save the reader from having to flip back to Chapter 3.

Many of the elements for this model (Figure 14.1) have been discussed in this book. This chapter will now present these components together to explain how these aggregate to form a potential guide for what might be involved if planning to separate from an abusive and controlling relationship.

Power and Control

The Power and Control Wheel was presented previously (see Figure 3.4), and the eight components from that model are identified in the Escaping Family Violence framework model (Figure 14.1). These components create what I call 'the snake pit'. In the 'snake pit', the victim lives in an environment in which some or all of these eight elements exist.

Knowledge

In the middle layer of the snake and ladders model is 'knowledge'. It is depicted separately but there is no ladder up to it because but isn't actually a separate component. Knowledge is gained when in or out of

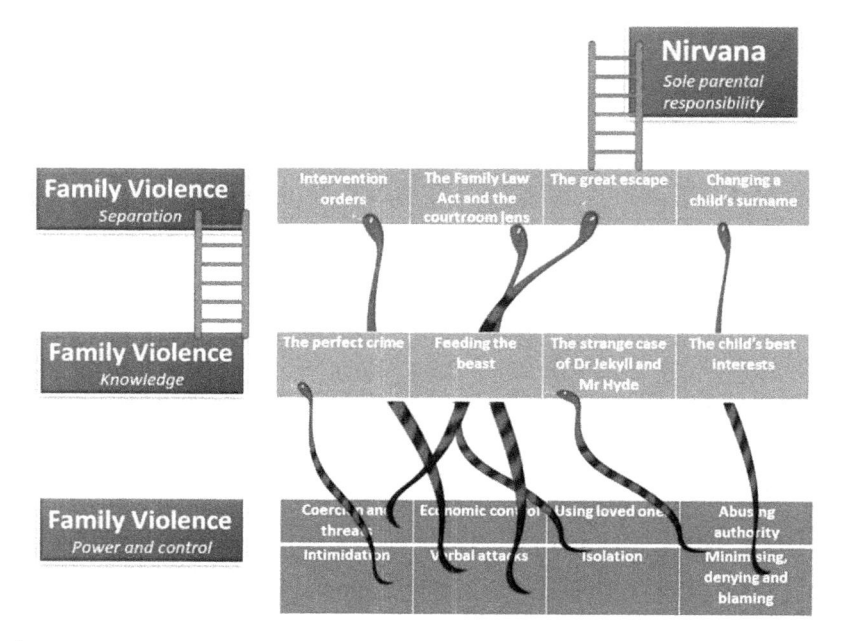

Figure 14.1 Escaping family violence framework

the 'snake pit'. Visually this layer is higher-order, and certainly, the more knowledge gained, the more someone may progress to the 'separation' level. Knowledge can highlight some of the elements in the 'snake pit'.

It is useful to keep in mind the types of tactics that perpetrators of family violence may use. For people who are in a relationship with a 'persuasive blamer' (Eddy & Kreger, 2011: 9), some of the things to expect might be: blaming you for their use of abuse/violence, spreading rumours against you, publicly humiliating you, and making false allegations against you in the family court (Eddy & Kreger, 2011).

There are four major components of knowledge:

- The perfect crime – people who are victims of family violence usually don't tell many, if any, people about what is happening to them. They often lie to cover it up. This makes it the perfect crime, because the victim covers up the crime and protects the perpetrator. Because the person may not tell people or have any form of evidence, there is often little or no proof that family violence has occurred. I know that in my situation, I did not speak of living with family violence. One of the reasons for this was that I was afraid that people would not let their children visit and play with my children. I did not want my children to be ostracised. There was not a single person who knew everything about what was happening. A small number of people knew a small number of things. One of the few people who knew the most, read a draft version of the Overture of this book and was shocked and said he wished he had done more to help me as he had no idea what I was going through. As mentioned earlier in this book, a large organisation reported that not one person had used their family violence leave. There is a lot of secrecy.

- Feeding the beast – victims may think that if they put more effort into the relationship to give in more to the perpetrator's requests and wishes, it will be better. They think that if they do more of the things the person wants and do not express an opinion, and tell the person how wonderful they are, things will get better. This rewards the perpetrator for their behaviour and is likely to 'feed the beast' and make things worse.
- The book, *The Strange Case of Dr Jekyll and Mr Hyde* (Stevenson, 1886), is about dual personalities in which one is good while the other is evil. I liken the behaviour of perpetrators of family violence to being like 'Jekyll and Hyde', because the perpetrator behind closed doors is generally very different to the perpetrator outside the home. It is important to understand this duality and not judge the situation purely on the 'Jekyll' the outside world sees.
- The child's best interests – this is the underlying foundation of the Family Law Act in Australia. In other countries, it is called other things, but the same principle tends to apply – that decisions made about the child should be child-centred and based upon what is best for the child rather than what is best for each parent. In practice, decisions may not necessarily be in a child's best interests. At the very least, applications are best crafted with that lens in mind.

Separation

I believe that the best prospects of separation are based on a foundation of knowledge. Understanding the traits of the person and how systems operate, can assist a person to operationalise some of the elements within the separation phase. A person may be able to find the 'ladder' from knowledge to separation, but there will be 'snakes' in each of the four components within this level. It will be easy to slide back down. The four central components of the separation phase are seen as:

- Intervention Orders – these are called different things in different states and countries, such as restraining order, apprehended violence order (AVO), domestic violence order (DVO), or protective order. These are an order to protect a person from being exposed to certain actions from another person. They are important in family violence situations. Risks often escalate after separation, so understanding how to apply for an Intervention Order is important.

- The Family Law Act and the court lens – in Australia, there is a Family Law Act, but there are equivalent frameworks in other countries. As discussed earlier, what happens in court may not be what is expected and there is a discretionary component. It is important to keep in mind 'the court lens' (i.e. what happens in court), which may not align with outcomes expected based on the Family Law Act (or its equivalent in other countries).
- The Great Escape – as explained earlier in this book, escape does not necessarily happen at separation. Sometimes the abusive behaviour continues but is outside the house instead of inside it. Decisions made in the courts can often enable the perpetrator to continue their controlling tactics. The ladder is deliberately placed at this location where it is argued that the best escape will be through sole parental responsibilities.
- Changing a child's surname – this component is deliberately to the side of the ladder from escape. It is not a necessary component but may be important in some situations. The matters relating to changing a child's surname and the gender bias was discussed in Chapter 9.

It is useful to keep in mind the battles that might be faced in these processes. A protective order issued by police makes things simpler, although the perpetrator may then blame the victim for it being issued and try to convince them to ask the police to retract it. This happened to me when the police issued an Intervention Order against Mr Ex in late 2013. When I contacted them to ask about the process for removing it, because Mr Ex said I should do that, the police said legislation did not allow that when it was police-issued because all too often perpetrators of family violence use coercive control to force the victim to request the protective Intervention Order be removed. I felt a tremendous sense of relief that it was out of my hands.

Applying for a protective order is trickier. My own journey for applying for an Intervention Order was outlined in Journey One in the Overture. It is important to be prepared for a battle. Just because you speak the truth doesn't mean there is no difficulty. I share this scenario from an excellent book that I read in the early stages of separation (Eddy & Kreger, 2011: 43–44):

> After enough incidents of being shoved, hit and kicked by Sam, Sarah, with the help of her cousin, got up the nerve to go to court and ask for a restraining order. She didn't really want a divorce; she only wanted Sam to change. She got a restraining order based on her description of only one incident. She held back the full history of abuse, because she did not want to upset Sam too much. But after she got the temporary restraining order (TRO) papers, she changed her mind and never had them served on Sam, so they expired.

Finally, after more abuse, she again went to court, got a new TRO, and had the papers served on Sam; he was ordered to move out of the house and stay at least a hundred yards away from her. At their first full hearing, Sarah was surprised to see that Sam had an attorney (she had none).

Sam's attorney argued persuasively that the allegations against Sam were false and he should get custody of their son, Jay, now one year old. He alleged that Sarah was a depressed pill addict who hit the child, gave him tranquilizers to keep him quiet, and left him unattended to wander in the house while she slept all day.

Sam provided two declarations (signed statements filed with the court), one from a friend and one from his sister, who said Sarah had told her that the bruises were from being clumsy (which Sarah actually told her once). Both declarations swore that Sam had never been violent with anyone, that he was a very caring father, and that Sarah was mentally unstable.

None of this was true, but Sarah was in shock. She knew she had seen her doctor for sleeping pills and overslept on one occasion. She felt guilty and was unable to speak up in her own defence against Sam's aggressive attorney and his declarations. She had merely tried to protect herself and was now a target of blame – unprepared to defend herself and unable to explain the full story of Sam's abusive behaviour toward her.

The above scenario demonstrates how things can be turned against a victim. This story is not uncommon. It has the same themes in it as I encountered in Journey Three. I applied on behalf of the children for their names to change. Although granted, the ordeal of the appeals process resulted in allegations against me including: that the 5-year Intervention Order was granted because I had lied to the courts; that all he wanted was to talk to the children and I had prevented such contact; and that he was such a good father. Like the case above, Mr Ex had filed two affidavits from his family members that stated that he was a good father (the affidavits were identical; a key indicator in my view that they had been written *for* those people rather than *by* them).

There are many difficulties to face. There are 'snakes' along the pathway to separation, which sends you back down to the snake pit. Keep going. There are ladders to the next level.

Nirvana

Equal Shared Parental Responsibility was discussed in Chapter 9 and was also discussed in the Overture (Journey Two). I have made the point previously in this book that there is no true escape from family violence as such (i.e. it tends to live on in memories and other ways as a minimum). However, I propose that with all options of how a post-separation life could be, having sole parental responsibilities will be the most like nirvana to aim for. If you can ensure that an abusive and controlling person is not involved in the main long-term decisions to do with your child, it will provide some type of freedom. You won't have to get their permission if you want to change the child's school, and you will be able to relocate if you need to. You can even go away from home on a holiday and get a passport for your child. There are likely to be visitation rights still but, given the options that currently exist for society, having sole parental responsibilities will reduce some of the opportunities for control. There is no 'snake' returning the person to the 'snake pit' at this point.

The Great Escape: Perspectives from an Australian Woman

One woman I spoke to as part of an ethics-approved research project regarding the connection between travel and family violence said that she 'felt perpetually abused by the court system'. She spoke of living in fear for years after separation and told how she had a recurring dream of the ex-husband taking their son and she couldn't save him. She felt that her ex-husband 'was supported by the family court'. She said: 'I wanted to get away from him but I had to live close to my ex. Therefore he dictated where I lived.' She had equal shared parental responsibilities that she found crippling. She spoke of her ex-husband having guns and how her son (aged around 7 or 8 at the time) had memorised the gun safe code. Several times she referred to experiencing 'continued abuse through the family court system'. She could not relocate and she could not go on a long holiday out of the region.

The Great Escape: Perspectives from a European Woman

This story was shared with me by a European woman who escaped an abusive and controlling marriage. As someone who has managed 'the great escape' but not nirvana, her experiences with separation show how she is 'free' but not 'free' and how, because of decisions made by the courts, she cannot reach nirvana. She cannot go on long holidays out of the region. Her thoughts on terminology such as 'survivor' mirror my own. These words below are presented virtually verbatim, with only a small number of minor grammatical edits:

> I refuse to continue labelling myself as a victim, or even to use what is supposed to be a more optimistic term, 'survivor of abuse'. Because the System will just happily keep us there, for ever, or for as long as we have to keep facilitating contact with our exes, which can be a very long time. The System just keeps us crawling on our knees with the hope of simply surviving.
>
> After all this time in court and using all the agencies in the System, I have come to realise that I am on my own, like all the others who have suffered abuse. I now understand that there is no real interest to change things, and that the System (of support) is ironically unsupportive.

At least now I have stopped making the noise in the wrong direction, I have stopped wasting my energy where I know it's going to be fruitless. I have realised that I need to simply tough it up. And that's why the label of victim simply doesn't work when there is no real support system in place. That term freezes you and paralyses you into this victim role, where you have to keep constantly second guessing yourself to make sure that you make absolutely no mistake, so that it clearly shows that he is an abuser and you are a victim. But even when keeping being polite, when you keep being respectful in your communication, he'll continue abusing you. So what this term does, in our current society which fails to support the victims, is to perpetuate the cycle of abuse by only offering us (victims) pity, a shoulder to cry on, to make us feel that we are understood and that what is happening isn't right. But then, it keeps throwing us back to the abusers. Thank you very much System, I've seen what you have to offer us and I refuse to live that life.

The Great Escape: Perspectives from a Woman Who Became a Family Violence Program Developer

Among my reading, I stumbled upon an article about family violence, and read the comments from various people about that article. Many spoke painfully about the secondary victimisation as a result of the courts. This comment, made 6 December 2021, is worth sharing in this book:

As a professional DV [domestic violence] program developer, executive, trainer, writer and activist … I raised four surviving children with a very violent, manipulative and hate-filled abuser, who was also the charming, wonderful son, brother, neighbor, friend, community member, politician and business owner/operator. I developed, ran and administered the business, managed and developed his political campaign, did all of the work for his participation in civic groups, and cared for the home, children and all else, all while volunteering for scouting, PTA and lots of other obligations. I also cared for my aging grandparents, and made many of his mother's clothes, designed and helped build and painted his mother's new home, and cared for and fed his brothers who lived with us while working for our company.

After 16 years of marriage (from my age of 15, in 1958, after he raped me when I was 14), I got one of the first 'orders of protection' issued in my region in the early 1970s. There were no shelters, rape crisis centers or any form of advocacy for victims of male terrorism. I was demonized by the friends, family and colleagues of this man, as well as some of my own relatives, and he was held up as a wonderful person. The sheriff's deputies took him around in their patrol cars rather than leave him in jail on the rare occasions when some judge held him accountable for a few days … I was left in poverty with my four children, avoiding his stalking and continuing abuse, until he died suddenly at age 39 of a heart attack in early 1980.

Meantime I finished college, struggled through, and developed more career skills. After working in higher education, I was hired by a DV program I had helped to start. My years of activism, protests, and helping to start DV programs and a rape crisis hotline were not important to this program, owned by a church and a large board of middle-class liberals. I left that program after about two years to start, develop and lead a program in a bordering county and we became nationally known for some of our cutting-edge work.

During all of this my children became adults, as they struggled with the effects of what their father had wrought, including raping my youngest daughter after the separation, when she was nine years old! After that too-long narrative I wanted to share about one of my two sons who inexplicably became a pale imitation of his father, resumed his dead father's demonization of me and said his sister was a liar regarding his father's rape of her at age nine. He has caused me more heartache than I can describe and remains one of my worst issues. I will be 70 years old in February and feel as though my whole life is in some way a long description of what domestic violence is and becomes.

The Great Escape: Perspectives from an Australian Woman

An Australian woman wrote the following piece, anonymously, that was published in *The Sydney Morning Herald* (Anonymous, 2022):

My ex-boyfriend never hit me, but when I tell people about the abuse I am constantly hit with confused looks, disregard, and a lack of validation. He didn't hit you, they say. So it wasn't that bad then? Sometimes I wish he had hit me. It would have made it easier to identify the abuse and understand the amount of danger I was in. It would also mean the confused looks would be replaced with believing faces.

My abuser was smart. He was smart enough to never threaten me in writing and only punch near my head. He was smart enough to only throw things close to me and drive dangerously at high speeds while I begged him to stop. He was smart enough to tell me that his anger was my fault. If I was just more agreeable, more available, offered more sex, smiled more, he wouldn't be so angry all the time. He was also smart enough to never hit me.

The chronic self-doubt he created within me, overrode the proof that was always there - just not in the form of a bruise on my face. I am a victim-survivor of domestic violence. It has taken me a long time and a lot of counselling to understand and accept that I am. I denied and downplayed it because no one wants that title. I did not want to believe it, but I was also trained not to. When the abuse is not clear-cut, you're trained - by society, by your abuser - that what you are feeling isn't valid or real. You're just an erratic, distraught woman screaming in a corner, claiming abuse. You're crazy. That is what he called me. And as you're slowly convinced that your feelings aren't valid, that your thoughts aren't true, you begin to second-guess your intuition. It took me a long time witnessing his escalating violence before I did listen to it again.

When I was contemplating leaving that relationship, counsellors, support workers and the staff at 1800 Respect explained the numerous forms in which abuse can rear its ugly head. Emotional, verbal, social, financial, spiritual, psychological, and sexual. Perpetrators even use the court system to scare and control the victim. My perpetrator abused me in all of these ways but it had taken me years to get to this place, where I had terms to validate my experience and people who told me that I wasn't crazy. That my concerns weren't anxieties, but the truth.

Imposter syndrome is something we usually discuss in relation to professional success. It has been defined as 'a collection of feelings of inadequacy that persist despite evident success'. Imposters suffer from a 'chronic self-doubt' that overrides 'any external proof of their competence'. I had imposter syndrome, but in relation to the abuse playing out in my relationship. The chronic self-doubt he created within me, overrode the proof that was always there - just not in the form of a bruise on my face.

The language around domestic violence is still catching up to the reality of the experience. We may recognise and reprimand physical abuse, but the subtle pattern of controlling and coercive behaviours is not fully understood by society. And when I was in the depths of the abuse, the lack of understanding from the police, the court system, my friends and society-at-large coalesced to create the imposter syndrome within me. I thought my perpetrator was right. I thought I was crazy. Because if I wasn't, the police and my friends would believe me.

After I lost my home, my job, my friends and my pets as a result of his actions, I sat in a refuge with other women who had also lost their safety, their security, and their sense of self, at the hands of abusive men. Many of them had the physical evidence marked on their bodies in the shape of purple and green bruises. Many of them had far worse stories than mine. But as I sat in the refuge kitchen, teary-eyed and questioning myself and my story again, a kind lady offered me a cup of tea. She sat down beside me and said eight simple words: 'I believe you. You deserve to be here.'

Those eight words allowed me to trust my intuition again. Those eight words changed my life. And through the expertise, awareness, and understanding of fellow victim-survivors and skilled workers like this woman, I slowly found myself again. They paid attention to my story, they didn't judge, and - most importantly - they believed me. So next time a woman tells you she is being abused, instead of listening to the man saying she is crazy, vindictive and spiteful, maybe just listen. You could save a life.

The Great Escape: Perspectives from a UK Woman

A UK woman who has managed the great escape only to find herself constantly going back to court, wrote this piece to share her experiences of a life after 'escape' (Smith, 2021):

I use a pseudonym to protect my identity, not from thugs or criminals, as you may be thinking, nor from my abuser (yes, I have an abuser). It is to keep me safe from the very people who are supposed to protect me: our judges. If you go through family court proceedings you are not allowed to share information about what happens in court, auspiciously to protect the identity of the children. However, as we know from other areas of life, a lack of transparency means any opportunity for scrutiny also disappears. As a result, the very baseline of our democracy vanishes, and with this, very often, any common sense.

I hear of mums who are forced by the judge to return to the family home where they've faced abuse for years, or who lose custody of their children because they spoke out about the violence they've endured. Without this transparency, nobody can be in any way certain that what is happening in our courts bears any resemblance to justice.

I chose a very nondescript name to reflect how painfully common the issues I face with the family court are. Whenever I share them with friends or neighbours, or through my social network support sites, I hear other stories very similar to mine, and often much worse.

An application to the family court costs £255. This is not that much money, and since it is possible to attend court without a solicitor, it makes it pretty much accessible to everyone. Up to here, this is good news of course. As a parent, nothing should stand in your way when trying to make things right for your children. But what if this is used by the wrong hands? What if someone keeps taking you back to court with the only intention being to make your life hell? It'd be the perfect weapon to control you, wouldn't it? Your life would get placed on hold, you wouldn't be able to make any plans as you wouldn't know when you'll have the kids, you'd live in constant fear that your children could be taken away from you.

You'd probably spend all your savings, most likely would get into debt to obtain legal advice, would possibly quit your job or reduce your hours and go onto benefits to give you enough time to prepare for the hearings. In these circumstances it becomes very hard to focus on normality like looking after your children, paying the bills, doing your job … having fun, what's that?

At the hearing your abilities as a mother, your true essence as a person, will be questioned again and again and you'll be pulled apart every single time. A proper rollercoaster of anxiety and stress over which you have no control. A perfect form of abuse.

You probably imagine, like most people, that once the divorce is finalised and there's an order in place, everyone can move on and carry on with their life. Or that there would be some sort of filter by the court not to allow this type of nonsense.

Ultimately, this is costing the taxpayer an absolute fortune that could be spent in putting in place a proper system that works. Let's face it, £255 doesn't even cover the price of processing your application by the clerk, let alone the wages of the judges who may end up dealing with it! It is not only that this is happening right in front of the eyes of the court system, but what is especially most concerning is that this system itself is enabling it, to the point that it's been defined as 'state-sanctioned abuse'.

Surely it is very easy to see when someone is abusing the system and constantly taking their ex back to court for no reason, or deliberately forcing them to make the same application again and again without good justification? You hear of mothers who just a couple of months after an order has been issued are taken back to court without any justification other than 'I changed my mind', mums who live in misery until their children turn 18.

How long will this abuse continue to take place?

Conclusion

This chapter has explained the complex components of the great escape, using the Escaping Family Violence Framework to outline the stages and issues that can arise. These stories tell of the ongoing hardship and pain for victims, even after leaving abuse. These stories capture the ongoing impact of abuse, even after separation. The victim may be limited with holidays outside of the area, and constantly ground down, which impacts the entire tourism system (i.e. for those employed in firms that serve tourists). With safe houses for victims of family violence already at capacity, 'too many victim survivors of family violence are forced to choose between their safety or the streets' (State Government of Victoria, 2018).

15 Conclusion

'At any given moment you have the power to say
this is not how the story is going to end.'

– Christine Mason Miller

Introduction

This final chapter summarises and synthesises the discussions
throughout this book. In doing so, this chapter also provides some
concluding thoughts about research gaps and issues. The book has presented two key aspects that create an underbelly of tourism – issues
relating to employment that can impact those working in tourism, and
issues relating to family violence that can impact those engaging in
tourism activities. Together, these two components create an underbelly of
tourism.

The Underbelly of Legal Processes

While the focus of this book has been tourism, the central
components are broader issues, also highlighted is the underbelly of
legal processes. I firmly believe that much of what is wrong is linked to
the underbelly of legal processes. Research in law is almost always based
on doctrinal research; that is, reading about the cases. The cases do not
reveal the underbelly of the legal processes.

This book has outlined processes in employment law and what I view
as a possible opportunity for bias in the mechanics. Young vulnerable
workers, often teenagers, employed casually in hospitality, fast food and
retail are at risk of being disadvantaged. These industries are among
the worst for casualisation and for forms of disadvantage such as being
employed in an organisation that is covered by an expired enterprise
agreement. While there are processes to enable an employee to apply to
the Fair Work Commission to terminate that agreement, the process is
far from straightforward. This is especially the case for agreements that
cover numerous employers and/or cover more than one state/territory.

I make this comment as more than 'an armchair critic' but as one who was involved in the process through my 17-year-old daughter being the applicant in a case seeking to terminate a 'zombie agreement'.

Children younger than 17 can go to court: criminal courts will have hearings with children as young as 10. While children under 10 are considered too young to be held responsible for their actions under criminal law, children between 10 and 14 can be charged with an offence if it is identified that the child understood what they did was an offence. Children over 14 but under 18 are charged with criminal offences and the matter is dealt with in the children's court. However, in family law, children under the age of 18 have no direct voice. They are not allowed in court. Affidavits may be struck out (they were in my case – refer to Journey Three in the Overture). Their voice can go through a children's lawyer.

So, to be clear, a 17-year-old can take on an international company and take them to the Fair Work Commission. A 10-year-old can be held responsible for their criminal actions. But a 17-year-old cannot enter a court and say they want to change their surname. A 17-year-old cannot say they do not want to spend time with parent X because they do not feel safe. Is it just me, or does that fail to make sense? As Pakistani activist Malala Yousofazai said: 'We realise the importance of our voice only when we are silenced'.

The Silence

In my view silence is a problem in the family law courts. This is not unique to Australia. I have heard this from women in other countries. Women afraid to speak. Women afraid that if they talk about what happened to them in court, they will be punished further. These are women in countries such as Australia and the United Kingdom. They are afraid of the courts. I am unclear on how things will progress if we are not prepared to hear what is wrong with the system. We simply have to do better.

The research priorities for family violence in the Australian state of Victoria are outlined as follows (State Government of Victoria, 2022):

- Primary prevention of family violence and violence against women – build evidence for a shared understanding and approach to stopping family violence and violence against women from occurring in the first instance.
- Children and young people as victim-survivors in their own right – recognise children and young people's unique experiences and intervene early and tailor programs to support recovery.
- Family violence as experienced by Aboriginal people and communities – enabling Aboriginal communities and organisations to lead or partner on research and ensuring access to what works in family violence from an Aboriginal perspective.

- Family violence as experienced by people from diverse communities – research to ensure consideration of the needs and experiences of people from diverse communities embedded into service design and delivery.
- Sexual violence and harm – deepen understanding of and better respond to sexual violence and harm within intimate partner relationships and the broader family.
- Adolescent family violence – research to support early intervention and tailor supports to the distinct needs of adolescents using violence in the home or in intimate partner relationships.
- Perpetrators and people who use violence – strengthen understandings of people who use violence and build the evidence base of effective approaches to support perpetrator accountabilities and behaviour change.

These are all critical areas and it is fantastic to see these important items listed. However, the judicial system and the education system are also important. I wonder why some of the things that might make a difference to the next generation are not on the list. Perhaps, it is because we are not allowed to speak of them and few are aware of them.

Future Research

Post-separation

Research examining the ongoing impacts of family violence post-separation seems important. It would be valuable to understand to what extent victims and their children are impacted after separation, and in what ways they are impacted. These impacts could be especially pronounced in rural and regional areas, where an inability to relocate or go on holidays might have more pronounced complications.

VFR Travel

With the importance of friends and relatives to victims, further examination of how VFR travel might be used to facilitate support and recovery might be valuable. Tourism has been shown to boost quality of life. As discussed in the book, court orders may preclude separated victims from taking international trips. Potentially, research examining the benefits of these trips to victims and children may assist with better judicial outcomes.

Burnout

This book highlights that victims of family violence might be constantly on edge as they live with abuse and may have abusive workplaces. There is no break. This might put them at a higher risk of burnout. For those working in high-paced service environments such as those that serve tourists, there might be considerable constant pressure (at work and home). This could also be relevant for victims in any work situation, not just those firms that serve tourists. However, the casualisation and pace of businesses in the tourism system may present higher risks. There is now greater awareness of the growing problem of burnout in the workplace, and its cost to the workplace. The six main causes of burnout are: poor relationships, workload, perceived lack of control, lack of fairness, lack of reward/recognition, and values mismatch (Moss, 2021). If we look at those top six items, some of them also exist for those living with abuse. It would seem plausible that if victims of family violence endure some of the top six drivers of burnout at home, and then also endure some at work, they are potentially at a heightened risk of burnout. This presents a problem, as economic independence is important in reducing the chances of victims returning to the abuser.

Psychological safety

This book briefly mentioned the importance of psychological safety. This is increasingly recognised as being important in the workplace, but it is relevant for any environment. While research has clearly demonstrated that fear inhibits cognitive functioning, some managers believe that fear is a powerful motivator. If we have managers with the wrong concept of motivation (i.e. using fear tactics) and employees living with fear, we as a society have significant issues. Research to better understand this seems important.

Situational factors

This book highlights that things can go wrong on holidays away from home. Flight delays, traffic problems, lost baggage, lack of sleep, poor weather and getting food poisoning are just some things that can go wrong. This can compound and lead to explosive behaviour from a perpetrator of family violence. However, this has not been examined. Even too much hot weather can affect people's behaviour. In what way these situational factors are connected to family violence is not understood, and this could be important research for the future.

Discrimination

Victims of family violence may experience discrimination. That discrimination might be in the workplace, where their abusive partner or ex-partner is considered to be a health and safety risk for all employees so the victim is dismissed. The victim may also be discriminated against in their local communities, where neighbours stop talking to the victim and/or the victims and their children are ostracised. Rental accommodation may be difficult to obtain if landlords decide that victims of family violence trying to establish themselves after separation might be considered to be a risk. Research to explore where these discrimination matters may exist would assist in presenting evidence to inform mitigation strategies to reduce the prospect of women returning to unsafe homes, or choosing to stay in those unsafe homes.

Ho-Ho-Ho! It's the Holidays

Holidays are not always 'Ho-ho-ho!'; especially when living with family violence. In fact, 'co-parenting with a domestic violator can be difficult at the best of times. The holidays, however, often amplify those struggles' (Cohen, 2020). This book has highlighted, through various examples and cases, that holidays are not as they would seem or as they should be for those who live with family violence. It is most unfortunate that, for some,

> [Why is it that] every year around this time we are triggered by our past trauma that somehow unpacks itself at the most inopportune time? We grew up hoping that nothing "bad" ever happens during the holiday season, in spite of the research studies highlighting how deadly a time of year this can be. (Cohen, 2020)

In this book, the reader has been introduced to various materials that show that holidays are not a time for rest and relaxation for those living with family violence. As was shown through a discussion of Maslow's Hierarchy of Needs, if a person is focused on their foundational needs, such as safety, they are unable to properly obtain the higher-order benefits associated with touristic experiences. A person may look at the view but not take it in. They may be at a tourist attraction but may not have any connection to it or get any enjoyment from it. They may not even remember being there. Their mind is preoccupied with their safety – and/or the safety of their children. Family violence does not take a holiday.

Conclusion

In recent years, there has been considerable focus on the problem of family violence. Universities are establishing research centres dedicated to family violence as well as developing courses in the field. Society is concerned with this problem. Family violence represents the main cause of homelessness for women and their children in Australia (White Ribbon Australia, 2022). According to White Ribbon Australia (2018), on average one woman is killed each week in Australia by a former or current partner. Globally, intimate partner violence (IPV) affects close to 1 in 3 women in their lifetime (Heise & Kotsadam, 2015).

This book has discussed the themes of control, abuse, bullying and family violence in the tourism system. Through doing so, it has revealed the underbelly of tourism. Centrally, two key components create a tourism underbelly. Firstly, loopholes in employment law allowing tourists and/or employees who service tourists to work in sub-standard conditions. In some cases, they are working below the minimum award and subjected to poor conditions, including bullying, power imbalance (i.e. control) and abuse. This book has also revealed a second component of the tourism underbelly: family violence. There are five tourism elements and, as discussed in this book, family violence impacts each and every one of these five tourism elements. In many cases, the abuse escalates when on holiday. Even if victims separate from an abusive relationship, holidays away from home may not be possible. Court orders or the abusive ex-partner may not give permission. Finances may be severely limited because the victim is left with the majority of the child-raising since they are the safe house. Coupled with the trend for children to live at home for longer, these financial burdens are significant and may prevent the victim from engaging in leisure activities such as holidays, even after separation. When children are minors, courts and/ or the ex-partner may prevent the separated victim from holidaying. The example of the woman who wanted to holiday with the children overseas to visit the maternal grandparents is just one example. Her request to go on an international holiday for more than seven days was denied because the ex-husband (a proven perpetrator of family violence) was only allowed seven days and the courts wanted to 'be fair' to the perpetrator.

This book has also revealed the difficulties of separation. The judicial system does not make it as easy or as attractive as people are led to believe. There is little knowledge of this, especially since people are forbidden to talk about it. The secret remains.

When I finally separated from Mr Ex, my youngest two children were almost 12. Sebastian was angry with me for months and would sometimes yell at me, 'Why did you make us live that for so long!? Why didn't you leave earlier?' He was angry with me because my decision to stay so long resulted in so many years of abuse. I tried to explain to him that I waited so long as it was the best chance we had of being free and safe. It is stories such as Carly's (from Hill (2019)) that worry me. While no child under 18 has a voice in court, younger children have no way of saying they do not want to spend time with the other parent on an allocated visitation day. The fact that my children were older meant they had at least that power. By the time I separated, I had 10 years of evidence including an Intervention Order applied for by the police, and a police statement referring to me being choked for years, and having been hit in the head resulting in a perforated eardrum, black swollen eye, and cut eyebrow. I stayed living with abuse because I knew the courts would not set me free. I had to wait and keep my eyes on the prize of freedom. Strategy is everything when it comes to escaping family violence. Escaping family violence was the longest and most strategic project I have ever done in my life. How dreadful that it is so difficult.

In closing, this book has outlined and drawn together an array of complex information. Several conceptual frameworks are presented in this book, which attempt to explain how a victim might be hidden (the iceberg), how the victim gets caught (the perpetrator's web), and how a victim might try to leave an abusive relationship (snakes and ladders). The book outlines how each of the five whole tourism system elements is impacted by control, abuse, bullying and family violence. For victims of family violence, holidays are not a time for rest and relaxation as they may be for others. Even holidays after separation may be limited or denied. It is hoped that the information in this book may help victims to escape safely, friends and family to support victims, young employees to fight toxic workplaces, and children to grow up without fear. This Charles Dickens' book title is so apt: 'no one is useless in this world who lightens the burdens of another' (Dickens, 2013). As written by my daughter in the Mother's Day card she gave me less than two weeks before I sent the manuscript of this book to the publisher:

> we know you are busy on your book, which we are very proud of to have such an inspirational mother who uses her experiences to inspire and potentially change the lives of others and save them as you saved us.

I hope that being able to present this educational book through an autoethnography lens will help result in change toward a safer society, where children have a stronger voice in the courts and we have more understanding and compassion for how family violence impacts victims and children. I hope this book helps lead to change. The film *Custody* set out to answer the question 'Can a violent husband be a good father?' Hopefully, in the future, more family court judges will consider that question when making orders.

Epilogue

'If you want to know where to find your contribution to the world, look at your wounds. When you learn how to heal them, teach others.'

– Emily Maroutian, *Thirty: A Collection of Persona Quotes, Advice, and Lessons*

This epilogue serves to reflect on the contents of the book, to reflect on the parts of my story captured through the book and in particular the Overture. This section serves to provide a comment on what has happened. In a sense, this book is hoping to do as the epigraph above states: I am hoping to contribute to the world, I am hoping that my journey has some purpose. I am hoping to teach others what I have learned. When I went through the three 'journeys' in court and realised I had outcomes that others had not been able to achieve or even knew how to approach, I thought – there has to be some purpose to this beyond only me. This has to benefit more than just my family. Maybe there is a way I can share what I have learned and can help others.

I think it can be true that 'in violence, we forget who we are' (McCarthy, 1961: 271). Certainly, the longer I was married, the longer I forgot who I was. As I mentioned in the Overture, I spent two-thirds of my adult life either in a hopeless marriage or trying to map through a hopeless family law system to separate from the hopeless marriage.

In the Overture I talk of three court journeys – Intervention Order, financial/parenting agreement, and changing the surnames of the children. In family violence it is very easy to forget who you are. Socrates said: 'To find yourself, think for yourself' (Plato, 399 BCE).

Indeed, in many ways my outlook while living with family violence helped me endure it. I remained hopeful. I always had in my mind a plan that, if things did not change, I would escape, but that escape had to be carefully executed. Even having a plan for a life without family violence made it better. I could see a different life in the future by visualising it and planning for it. I kept pieces of evidence. This gave me hope that, should things not change and I find myself having to force myself out of the situation, then I had the very best chance possible within the hopeless legal system I would need to operate within.

Just as Andy Dufresne in *The Shawshank Redemption* coped by having a plan to escape, so did I. I chipped away at it. It was slow. Very slow. It took many many years. But I did escape. Similarly, Andy Dufresne chipped away at his escape ... with a little rock hammer. Gradually, slowly, eventually, Andy created an escape tunnel ... over many years ... with a rock hammer. The plan and the process gave him hope and helped him to stay positive and keep his spirit. Hope can keep us strong and help us to do the impossible.

I do acknowledge, however, that even with hope, enduring family violence through a 17-year marriage, and then enduring battles through the family court, has had an impact. I reflect back on the time and feel a mixture of emotions. However, one emotion I do not feel, nor have I ever felt, is hate. My mother said to me when I was going through the third court battle, 'You must really hate him [Mr Ex].' I said to her, 'Not at all. Why would I bother putting my time and energy into doing that?' She was a bit confused by my response and so I explained further:

> I do not love him, I do not like him, I do not hate him. I do not anything him. I have absolutely no emotions at all for him – neither good nor bad. All I feel is numb. I do not wish him bad but I also not do wish him well. I wish him nothing.

As Viktor E. Frankl said, 'I do not forget any good deed done to me and I do not carry a grudge for a bad one' (Frankl, 1959: 162). I think that bothering with hate will only weigh someone down. Instead, I look at how my experiences and my learnings can be useful and what the purposes of those might be. I focus on how they can serve to add value, not what value those experiences took away. American psychologist Carl Rogers said: 'The good life is a process, not a state of being. It is a direction, not a destination' (Rogers, 2012: 186).

Living with family violence is awful; and living after separation from family violence can, unfortunately, remain awful, with the abuse and control continuing, but from outside the house instead of within it. Trying to find reason and optimism can at times feel impossible. Telling people to be optimistic is pointless because it cannot be ordered upon someone. Happiness cannot be forced and sometimes can feel like an endless challenge. Viktor Frankl, who found reasons for optimism despite spending time in a concentration camp, believes that people should not be pursuing happiness but should instead focus on a reason to be happy. He said:

> Happiness cannot be pursued, it must ensue. One must have a reason to 'be happy'. Once the reason is found, however, one becomes happy automatically. As we see, a human being is not in pursuit of happiness but rather in search of a reason to become happy, last but not least

through actualizing the potential meaning inherent and dormant in a given situation. (Frankl, 1959: 138)

While we cannot control what happened to us and change it, we can try to find ways to feel empowered by what happened. These things that happen can shape us in many ways. There will be difficulties but there will be gifts. People who have experienced family violence may find that they are very good at reading non-verbal communication. They have a good sense of people. Often, they can read people quite quickly. Their instincts can be heightened. This can be because reading what was coming was linked to living with family violence. It helped to know when the bad mood was heightening and when things were escalating. Trying to focus on positives and what is within our control can be helpful. Viktor Frankl said, about living in a concentration camp:

> A human being is not one thing among others; things determine each other, but man is ultimately self-determining. What he becomes – within the limits of endowment and environment – he has made out of himself. In the concentration camps, for example, in this living laboratory and on this testing ground, we watched and witnessed some of our comrades behave like swine while others behaved like saints. Man has both potentialities within himself; which one is actualized depends on decisions but not on conditions. (Frankl, 1959: 133–134)

I ask myself again, reflecting on my journeys – my marriage journey and my court journeys – would I do anything differently if I could go back in time? My answer is no. Would I have liked to have left earlier? Yes. Did I feel trapped? Yes. Was I afraid? Yes. Did the experience change me? Yes. Did it destroy me? No.

From my perspective, because of our legal processes, I was stuck living with family violence. To have separated earlier would have meant almost certainly that the outcome would have been worse. I would have been freed from living with family violence inside the home, but I l would still have had to deal with it outside the home. The children would have been younger and more vulnerable and had no voice to say no. I cannot say what may have happened but it may have been a lot worse. On balance, because the children were old enough to avoid forced time with their father, we had freedom that I believe we would not have otherwise had. I don't need to seek permission to go on a holiday outside the region.

My hope from this book is that a spotlight has been shone on the legal systems around the world. There are too many stories, globally, of victims of family violence finally separating only to find themselves going in and out of court to entertain their abusive ex-partner. The courts allow this. In Australia, the default of equal shared parental responsibilities means that victims are forced to communicate with their abusive and controlling ex-partner to 'agree' on matters for the children. A perpetrator can use this as an opportunity to continue to exercise their power and control. In such situations, it cannot possibly be in the children's best interests.

I blame the courts for contributing to family violence continuing. I blame them for people living with family violence in their homes longer than they should because they are too afraid of what the courts will grant the perpetrator. I blame the courts for people living with family violence outside the home because of the discretionary nature of the family courts meaning that a poor decision could be made that is not in the children's best interests. I believe the courts are responsible in part for the ongoing nature of family violence and its generational cycle. They are contributing to feeding the beast.

I look at the priority research areas of family violence and the spotlight is not on the courts. It is perhaps assumed that there is fairness and justice. I am hoping that this educational book shines a little light on the underbelly of tourism and the underbelly of the courts. I am hoping that if the bacteria are exposed to sunlight, some of them may die off. Viktor Frankl said: 'It is not freedom from conditions, but it is freedom to take a stand toward the conditions' (Frankl, 1959: 130).

As I mentioned in the Overture, I do not see myself as a survivor. My children and I live with what happened to us – the scars, both internal and visible. The memories do not go away. But we do have freedom, because of those court outcomes.

As a society, we do not fully understand the damage done to children by family violence. We do know that even living in a house with family violence, even if the children are not the target, family violence will still impact them: a parent who feels unsafe and threatened in their own home cannot function effectively as a parent. If we return to Maslow's hierarchy of needs, we recall that if our safety needs are not being met then we cannot reach for higher-order elements. A parent cannot be the very best parent they can be while they are focused on their safety needs. Living in fear negatively impacts the brain.

A note I want to finish on is that of forgiveness. I have spoken of not hating, and of living by two central themes – to accept and to be thankful. There is no point in going back in time. It happened. Accept it. Fighting with yourself and punishing yourself for not leaving, not seeing clearly, or not acting differently changes nothing. You end up punishing yourself. You have been punished enough already. Accept. Accept it happened. Then be thankful. There is always something to be thankful for. Find it, focus on it, and remind yourself of it. Accept, and be thankful. And now – forgiveness.

I mentioned earlier that my mother said to me that I must really hate Mr Ex and I said I did not. I wished him no ill will, I wished him no goodwill. I wished him nothing. Anything more than nothing takes my energy, which I do not choose to give. Not long after that conversation with my mother, I talked to her about forgiveness. My mother is a strong believer in forgiveness. I said to her: 'I do not forgive him. I do not need to. I do not wish him ill will but I will not forgive him. My lack of forgiveness does not weigh me down. He simply does not deserve forgiveness.'

My mother did not know what to say but chose not to argue with me about it. There were times I struggled with myself about this choice. I wondered if I should forgive him. But every time I asked myself that question and saw the scars on my daughter's arms, I felt his chosen behaviour did not warrant forgiveness.

In the epilogue of *The Wild Truth* (McCandless, 2014) Carine McCandless writes about how abusive her parents, particularly her father, had been, and how the behaviour of her abusive parents had resulted in her brother going on a venture that took his life. In her epilogue, McCandless explains that she gives lectures on 'truth' to try to share the message about family violence and always allows time for questions and answers at the end of her lectures. Carine wrote that after one such lecture a question came from a young man, who asked her: 'Have you ever been able to forgive your parents?' (McCandless, 2014: 255). McCandless said:

> I had spoken to thousands of students over the past several years. It was not the most personal question I had ever been asked, but it was by far the most difficult. And I was not sure that I could give him an honest answer, because I was still trying to figure that one out for myself.
>
> I struggle with the definition of forgiveness. I debate with myself as to whether it is a matter of compassion, of understanding, or of simply being willing and able to forget. But with forgetfulness comes recurrence. I wrestle with my faith, which instructs me to show mercy to those who have not asked for it and pardon those who have not earned it. As painful and complicated as it is, the conflict dissipates when I look at my children. I know in my heart and soul that my primary responsibilities – above all else – are to protect them and to teach them. Through any adversity, against all odds, and until my last breath, I will measure myself on how well I serve this purpose. (McCandless, 2014: 255)

This gave me comfort. I do not owe Mr Ex forgiveness. Forgetting can lead to recurrence. And so I am at peace. In truth, can a person who is not sorry be forgiven? I feel that we have a pack of forgiveness cards for each person in our lives and that once a person uses up every one of those forgiveness cards, there are no more to hand out to that person. I feel no requirement to forgive and forget as freedom can sometimes best be found by giving ourselves permission to grieve and then to let go.

There can be an abuse of power in the home, the education system, and the workforce. There can also be an abuse of power in judicial settings. I oppose the abuse of power and I oppose the power to abuse. Sometimes the judicial system gives abusers the power to abuse. I hope this book may result in less abuse of power and less power to abuse.

References

9 News (2022, April 15) Cancelled flights, missing baggage – more travel chaos as Easter long weekend begins. *Nine.Com.Au*. https://www.9news.com.au/national/easter-travel-delays-good-friday-sydney-melbourne-airports-lengthy-queues-long-waits-million-expected-to-fly/525e8d48-1636-4457-8cd4-29e44a8d10ba?app=applenews.

ABC News (2019, May 29) *Not just high house prices: The reasons more young adults live with their parents*. https://www.abc.net.au/news/2019-05-29/house-prices-and-why-young-australians-still-living-at-home/11110552.

ACTU (2020) *Fair Work Amendment (Supporting Australia's Jobs and Economic Recovery) Bill 2020*. http://journals.sagepub.com/doi/10.1177/1120700020921110%0Ahttps://doi.org/10.1016/j.reuma.2018.06.001%0Ahttps://doi.org/10.1016/j.arth.2018.03.044%0Ahttps://reader.elsevier.com/reader/sd/pii/S1063458420300078?token=C039B8B13922A2079230DC9AF11A333E295FCD8.

Alannah & Madeline Foundation (2014) *Our Story: Grant and Ashton*. https://www.youtube.com/watch?v=XMATXHDHFJg.

Alexander, R. (2018) *Family Violence in Australia: The Legal Response*. Alexandria: The Federation Press.

Anonymous (2021, July 1) My ex used the justice system as a form of coercive control – the law should not aid the abuse of women. *The Independent*. https://www.independent.co.uk/voices/domestic-violence-abuse-justice-system-coercive-control-b1876370.html.

Anonymous (2022, February 22) In the depths of abuse, self-doubt led me to believe my perpetrator was right. *Sydney Morning Herald*. https://www.smh.com.au/lifestyle/life-and-relationships/in-the-depths-of-abuse-self-doubt-led-me-to-believe-my-perpetrator-was-right-20220209-p59v1m.html.

Ariza-Montes, A., Arjona-Fuentes, J.M., Law, R. and Han, H. (2017) Incidence of workplace bullying among hospitality employees. *International Journal of Contemporary Hospitality Management* 29 (4), 1116–1132. https://doi.org/10.1108/IJCHM-09-2015-0471.

Attorney-General's Department (2021) *Appointments to the Fair Work Commission*. https://ministers.ag.gov.au/media-centre/appointments-fair-work-commission-01-04-2021.

Australian Human Rights Commission (2011) *Workplace bullying: Violence, Harassment and Bullying Fact sheet*. https://humanrights.gov.au/our-work/employers/workplace-bullying-violence-harassment-and-bullying-fact-sheet.

Australian Human Rights Commission (2017) *Family violence linked to heightened self-harm among children*. https://humanrights.gov.au/about/news/family-violence-linked-heightened-self-harm-among-children.

Australian Human Rights Commission (2022) *What is bullying?: Violence, Harassment and Bullying Fact Sheet*. https://humanrights.gov.au/our-work/commission-general/what-bullying-violence-harassment-and-bullying-fact-sheet.

Backer, E. (2007) VFR Travel – An examination of the expenditures of VFR travellers and their hosts. *Current Issues in Tourism* 10 (4), 366–377.

Backer, E. (2012) VFR travel: It *is* underestimated. *Tourism Management* 33 (1), 74–79. https://doi.org/10.1016/j.tourman.2011.01.027.

Backer, E. (2018) VFR travel: Do visits improve or reduce our quality of life? *Journal of Hospitality and Tourism Management, Special Issue on CAUTHE 2017 Conference: Time for big ideas? Rethinking the field for tomorrow*. https://doi.org/https://doi.org/10.1016/j.jhtm.2018.04.004.

Backer, E. and Barry, B. (2013) Empirical testing of the theory of partial industrialisation in tourism. *Journal of Hospitality and Tourism Management* 20, 43–52. https://doi.org/10.1016/j.jhtm.2013.06.001.

Backer, E. and Morrison, A.M. (2017) VFR Travel Special Issue. *International Journal of Tourism Research*.

Baggio, R. (2008) Symptoms of complexity in a tourism system. *Tourism Analysis* 13 (1), 1–20.

Bain, J.S. (1968) *Industrial Organization* (2nd edn). Chichester: John Wiley & Sons.

Bancroft, L. (2002) *Why Does He Do That? Inside the Minds of Angry and Controlling Men*. London: Penguin Books.

Bancroft, L. (2022a) *Kids who side with the abuser, Part 1*. https://lundybancroft.com/kids-who-side-with-the-abuser-part-1/?fbclid=IwAR2Z4dmuimDskyh3qCFLobRxDRrH0YVuvMfq9Ycvp3mHSmCIYSaacxOT6dg.

Bancroft, L. (2022b) *Narcissists versus Abusers*. Domestic Abuse & Custody. https://lundybancroft.com/narcissists-vs-abusers/.

Bancroft, L., Silverman, J. and Ritchie, D. (2011) *The Batterer as Parent* (2nd edn). Thousand Oaks, CA: Sage Publications.

Benson, H., Skolnik, L., Tipton, S. and Johnson, L.M. (2016) *DNA Lyrics*. Musixmatch. https://www.google.com/search?q=lia+marie+johnson+dna&rlz=1C1GCEB_enAU946AU946&sxsrf=ALiCzsYYSiAJzU4baZ6cTwg6N5DsHuluOA%3A1666431576562&ei=WLpTY4zoIfjC4-EPmbqGmAY&oq=song+lyrics+dna+li&gs_lcp=Cgdnd3Mtd2l6EAMYADIGCAAQFhAeMgYIABAWEB4yBQgAEIYDOgoIABBHENYEYEELA.

Bertalanffy, L. (1928) *Kritische Theorie der Formbildung. Modern Theories of Development*. (T. by J.H.W. (1934) M.T. of D.O.O.U. Press. (ed.)). Borntraeger.

Bertalanffy, L. (1968) *General System Theory: Foundation, Development, Applications*. New York: George Braziller Inc.

Bertalanffy, L. (1972) The history and status of general systems theory. In G. Klir (ed.) *Trends in General Systems Theory* (pp. 21–41). Chichester: Wiley & Sons.

Blumer, A., Ehrenfeucht, A., Haussler, D. and Warmuth, M. (1987) Occam's Razor. *Information Processing Letters* 24, 377–380.

Boutilier, S., Jadidzadeh, A., Esina, E., Wells, L. and Kneebone, R. (2017) The connection between professional sporting events, holidays and domestic violence in Calgary, Alberta. *The School of Public Policy Research Papers* 10 (12).

Bove, T. (2022, March 26) Adults are living with their parents at unprecedented levels as crushing debt, a runaway housing market, and the pandemic make independence impossible. *Fortune*. https://fortune.com/2022/03/25/more-adults-living-with-parents-than-ever-pew-research-pandemic-covid-great-depression/.

Brooks, S. (2013) *Worst holiday travel experiences*. Sheknows. https://www.sheknows.com/living/articles/1021939/worst-holiday-travel-experiences/.

Broughton, S. and Ford-Gilboe, M. (2017) Predicting family health and well-being after separation from an abusive partner: Role of coercive control, mother's depression and social support. *Journal of Clinical Nursing* 26 (15–16), 2468–2481. https://doi.org/10.1111/jocn.13458.

Butler, P. (2020, October 19) "Boomerang" trend of young adults living with parents is rising – study. *The Guardian*. https://www.theguardian.com/society/2020/oct/18/boomerang-trend-of-young-adults-living-with-parents-is-rising-study.

Butler, R. (1980) The concept of a tourist area cycle of evolution: Implications for management of resources. *Canadian Geographer* 24, 5–12.

Cambridge Dictionary (n.d.) *holiday*. Retrieved April 3, 2022, from https://dictionary.cambridge.org/dictionary/english/holiday.

Carver, J. (2019) *Love and Stockholm Syndrome: The Mystery of Loving an Abuser*. Councelling Resource. https://counsellingresource.com/therapy/self-help/stockholm/.

Cohen, R. (2020) *Narcissistic Ex means Hellish Holidays*. The Court Said. https://thecourtsaid.org/2020/12/22/holiday-health-warning/.

Collard, S. (2018, December 19) A dark Christmas looms as the busiest time of the year for domestic violence shelters. *ABC News*. https://www.abc.net.au/news/2018-12-19/domestic-violence-rates-spike-at-christmas/10629006.

Corporate Finance Institute (2022a) *Monopoly*. https://corporatefinanceinstitute.com/resources/knowledge/economics/monopoly/.

Corporate Finance Institute (2022b) *Oligopoly*. https://corporatefinanceinstitute.com/resources/knowledge/economics/oligopoly/.

Council of Australian Governments (2015) *National Outcome Standards for Perpetrator Interventions*. National Plan to Reduce Violence Against Women and their Children.

Crompton, J. (1979) Motivations for pleasure vacation. *Annals of Tourism Research*, Oct/Dec, 408–423.

Curtale, R. (2018) Analyzing children's impact on parents' tourist choices. *Young Consumers* 19 (2), 172–184. https://doi.org/10.1108/YC-07-2017-00715.

Dearden, L. (2018, September 8) Domestic abuse reports soared during the World Cup, police figures show. *The Indepdent*. https://www.independent.co.uk/news/uk/crime/world-cup-2018-domestic-abuse-violence-rise-police-football-linked-crime-a8529056.html.

Deighton, K. (2018, June 28) 'If England get beaten, so will she' – posters bleed World Cup fever into domestic violence. *The Drum*. https://www.thedrum.com/news/2018/06/28/if-england-get-beaten-so-will-she-posters-bleed-world-cup-fever-domestic-violence.

Denham, A.C., Frasier, P., Hooten, E., Belton, L., Newton, W., Gonzalez, P., Begum, M. and Campbell, M.K. (2007) Intimate partner violence among Latinas in Eastern North Carolina. *Violence Against Women* 13 (2), 123–140.

Department of Education and Training (2018) *Protect: Identifying and Responding to all forms of abuse in Victorian School*. https://www.education.vic.gov.au/Documents/about/programs/health/protect/ChildSafeStandard5_SchoolsGuide.pdf.

Dickens, C. (2013) *Charles Dickens' Doctor Marigold: No One Is Useless in This World Who Lightens the Burdens of Another*. Word to the wise.

Domestic Abuse Intervention Programs (2017) *The Duluth Model*. https://www.theduluthmodel.org/wheels/.

Doxey, G. (1976) When enough's enough: The natives are restless in Old Niagara. *Heritage Canada* 2 (2), 26–27.

Eddy, B. and Kreger, R. (2011) *Splitting: Protecting Yourself while Divorcing Someone with Borderline or Narcissistic Personality Disorder*. Oakland, CA: New Harbinger Publications.

Edmondson, A.C. (2019) *The Fearless Organization: Creating Psychological Safety in the Workplace for Learning, Innovation, and Growth*. Chichester: Wiley & Sons.

Employer Services (2022) *"Disgrace": Fair Work Commission takes aim at hospitality employer's ancient EBA*. https://employerservices.com.au/disgrace-fair-work-commission-takes-aim-at-hospitality-employers-ancient-eba/.

Fair Work Claims (2019) https://www.fairworkclaims.com.au/workers-ripped-off-with-zombie-workplace-agreements/.

Fair Work Commission (2022a) *Application to terminate the IPCA (VIC, ACT & NT) Agreement 2011*. https://www.fwc.gov.au/hearings-decisions/major-cases/application-terminate-ipca-vic-act-nt-agreement-2011.

Fair Work Commission (2022b) *Fair Work Commission*. Agreements. https://www.fwc.gov.au/search/document/agreement.

Family Court of Australia (2018) *Exposure to family violence and its effect on children*. http://www.familycourt.gov.au/wps/wcm/connect/fcoaweb/reports-and-publications/publications/family+violence/exposure-to-family-violence-and-its-effect-on-children#.

Farrell, P. and McDonald, A. (2018) *Merivale staff seek to kill off WorkChoices-era pay agreement over weekend penalty rates*. ABC News. https://www.abc.net.au/news/2018-11-12/merivale-staff-move-to-kill-off-pay-agreement/10467566.

Fast Company (2014) *The Best (And Worst) Countries For Workers*. https://www.fastcompany.com/3031015/the-best-and-worst-countries-for-workers.

Florida State University (n.d.) *Self-Harm & Cutting*. Retrieved March 15, 2022, from http://www.youtube.com/watch?v=7Y3KaAeBQ6Y&feature=youtube_gdata_player.

Fodness, D. and Murray, B. (1999) A model of tourist information search behavior. *Journal of Travel Research* 37 (3), 220–230. https://doi.org/10.1177/004728759903700302.

Foundation for Alcohol Research & Education (2018, June 22) Domestic violence surge: state of origin game leaves women and children battered and bruised. *Media Release*. https://fare.org.au/domestic-violence-surge-state-of-origin-game-leaves-women-and-children-battered-and-bruised/.

Frankl, V.E. (1959) *Man's Search for Meaning*. Boston: Beacon Press.

French, R. (2010) *Procedural Fairness – Indispensable to Justice?* https://www.hcourt.gov.au/assets/publications/speeches/current-justices/frenchcj/frenchcj07oct10.pdf.

Gallant, D. and Humphreys, C. (2019) *Football finals and domestic violence*. https://pursuit.unimelb.edu.au/articles/football-finals-and-domestic-violence.

Getz, D. (1986) Models in tourism planning. *Tourism Management* 7, 21–32.

Gilbert and Tobin Law (2022) *High Court changes direction on independent contractors*. https://www.gtlaw.com.au/knowledge/high-court-changes-direction-independent-contractors.

Gilbert, C. (1990) Conceptual issues in the meaning of tourism. In C. Cooper (ed.) *Progress in Tourism, Recreation and Hospitality Management* (Volume 2, pp. 4–27). London: Belhaven Press.

Gilfillan, G. (2018) Characteristics and use of casual employees in Australia. *Research Paper Series 2017-18, January*, 1–15. https://parlinfo.aph.gov.au/parlInfo/download/library/prspub/5742396/upload_binary/5742396.pdf.

Gilmore, J. (2018, December 6) Family violence is about to spike, here's how to help yourself or a friend. *The Sydney Morning Herald*. https://www.smh.com.au/lifestyle/life-and-relationships/family-violence-is-about-to-spike-here-s-how-to-help-yourself-or-a-friend-20181205-p50kbw.html.

Glass, N., Laughon, K., Campbell, J., Wolf, A.D., Block, C.R., Hanson, G., Sharps, P.W. and Taliaferro, E. (2008) Non-fatal strangulation is an important risk factor for homicide of women. *Journal of Emergency Medicine* 35 (3), 329–335. https://doi.org/10.1111/j.1743-6109.2008.01122.x.Endothelial.

Global People Strategist (2019) *5 Countries with the Best Employment Laws*. https://www.globalpeoplestrategist.com/5-countries-with-the-best-employment-laws/.

Goodall, Z. and Spark, C. (2020) Naming rights? Analysing child surname disputes in Australian courts through a gendered lens. *Feminist Legal Studies* 28 (3), 237–255. https://doi.org/10.1007/s10691-020-09443-1.

Goodman, G.S., Luten, T.L., Edelstein, R.S. and Ekman, P (2006) Detecting lies in children and adults. *Law and Human Behavior* 30 (1), 1–10. https://doi.org/10.1007/s10979-006-9031-2.

Gordon, S. (2022) *What is Gaslighting?* Verywellmind. https://www.verywellmind.com/is-someone-gaslighting-you-4147470.

Gratz, K.L. (2003) Risk factors for and functions of deliberate self-harm: An empirical and conceptual review. *Clinical Psychology: Science and Practice* 10 (2), 192–205. https://doi.org/10.1093/clipsy/bpg022.

Hall, B. (2019, September 20) A fraction of fathers lose access to their kids: why the Family Court isn't anti-men. *Sydney Morning Herald*. https://www.smh.com.au/politics/federal/a-fraction-of-fathers-lose-access-to-their-kids-why-the-family-court-isn-t-anti-men-20190919-p52syn.html.

Hall, C.M. (2007) *Introduction to Tourism in Australia: Development, Issues and Change*. Sydney: Pearson Education Australia.

Hall, C.M. and Butler, R. (1995) In search of common ground: Reflections on sustainability, complexity and process in the tourism system. *Journal of Sustainable Tourism* 3 (2), 99–105.

Hall, C.M. and Page, S. (2010) The contribution of Neil Leiper to tourism studies. *Current Issues in Tourism* 13 (4), 299–309.

Hanks, P. (ed.) (1986) *The Collins English Dictionary* (2nd edn). Collins.

Hanson, D., Hitt, M.A., Ireland, R.D. and Hoskisson, Robert, E. (2014) *Strategic Management: competitiveness & globalisation* (5th edn). Melbourne: Cengage Learning Australia.

Harkison, T. (2022) Luxury tourism and hospitality employees: Their role in service delivery. In A.S. Kotur and S.K. Dixit (eds) *The Emerald Handbook of Luxury Management for Hospitality and Tourism* (pp. 199–219). Bingley: Emerald Group Publishing. https://doi.org/doi.org/10.1108/978-1-83982-900-020211010.

Heise, L.L. and Kotsadam, A. (2015) Cross-national and multilevel correlates of partner violence: An analysis of data from population-based surveys. *The Lancet Global Health* 3 (6), e332–e340. https://doi.org/10.1016/S2214-109X(15)00013-3.

High Court of Australia (2022a) *Construction, Forestry, Maritime, Mining and Energy Union & Anor v Personnel Contracting Pty Ltd [2022] HCA 1 Judgement Summary*. https://cdn.hcourt.gov.au/assets/publications/judgment-summaries/2022/hca-1-2022-02-09.pdf.

High Court of Australia (2022b) *ZG Operations & Anor v Jamesk & Ors [2022] HCA 2 Judgement Summary*. https://cdn.hcourt.gov.au/assets/publications/judgment-summaries/2022/hca-2-2022-02-09.pdf.

Hill, J. (2019) *See What You Made Me Do*. Melbourne: Black Inc.

Hill, J. (2022) *Meet the survivors reshaping the system*. Primer. https://primer.com.au/victim-survivors-reshaping-the-system/.

Holding Redlich (2022) *The primacy of the contract: High Court revises approach to determining independent contracting*. Workplace Relations and Safety. https://www.holdingredlich.com/the-primacy-of-the-contract-high-court-revises-approach-to-determining-independent-contracting.

Hotchkiss, S. (2002) *Why is it Always About You? The Seven Deadly Sins of Narcissism*. New York: Free Press.

House, A. (2019) *Merivale reviews viability following termination of enterprise agreement*. Drinks Trade. https://www.drinkstrade.com.au/merivale-reviews-viability-following-termination-of-enterprise-agreement.

Human Resources Director (2019) *The best countries for promoting workers' rights*. HCA Mag. https://www.hcamag.com/au/news/general/the-best-countries-for-promoting-workers-rights/170414.

Hunter, R. (2006) Narratives of Domestic Violence. *Sydney Law Review* 28, 733–776.

HWL Ebsworth Lawyers (2022) *EMPLOYEE OR INDEPENDENT CONTRACTOR? THE PARAMOUNT IMPORTANCE OF THE WRITTEN CONTRACT IN DETERMINING THE RELATIONSHIP BETWEEN PARTIES IS NOW FIRMLY ESTABLISHED*. https://hwlebsworth.com.au/employee-or-independent-contractor-the-paramount-importance-of-the-written-contract-in-determining-the-relationship-between-parties-is-now-firmly-established/.

IPCA (2020) *IPC Asia Pacific*. https://www.ipcasiapacific.com/.

Iso-Ahola, S. (1982) Toward a social psychological theory of tourism motivation: A rejoinder. *Annals of Tourism Research* 9 (2), 256–262.

Jackson, R. (1990) VFR tourism: Is it underestimated? *Journal of Tourism Studies* 1 (2), 10–17.

John, S. (2020) *This is the Fast-Food Chair With the Most Locations in America*. Eat This, Not That! https://www.eatthis.com/fast-food-chain-with-most-locations/.

Johnson, L.M. (2016) *Lia Marie Johnson – DNA (Official Video)*. YouTube. https://www.youtube.com/watch?v=4Y7pRYhvOBU.

Karp, P. (2018) *Coalition stacking Fair Work Commission with mates, Labour says.* The Guardian. https://www.theguardian.com/australia-news/2018/dec/07/coalition-stacking-fair-work-commission-with-mates-labor-says.

Kelleher, S.R. (2022, April 26) Delta Flight Attendants Will Be Paid During Boarding—A First For U.S. Airlines. *Forbes.* https://www.forbes.com/sites/suzannerowankelleher/2022/04/26/delta-flight-attendants-union/?utm_campaign=forbes&utm_source=facebook&utm_medium=social&utm_term=Valerie&fbclid=IwAR1FN08_SwT9_mX1oBdkqnfjKwf4ioSKdJTnKyf3MZuNeGBoxx1ySk6w1Os&sh=6360a38125b2.

Khadem, N. (2019) *Australia has a high rate of casual work and many jobs face automation threats: OECD.* ABC News. https://www.abc.net.au/news/2019-04-25/australia-sees-increase-in-casual-workers-ai-job-threats/11043772.

Khoema (2020) *McDonald's vs Subway: Which Has the Bigger Restaurant Chain?* https://knoema.com/infographics/yhawhcb/mcdonald-s-vs-subway-which-has-the-bigger-restaurant-chain.

Kivela B. (2020) *"The Harm Report": Assessing risk of harm to children and parents in private law cases.* Rayden Solicitors. https://raydensolicitors.co.uk/blog/the-harm-report-assessing-risk-of-harm-to-children-and-parents-in-private-law-cases/.

Klir, G.J. (1972) *Trends in General Systems Theory.* Wiley & Sons.

Krakauer, J. (1996) *Into the Wild.* London: Pan Macmillan.

Law Insider (2022) *Batterer definition.* https://www.lawinsider.com/dictionary/batterer.

Lehto, X.Y., Morrison, A.M. and O'Leary, J.T. (2001) Does the Visiting Friends and Relatives' typology make a difference? A study of the international VFR market to the United States. *Journal of Travel Research* 40 (2), 201–212. https://doi.org/10.1177/004728750104000211.

Leiper, N. (1979) The framework of tourism: Towards a definition of tourism, tourist, and the tourist industry. *Annals of Tourism Research* Oct/Dec, 390–407.

Leiper, N. (1990) Partial industrialization of tourism systems. *Annals of Tourism Research* 17 (4), 600–605.

Leiper, N. (2004) *Tourism Management* (3rd edn). London: Pearson Education.

Leiper, N. (2008) Why "the tourism industry" is misleading as a generic expression: The case for the plural variation, "tourism industries." *Tourism Management* 29 (2), 237–251. https://doi.org/10.1016/j.tourman.2007.03.015.

Leiper, N., Stear, L., Hing, N. and Firth, T. (2008) Partial Industrialisation in tourism: A new model. *Current Issues in Tourism* 11 (3), 207–235.

Leung, A.K.C. and Barankin, B. (2017) An adolescent with a self-inflicted forearm/wrist cutting injury. *Consultant 360,* 57 (11), 1–5. https://www.consultant360.com/articles/adolescent-self-inflicted-forearmwrist-cutting-injury.

Macmillan Dictionary (2022) *Survivor.* https://www.macmillandictionary.com/dictionary/british/survivor.

Markey, R. and McIvor, J. (2018) Regulating casual employment in Australia. *Journal of Industrial Relations* 60 (5), 593–618. https://doi.org/10.1177/0022185618778084.

Marsh, S (2018) *Fast food worker threatened with death over cold cheeseburger.* Nine News. https://www.9news.com.au/national/fast-food-industry-87-percent-of-workers-abused-on-the-job/88c19b61-c257-4442-8eb8-08238893d86a.

Maslow, A.H. (1943) A theory of human motivation. *Psychological Review* 50 (4), 370–396.

McCabe, S. (2009) Who needs a holiday: Evaluating social tourism. *Annals of Tourism Research* 36 (4), 667–688.

McCandless, C. (2014) *The Wild Truth.* London: HarperElement.

McCarthy, M. (1961) *On the Contrary: Articles of Belief 1946-1961.* New York: Warbler Press.

McDonald, R., Jouriles, E.N., Ramisetty-Mikler, S., Caetano, R. and Green, C.E. (2006) Estimating the number of American children living in partner-violent families. *Journal of Family Psychology* 20 (1), 137–142. https://doi.org/10.1037/0893-3200.20.1.137.

McKercher, B. (1999) A chaos approach to tourism. *Tourism Management* 20, 425–434.

McPherson, E. (2020) *The "zombie agreement" loophole leaving Subway workers trapped*. Nine News. https://www.9news.com.au/national/subway-australia-staff-speak-out-about-loophole-creating-unfair-wages/b5235084-1c3d-48b1-b076-ec4b5230261b.

Meyer, S. (2015) *Hitting Home: why separation is often the most dangerous time for a victim of domestic violence*. The Conversation. https://theconversation.com/hitting-home-why-separation-is-often-the-most-dangerous-time-for-a-victim-of-domestic-violence-50650.

Mirriam-Webster (2022) *Merriam-Webstar Dictionary*. https://www.merriam-webster.com/dictionary/nominal.

Morrison, A., Woods, B., Pearce, P., Moscardo, G. and Sung, H. (2000) Marketing to the visiting friends and relatives segment: An international analysis. *Journal of Vacation Marketing* 6 (2), 102–118.

Moss, J. (2021) *The Burnout Epidemic*. Cambridge, MA: Harvard Business Review Press.

Murphy, P.E. (1985) *Tourism: A Community Approach*. London: Routledge.

Myers, D. (2017) *5 things you didn't know about Subway*. Fox News. https://www.foxnews.com/food-drink/5-things-you-didnt-know-about-subway.

Norkey, T. (2018) *20 Things That Make No Sense About Spider-Man: Into The Spider-Verse*. Screenrant. https://screenrant.com/spider-man-into-the-spider-verse-makes-no-sense-plot-holes/.

NSW Government Communities & Justice (2019) *The effects of domestic and family violence on children and young people*. https://www.facs.nsw.gov.au/domestic-violence/about/effects-of-dv-on-children.

Oppenheim, M. (2021, June 22) Domestic abuse victims 'silenced' by family courts and forced into letting dangerous exes see children, warn campaigners. *Independent*. https://www.independent.co.uk/news/uk/home-news/domestic-abuse-family-courts-children-b1870605.html?r=34219.

Our Watch (2018) *Understanding violence facts and figures*. Understanding Violence: What's Happening in Australia. https://www.ourwatch.org.au/understanding-violence/facts-and-figures.

Parliament of Australia (2011) *Domestic Violence in Australia – an overview of the issues*. https://www.aph.gov.au/about_parliament/parliamentary_departments/parliamentary_library/pubs/bn/2011-2012/dvaustralia#_Toc309798373.

Peetz, D. (2020) What do the data on casuals really mean? *Journal of Industrial Relations* 64 (5), 734–758.

Perkins, M. and Butt, C. (2018, December 20) "He's beating me again. Please help": Family violence soars over Christmas period. *The Age*. https://www.theage.com.au/national/victoria/he-s-beating-me-again-please-help-family-violence-soars-over-christmas-period-20181219-p50n9l.html.

Pescud, M. (2018) *Whether teams win or lose, sporting events lead to spikes in violence against women and children*. The Conversation. https://theconversation.com/whether-teams-win-or-lose-sporting-events-lead-to-spikes-in-violence-against-women-and-children-99686.

Plato (399 B.C.E.) *Apology of Socrates* (Translated by Benjamin Jowett (ed.)). Auckland: The Floating Press.

Plato (380 B.C.E.) The Republic. In Translator B. Jowett (Ed.) *The Republic* (eBook Octo). https://doi.org/10.4324/9781912281992.

Porter, M. (1979) How competitive forces shape strategy. *Harvard Business Review* March.

Price, J. (2022, October 7) Children victims, survivors of domestic violence need to be heard and supported to end intergenerational trauma. *The Courier*. https://www.thecourier.com.au/story/7930784/the-only-way-to-end-the-cycle-of-domestic-violence-in-this-country/?cs=12&fbclid=IwAR3Ru9ObPgGyGhmOdEFsDD2oYdjPZVoyi6jbjSzIdyINDVpIlMR-75ycwG8.

Puddy, R. (2022) *SDA union takes McDonald's to court over allegedly denying paid rest breaks*. ABC News. https://www.abc.net.au/news/2022-01-30/union-takes-mcdonalds-to-court/100789788.

Ram, Y. (2018) Hostility or hospitality? A review on violence, bullying and sexual harassment in the tourism and hospitality industry. *Current Issues in Tourism* 21 (7), 760–774. https://doi.org/10.1080/13683500.2015.1064364.

Reardon, T. (2021) *An Expert Guide to Sole Parental Responsibility in Australia*. Unified Lawyers. https://www.unifiedlawyers.com.au/blog/sole-parental-responsibility-guide/.

Richards, K. (2011) Children's exposure to domestic violence in Australia. *Trends and Issues in Crime and Criminal Justice*, 419.

Rogers, C. (2012) *On Becoming a Person: A Therapist's View of Psychotherapy*. Boston: Houghton Mifflin Harcourt.

Safe Steps (2022) *What is Family Violence*. https://www.safesteps.org.au/understanding-family-violence/what-is-family-violence/.

Sarwar, A. and Muhammad, L. (2020) Impact of employee perceptions of mistreatment on organizational performance in the hotel industry. *International Journal of Contemporary Hospitality Management* 32 (1), 230–248. https://doi.org/10.1108/IJCHM-01-2019-0046.

Saunders, P. and Bedford, M. (2018) *New estimates of the costs of children*. https://aifs.gov.au/publications/issue/new-estimates-costs-children.

Schänzel, H. and Yeoman, I. (2015) Trends in family tourism. *Journal of Tourism Futures* 1 (2), 141–147.

Schänzel, H., Yeoman, I. and Backer, E. (2012) Introduction: Families in tourism research. In H. Schänzel, I. Yeoman and E. Backer (eds) *Family Tourism: Multidisciplinary Perspectives* (pp. 1–14). Bristol: Channel View Publications.

Sena, M. (2022) *Fast food industry analysis 2020 - costs & trends*. Franchise Help. https://www.franchisehelp.com/industry-reports/fast-food-industry-analysis-2020-cost-trends/.

Senge, P.M. (2006) *The Fifth Discipline: The Art & Practice of the Learning Organisation* (2006). New York: Random House.

Skyttner, L. (2001) *General Systems Theory: Ideas and Applications*. London: Imperial College Press.

Slater and Gordon Lawyers (2022) *What is the definition of abuse?* https://www.slatergordon.com.au/abuse-law/what-is-the-definition-of-abuse.

Small Business Prices (2022) *2021 Worker's Rights Index: Best & Worst Countries*. https://smallbusinessprices.co.uk/workers-rights-index/.

Smith, M. (2021, July 20) "State-sanctioned abuse" – why the family court system is failing. *The Herts Advertiser*. https://www.hertsad.co.uk/lifestyle/family-court-system-on-trial-8107428.

Sovereign Hill (2022) *Sovereign Hill About Us*. https://sovereignhill.com.au/about-sovereign-hill.

Spence, H. and Abtrobus, B. (2022, April 16) Luggage left behind in chaotic airport crush over Easter weekend. *News.Com.Au*. https://www.news.com.au/travel/travel-updates/half-a-km-long-chaos-at-airports-continues-over-easter/news-story/78624b98e5e19ba2550c001537143c21.

Stacey, M. (2021, October 12) Manual strangulation is the biggest sign domestic abuse will turn deadly, experts say. *13WTHR*. https://www.wthr.com/article/news/crime/manual-strangulation-is-the-biggest-sign-domestic-abuse-will-turn-deadly-experts-say/531-0a9a92c8-a0da-418a-b81e-a3d80ddacf38.

Stark, E. (2007) *Coercive Control: How Men Entrap Women in Personal Life*. Oxford: Oxford University Press.

State Government of Victoria (2018) *Family violence housing support*. State Government of Victoria. https://www.vic.gov.au/affordablehousing/housing-services/family-violence-housing-support.html.

State Government of Victoria (2022) *Victorian Family Violence Research Agenda 2021-2024*. Vic.Gov.Au. https://www.vic.gov.au/victorian-family-violence-research-agenda-2021-2024.

Stear, L. (2002) Studying Highly Industrialised Tourism Systems. University of Technology, Sydney

Stevenson, R. (1886) *The Strange Case of Dr. Jekyll and Mr. Hyde*. Auckland: The Floating Press.

Swarbrooke, J. (2002) *The Development and Management of Visitor Attractions* (2nd edn). Oxford: Elsevier.

Sweet, P.L. (2019) The sociology of gaslighting. *American Sociological Review* 84 (5), 851–875. https://doi.org/10.1177/0003122419874843.

The Australasian Institute of Judicial Administration (2017) *National Domestic and Family Violence Bench Book*. AIJA. http://dfvbenchbook.aija.org.au/dynamics-of-domestic-and-family-violence/myths-and-misunderstandings/.

The Courier (2022, March 5) Seriousness increases when children see family violence. *The Courier*, 15.

The Fair List (2021) *Zombie Enterprise Agreements*. https://thefairlist.org/zombie-enterprise-agreements/.

The Network la Red (2018) *What is partner abuse?* https://www.tnlr.org/en/what-is-partner-abuse/.

Tonkin Legal Group (2020) *Dealing with Family Violence at Christmas*. https://www.tonkinlaw.com/resources/dealing-with-family-violence.

Tremblay, P. (1998) The economic organization of tourism. *Annals of Tourism Research* 25 (4), 837–859.

Truong, K. (2018, August 9) What You Need To Know About Domestic Violence & Big Sporting Events. *Wellness*. https://www.refinery29.com/en-us/domestic-violence-sports-events-study.

Tuohy, W. (2021) 'You still battle': Rosie Batty on five years of family violence action. *The Age*, 28 March. https://www.theage.com.au/national/you-still-battle-rosie-batty-on-five-years-of-family-violence-action-20210320-p57cic.html.

Tuohy, W. (2022a, February 22) One-third of family violence killers are 'very functional', middle-class: new research. *Sydney Morning Herald*. https://www.smh.com.au/national/one-third-of-family-violence-killers-are-very-functional-middle-class-20220221-p59y68.html.

Tuohy, W. (2022b, April 7) 'The last place you expect it': Tiny money transfers used to send family violence abuse. *The Age*. https://www.theage.com.au/national/the-last-place-you-expect-it-tiny-money-transfers-used-to-send-family-violence-abuse-20220407-p5abka.html?btis&fbclid=IwAR23p5SLEsyfwHN-MHjzHYC-gRZeh8htkCVAHzCkpxOLCm9onjNRjh4ICJg.

United Nations (2022) *What is Domestic Abuse*. https://www.un.org/en/coronavirus/what-is-domestic-abuse.

Walk Through India (2010) *Top six Ancient Indian board and Dice games that are still played today*. http://www.walkthroughindia.com/miscellaneous/top-six-ancient-indian-board-and-dice-games-that-are-still-played-today/.

Wattenberg, G. and Roberge, M. (2008) *Shattered song by O.A.R.* Lyrics. https://www.google.com/search?q=OAR+shattered+song+lyrics&rlz=1C1GCEB_enAU946AU946&sxsri=ALiCzsaSDgBruwAYcv7JyKSaqMvDOvEx8A%3A1666300358838&ei=xrlRY9vkMu-s3LUPvZqT8AM&ved=0ahUKEwjb3-jH3O_6AhVvFrcAHT3NBD4Q4dUDCA8&uact=5&oq=OAR+shattered+song+lyrics&gs_lcp=.

White Ribbon Aautralia (2018) Prevalence [domestic violence statistics]. https://www.whiteribbon.org.au/Learn-more/Get-the-facts/Facts-and-Statistics/Prevalence.

White Ribbon Australia (2022) Prevalence. [domestic violence statistics]. https://www.whiteribbon.org.au/understand-domestic-violence/facts-violence-women/domestic-violence-statistics/.

Wilkins, R. and Vera-Toscano, E. (2019, August 1) HILDA: Children staying at home longer is now a confirmed sustained trend in Australia. *AdNews*. https://www.adnews.com.au/news/hilda-children-staying-at-home-longer-is-now-a-confirmed-sustained-trend-in-australia.

Wilson, I. and Taft, A. (2015, February 24) Alcohol's link to domestic violence is in focus – now what? *The Conversation*. https://theconversation.com/alcohols-link-to-domestic-violence-is-in-focus-now-what-37696.

Witchel, A. (1998) How a rogue turns himself into a saint: The blarney fails to hide an emotional directness. *New York Times*, July 29. https://www.nytimes.com/1998/07/29/books/lunch-with-malachy-mccourt-rogue-turns-himself-into-saint-blarney-fails-hide.html.

Women Against Crime (2022) *Domestic Violence and the Holidays: What You Should Know*.https://womenagainstcrime.com/domestic-violence-and-the-holidays-what-you-should-know/.

World Health Organization (2012) *Understanding and addressing violence against women.* https://apps.who.int/iris/bitstream/handle/10665/77432/WHO_RHR_12.36_eng.pdf.

Zentveld, E. (2020, July 29) Should the voice of children be stronger? *The Courier*. https://www.thecourier.com.au/story/6853160/should-the-voice-of-children-be-stronger/.

Zentveld, E. (2021, April 13) When it comes to family violence, we need to think of the children. *The Courier*. https://www.thecourier.com.au/story/7206565/when-it-comes-to-family-violence-we-need-to-think-of-the-children/.

Zentveld, E., Labas, A., Edwards, S. and Morrison, A.M. (2022) Now is the time: VFR travel desperately seeking respect. *International Journal of Tourism Research* September 2021, 1–15. https://doi.org/10.1002/jtr.2509.

Zhou, Y., Mistry, T.G., Kim, W.G. and Cobanoglu, C. (2021) Workplace mistreatment in the hospitality and tourism industry: A systematic literature review and future research suggestions. *Journal of Hospitality and Tourism Management*, 49 (December), 309–320. https://doi.org/10.1016/j.jhtm.2021.09.024.

Index

Figures and boxes are shown in *italics*, tables in **bold**.